OLIVER FORD DAVIES

r   d Davies played his first Shakespeare leads,
llo and Falstaff, when a student at Oxford. He then
ne a history lecturer at Edinburgh University and a
nal drama critic for *The Guardian* and the BBC. In
he began as a professional actor at the Birmingham
and went on to leading parts in the regions and the
t End in plays as diverse as *The School for Scandal*,
ght at 8.30, *Hadrian VII* and *Long Day's Journey into
t*.

ce 1975 he has appeared in twenty-six productions
the Royal Shakespeare Company, including fifteen
akespeares. His work at the National Theatre has
ged from *Hamlet* to the 1993 David Hare trilogy to
ileo in 2006. For his role as Lionel Espy in Hare's
ing Demon he won the Olivier Award for Best Actor.
ce 1997 he has played at the Almeida Theatre in *Ivanov*
first British production of Chekhov to visit Moscow),
*   *ndello's *Naked* (with Juliette Binoche), *Richard II*
and *Coriolanus* (with Ralph Fiennes), and the title role
in *King Lear* in 2002 (the subject of his first book,
Playing Lear).

His films range from *Sense and Sensibility* to *Star Wars
Episodes I*, *II* and *III*, and his many television appearances
include five series as Head of Chambers in *Kavanagh QC*.
He has also written plays for the theatre, television and
radio.

Other Titles in this Series

ACTING AND REACTING
Tools for the Modern Actor
Nick Moseley

ACTIONS: THE ACTORS' THESAURUS
Marina Caldarone and Maggie Lloyd-Williams

THE ACTOR AND THE TARGET
Declan Donnellan

THE ARTICULATE BODY
The Physical Training of the Actor
Anne Dennis

BEYOND STANISLAVSKY
The Psycho-Physical Approach to Actor Training
Bella Merlin

THE COMPLETE STANISLAVSKY TOOLKIT
Bella Merlin

FINDING YOUR VOICE
A Step-by-Step Guide for Actors
Barbara Houseman

HOUSE OF GAMES
Making Theatre from Everyday Life
Chris Johnston

THE IMPROVISATION GAME
Discovering the Secrets of Spontaneous Performance
Chris Johnston

LABAN FOR ACTORS AND DANCERS
Putting Laban's Movement Theory into Practice
Jean Newlove

LABAN FOR ALL
Jean Newlove and John Dalby

OTHER PEOPLE'S SHOES
Thoughts on Acting
Harriet Walter

SINGING WITH YOUR OWN VOICE
Orlanda Cook

SO YOU WANT TO BE AN ACTOR?
Prunella Scales and Timothy West

SO YOU WANT TO BE A THEATRE DIRECTOR?
Stephen Unwin

THROUGH THE BODY
A Practical Guide to Physical Theatre
Dymphna Callery

PERFORMING SHAKESPEARE

Oliver Ford Davies

Foreword by Stanley Wells

NICK HERN BOOKS
London
www.nickhernbooks.co.uk

A NICK HERN BOOK

Performing Shakespeare
first published in 2007
by Nick Hern Books Limited,
14 Larden Road, London W3 7ST

British Library cataloguing data for this book
is available from the British Library

Author photo: Fatima Namdar
Cover design: Ned Hoste, 2h

Typeset by Country Setting,
Kingsdown, Kent CT14 8ES

Printed and bound in Great Britain
by Cromwell Press, Trowbridge

ISBN 978 1 85459 781 6

CONTENTS

For Robert Davies

FOREWORD

Stanley Wells

Shakespeare has achieved such great fame as a poet and dramatist that it is easy to forget that – unlike most playwrights – he was also an actor. Very likely he acted before he started to write plays. He kept company with actors. He acted in plays written by other dramatists, including Ben Jonson, as well as in his own. He wrote parts with specific actors in mind, and he went on acting long after he became established as his company's leading playwright. He left money to actors in his will, and it was two of his long-standing actor friends, John Heminges and Henry Condell, who, after he died, assembled his plays in the First Folio. Those plays were written from within, by a practitioner who knew how much he could ask of his actors, and who was aware of the specific strengths and limitations of those who would first perform them.

Shakespeare knew too that his actors would make a creative contribution to theatrical realisation of what he wrote. There is an unwritten dimension to his plays which allows for the collaboration of his actors. I very much share Oliver Ford Davies' view that 'Shakespeare deliberately left major decisions to his actors', that 'the completion of character lies in the actor's ability and personality'. While Shakespeare can cause his characters to express their inmost thoughts with matchless eloquence, he can also ask his actors to convey wordless emotion at crucial points of the action through such elementary signifiers as the 'O, O, O!' with which Lady Macbeth sighs out her heart in her sleepwalking scene, or the almost inarticulate cries of Othello over the dead Desdemona: 'O Desdemon! Dead Desdemon! Dead! O! O!' Performers share in the act of artistic creation; and this is one of the reasons why we can go on seeing the plays again and again, experiencing them afresh in every varied incarnation.

It is fitting then that this guide to the performing of Shakespeare's plays should be written by a long-practised and widely experienced member of the acting profession. Oliver Ford Davies has played an ample range of Shakespearean roles great and small. He knows the texts of the plays inside out, and he has seen and thoughtfully observed performances of them in a wide range of production styles. He has talked, too, to many of the leading Shakespeare actors of our time, and has supplemented his views with theirs in the interviews printed here. Also he has read widely and with understanding. He recognises that an actor's innate talents can be valuably supplemented by knowledge of the original publication of Shakespeare's plays, of the circumstances of their composition and of their early performance, of the language of his time and his principles of versification. He is able to warn his readers against commonly held superstitions such as the idea that the punctuation and capitalisation of the Folio offer reliable guides to performance, or that there is any point in trying to reproduce archaic spellings preserved by editors. His book will be an invaluable guide to those who act and to all who wish to gain deeper insights into the performance of Shakespeare's plays.

Stanley Wells is Emeritus Professor of Shakespeare Studies and former Director of the Shakespeare Institute, Stratford-upon-Avon. He is General Editor of the Oxford and the Penguin editions of Shakespeare, co-editor of the *Oxford Companion to Shakespeare*, and author of many books, including *Shakespeare: A Dramatic Life*, *Shakespeare for All Time* and *Shakespeare and Co.* He is Chair of the Shakespeare Birthplace Trust, Honorary Governor Emeritus of the Royal Shakespeare Company, and a member of the Board of Directors of the Globe Theatre, London.

ACKNOWLEDGEMENTS

I owe a great deal to the Shakespeare productions I have seen over the years, starting with the Old Vic in the 1950s. In 1959, when visiting Stratford with a university production of Jonson's *Bartholomew Fair*, I stood at the back of the stalls in the Shakespeare Memorial Theatre to see Laurence Olivier, Edith Evans, Charles Laughton, Paul Robeson, Sam Wanamaker, Vanessa Redgrave and Albert Finney. Then in 1962 came the defining production of the early RSC, Peter Brook's *King Lear* with Paul Scofield.

There have been many writers and critics whom I've admired and learnt from, but I have been more directly influenced by the actors and directors that I have worked with. Watching a performance being slowly brought into being teaches you so much more than the finished article. Among my many Shakespeare colleagues, I am especially grateful to John Barton, Adrian Brine, Michael Bryant, Anna Calder-Marshall, Ian Charleson, Tony Church, Nevill Coghill, Richard Cotterell, Brian Cox, Graham Crowden, Howard Davies, Judi Dench, Peter Dews, Richard Eyre, Ralph Fiennes, Michael Gambon, Patrick Garland, Richard Griffiths, Terry Hands, Ronald Harris, Alan Howard, Geoffrey Hutchings, Emrys James, Barbara Jefford, Gemma Jones, Felicity Kendal, Jonathan Kent, Jane Lapotaire, Daniel Massey, Joe Melia, Andrée Melly, Roger Michel, Richard Moore, Adrian Noble, Trevor Nunn, Anthony Page, Richard Pasco, Michael Pennington, Anthony O'Donnell, John Shirley and Juliet Stevenson. My greatest thanks go to my earliest influence, my father Robert Davies (1892–1974).

I owe a special debt to Stanley Wells for his foreword, and to Judi Dench, Barbara Jefford, Adrian Lester, Ian McKellen, Simon Russell Beale, Josette Simon, Juliet Stevenson and Harriet

Walter for being such helpful interviewees. I am very grateful to friends and family who have read this book in draft: Jenifer Armitage, Stephen Boxer, Michael Cordner, Miranda Davies, Nick de Somogyi and Robert Smallwood. They have made invaluable suggestions and corrected many errors. I owe a great deal to Nick Hern, who published my book *Playing Lear* in 2003. He suggested this book to me, commissioned it, and waited patiently for three years, while I played, among others, Oliver Cromwell, Charles Darwin and Philip Larkin. He has been an invaluable counsellor and editor, and his colleague Matt Applewhite has been a meticulous proofreader. The mistakes and rash judgements that remain are of course entirely mine.

My final thanks go to the theatre in Britain, and in particular the Royal Shakespeare Company, which despite many difficulties still manages to present so many of the plays of Shakespeare.

INTRODUCTION

This book is for anyone who wants to perform Shakespeare – student, professional or amateur. At the same time it's not simply a 'how to' book, as it discusses many of the issues writers and critics have raised in recent years. It concentrates on acting Shakespeare's text, while not denying that wholesale rewritings, whether in a Japanese *King Lear* or an African *Macbeth*, have proved Shakespeare an enormous inspiration in modern theatre and film.

My main reason for writing is the absence of any book by an *actor* on the whole wide range of performing in Shakespeare. As an actor I feel there is some accumulated experience that is worth setting down, if only to support, and hopefully guide, other actors' process of discovery. The book is inevitably a personal view, but it is not a succession of reminiscences. I have acted in most of Shakespeare's plays over the past forty years (partly during my twelve years with the Royal Shakespeare Company) – some plays more than once, and these include *Hamlet*, *King Lear*, *Twelfth Night*, *Romeo and Juliet*, *Richard II*, *As You Like It*, *Henry IV*, *Henry V*, *Coriolanus* and *Measure for Measure*. Those that have so far eluded me include *Richard III*, *Pericles*, *Cymbeline*, *King John* and (surprisingly) *Macbeth*. My examples are largely drawn from the more popular plays since, fond as I am of *Timon* and the three *Henry VI*s, they won't be familiar to most readers.

I am aware that dividing the acting process into Preparation, Rehearsal and Performance is to some extent an illusion since they overlap so much, and that placing topics like Politics, Sex or Character into one chapter rather than another may seem arbitrary. But I was anxious to give the development of a performance some sense of structure, even if the actor's best ideas come at the most unexpected moments. I didn't want to weigh the book down with too many footnotes, giving the exact reference for every actor's brief remark, but I have provided fairly comprehensive Notes on Sources, a Bibliography and Index. I have often used the term 'Elizabethan', when 'Elizabethan and Jacobean', or even 'Jacobethan' (terrible word) would be more correct, if unwieldy. Throughout the book I have used for quotations and line references *The Norton Shakespeare* (based on the Oxford edition), general editor Stephen Greenblatt, New York and London: W.W. Norton & Co., 1997.

The question of the performer's gender is tricky. I have used the word 'actor' throughout, just as I would if we were doctors or plumbers. I dislike continually referring to the actor as 'he', but I find the terms 'he/she' or 's/he' clumsy. I have therefore experimented with using 'she' and 'he' in alternate chapters, and hope this won't prove confusing.

Of course I hope you will read the whole book. But I have arranged it in such a way that if your interest lies in language, rehearsal, or actor interviews you can cut straight to them – and then perhaps give the other chapters a chance as well . . .

PERFORMING SHAKESPEARE

I

THE ELIZABETHAN ACTOR

An actor's art can die, and live to act a second part.
1623 folio

Why bother with what actors did four hundred years ago? If you feel this strongly, skip this chapter, but I think you will be missing a valuable source of help. Shakespeare was an acting member of a permanent company – unlike, say, Congreve, Wilde or Stoppard – and wrote for a particular theatre, audience and group of actors. Hard evidence is scanty, but there are signs that he tailored his plays to suit his chosen stages and company of actors. To have some knowledge of the Elizabethan stage must be a help in understanding how to interpret and perform the plays.

THE ROOTS OF ELIZABETHAN THEATRE

The tradition of acting in plays went back many centuries, and by the sixteenth century took several forms. There were various kinds of religious plays – morality plays, saint plays and biblical plays – promoted by towns and parishes and performed by local amateurs, sometimes supplemented by travelling actors we might call semi-professional. The most ambitious of these were the mystery cycles, presented by the great civic authorities, often with elaborate stage effects. But Catholic doctrine was inevitably an integral part of these scripts, and so they increasingly fell foul of both the state and local Protestant authorities. The last York cycle was performed in 1575, the Coventry cycle in 1579, and in 1581 the government prohibited them altogether. The morality tradition lived on, however, and can be seen in Marlowe's Good and Bad Angels in *Dr Faustus*, and in Shakespeare's Father and Son who flank Henry VI after the Battle of Towton.

There was a strong tradition of touring players, entertainers and minstrels – would-be professionals who could turn their hands to other things when times were hard. Civic authorities also funded plays and entertainments, either based on local figures such as Robin Hood or to celebrate the various Christian festivities. Schools and universities were active in promoting drama, because public speaking and the art of rhetoric were fundamental to Tudor education. There was a tradition of boy choristers performing at court and in aristocratic households, often in large-cast plays with music that had religious or political agendas. In 1576 the Chapel Children moved to a theatre in Blackfriars and were the predecessors of Hamlet's 'eyrie of children, little eyases', strong competition for the adult companies. Finally there were acting companies attached to the court and aristocratic households. Encouraged by Henrys VII and VIII a new theatrical tradition emerged after 1500, rooted in the emerging tide of humanism. These 'interludes' were classically inspired allegories like John Skelton's *Magnificence* (1515–18) or romantic comedies such as Nicholas Udall's *Ralph Roister Doister* (1530?). They contained characters, themes, and an emphasis on internal moral struggle that greatly influenced Elizabethan playwrights. These early Tudor household players were at first part-timers, with other household and musical duties. Gradually they formed more independent groups, touring a great deal, but always under the umbrella of aristocratic patronage. This patronage enabled them to travel unhindered by the Elizabethan proclamations against wandering vagabonds, as well as giving them some protection at court and in government; in return their patron gained both prestige and entertainment at his various feasts and gatherings. In the 1570s and 1580s there were about a dozen such troupes. By 1594, as a result of amalgamations, the main permanent troupes were the Lord Chamberlain's Men based at the Theatre in Shoreditch, the Lord Admiral's Men at the Rose in Southwark, and the Queen's Men formed in 1583 to tour and make court appearances.[1]

Shakespeare therefore could have become hooked on theatre from many different sources. He would have studied rhetoric and acted in plays at the King's New School in Stratford. He would have seen the many touring companies which his father, as town bailiff in 1569, had to license as well as attending the first performance. He could have seen the entertainments at the Queen's visit to nearby Kenilworth in 1575, and he might even have seen the last Coventry mystery cycle when he was fifteen. If he was the 'William Shakeshafte', who was working in 1581 as a tutor in Lancashire, he would have come into contact with Lord Strange's acting company when they toured there, and that might have given him the patronage that took him to London some time after 1585 (when his last, twin children were born) and propelled him into acting and writing at both the Theatre and the Rose by 1590. There is some speculation that he may have joined the Queen's Men when they visited Stratford in 1587, shortly after the murder of one of their players, William Knell. His acting skills could therefore have been honed at school, in local festivities, and through a connection with one of the touring companies. All this is conjecture . . . but at the same time, Shakespeare's extraordinary theatrical talent must have been nurtured *somewhere*.

THE ACTORS

We have the names of nearly a thousand actors between 1560 and 1640. Where did they all come from? Some were entertainers – minstrels, jugglers, tumblers like Richard Tarlton – or comedians and dancers of jigs, like Will Kemp who played Dogberry and was probably the first Falstaff. Some actors were tradesmen, from goldsmiths to butchers, who abandoned the professions their fathers had carved out for them. Theatrical dynasties were already being established. Richard Burbage (1568–1619), Shakespeare's star actor, followed his father on to the stage and was acclaimed by the age of sixteen. The female parts were played by boys, who were usually apprenticed from the age of ten upwards to an individual player and maintained by him. John Heminges apprenticed ten such through his long career. In their late teens, when they could no longer speak in a convincingly high register, they might graduate to male parts (see pp. 20–1). Then there must have been those who simply hung around the theatres doing odd jobs, hoping to worm their way into playing. If Shakespeare arrived from Stratford with no professional experience he may have been among those hopefuls (one tradition has him holding horses for visiting gentry).[2]

We have no record of how actors were auditioned or assessed. Some bought a share in a company: in the 1590s £50 seems to have been the going rate, and this is what Shakespeare paid in 1594 when he passed from Lord Strange's company into the newly re-formed Lord Chamberlain's Men. We don't know how he raised such a large sum (many thousands in modern terms). It may have been through an aristocratic patron like the Earl of Southampton, but it more likely reflects the success of his early plays and of his poems, *Venus and Adonis* and *The Rape of Lucrece*. By 1594, when he was thirty, he had already written the three *Henry VI*s, *The Two Gentlemen of Verona*, *Titus Andronicus*, *The Taming of the Shrew*, *Richard III*, and possibly *The Comedy of Errors* and *Love's Labour's Lost*. The eight 'sharers' of the Lord Chamberlain's Men (all of whom were actors in the company) provided capital which helped buy plays, costumes and other equipment, and pay the rent. In return they took a cut of box-office takings. They needed to hire staff as musicians, stage-keepers, book-keepers, property makers, etc., and also as performers. Shakespeare's plays needed between twelve and sixteen actors, so the eight sharers and perhaps three boys would need to hire several men to make up the cast, probably doubling and trebling the smaller parts. Hired men were usually paid ten shillings a week in London and five shillings on tour. The stage may have been an exclusively male world, but not the theatre at large. Women were engaged in making costumes, hats and properties, and as dressers, hairdressers, doorkeepers, ticket-sellers, vendors of food, drink and tobacco – and most important for profligate actors, as pawn-brokers.[3] It is also possible that they wrote, or co-wrote, plays under male pseudonyms.

The Chamberlain's Men thought of themselves as a 'brotherhood', and remained very loyal to their company. They intermarried, lent one another money, and certainly while Shakespeare and Burbage were alive there seems to have been little internal discord. Burbage was acknowledged their star and played Richard III, Hamlet, Othello, Lear and other leads until his death in 1619. Will Kemp was their first star comic, and after he left the company in 1599 Robert Armin probably played Feste and the other professional fools. We know the names of almost all the other actors, but we have no reliable guide to what they played. Contemporary accounts almost never single out individual actors, so although a tradition has grown up that Shakespeare had no great talent as a performer, there is little evidence either way. He may have been the great Claudius or Iago of his day, or he may have played a line of parts that included, for example, Benvolio, Grumio, Gaunt, Polonius and Duncan.[4] It's possible that he retired as an actor sometime after 1603, certainly by 1611, but it's significant that he remained an actor into his 40s, when other playwrights like Ben Jonson and Anthony Munday gave up performing as soon as they could. Perhaps the success of *Hamlet* was partly due to the author keeping an eye on everything on stage as the Ghost, Polonius or the Gravedigger – or possibly all three?

THE THEATRES

The Red Lion (1567) in Stepney is the first recorded London theatre, though it was almost certainly a converted inn and survived for only a few months. James Burbage, Richard's father, constructed the first purpose-built theatre in 1576, called simply the Theatre, and it was here in Shoreditch that many of Shakespeare's early plays, like *Romeo and Juliet*, were first seen. His very first plays, like *1 Henry VI*, were probably presented at the Rose, built by Philip Henslowe in Southwark in 1587. All these theatres were built in the 'liberties' outside the City boundaries, because rents were cheaper and there was no interference from mayoral regulations or city neighbours.

In 1596 Burbage converted part of the old Blackfriars monastery into a small indoor theatre for the Chamberlain's Men when their lease on the Theatre ran out in 1597. Unfortunately a local petition about traffic, noise and undesirables caused the privy council to forbid its adult use, and it reverted to a more amenable boys' company. After a difficult two years hiring other venues the company took the timbers from the Theatre – much to the landlord's fury – across the river, and used them to build the Globe close to the Rose in Southwark. It's intriguing to think that if Burbage's original Blackfriars scheme had succeeded, the Globe might never have been built, and all Shakespeare's mature work would have been first presented in an intimate indoor theatre (66 by 46 feet, with a 30-foot-wide end-on stage), and might have taken a somewhat different form.[5]

The Globe opened in 1599 and was, however, a great success. Using knowledge gained at the Theatre and the Rose, the company devised an extremely flexible space. The outer walls were probably hexagonal, about 100 feet in diameter and 36 feet high. The inner walls afforded a depth of 12 feet for three levels of tiered benches topped by a thatched roof (the cause of the 1613 fire). The stage jutted out into the central yard, where the groundlings could partly surround it. If it was similar to the smaller Fortune, built the following year, it had a stage 43 feet wide by 27 ½ feet deep and about 5 feet high. This stage was large enough for leading players to stand centre, and commentators (clowns or characters like Iago) to prowl the edges making quips and asides to the audience. Recent discoveries from the foundations of the Rose suggest that its stage was not a simple rectangle, but tapered from 36 feet to 26 feet at the front and was only 15 feet deep. The problems of how to keep actors apart and how to make one scene flow into another were solved with great ingenuity. At the back of the stage was a central 'discovery space' where, behind a curtain, characters could be revealed – Polonius eavesdropping perhaps, or Miranda and Ferdinand playing chess. On either side were doors, enabling characters to enter and exit 'severally'. Behind was the dressing room, or 'tiring house'. Above on a second level was a gallery, divided into sections, which could serve for Juliet's balcony and characters 'aloft', probably housed the musicians (viol, lute, oboe and trumpets), and provided some special seating for 'lords' at a shilling a time (suggesting that the actors may have been conscious that they were playing to some extent in the round). Above that was a window, known as the 'top', from which Brabantio might look out or Prospero spy 'invisible'. At the back of this highest level was a room where storm and other effects could be created (cannon-balls rolling round a trough to create thunder).

A canopy covered part of the acting area, with the painted 'Heavens' on its underside, which were 'hung with black' for tragedy. This canopy was probably supported by two pillars, their existence, position and width still a matter of much dispute, which could serve as trees or places to hide. In the stage floor was a trap, which could have provided a prison for Barnardine or a grave for Ophelia. There was cellarage below the stage for Hamlet's 'old mole' to make his groans. Various large props – beds, thrones, tables – could be pushed on by attendants, but essentially word and action rather than scenery conveyed a sense of place. Shakespeare was writing specifically for this space, which imposed itself on both the writing and the performance of the plays. His stage directions make it clear that the scene was both the prescribed location and the Globe. The audience were never in any doubt that they were in a theatre.

The company shareholders became the owners ('house-holders') of the Globe. English actors had never owned their own building before, and sadly never would again on the same principles of commonwealth. It was probably the most co-operative and democratic organisation of its time. Decisions about repertoire, casting and finance were taken collectively by the sharers – something modern actors might ponder on. When James I came to the throne in 1603, he decided to take all the companies under royal patronage. The Chamberlain's became the King's Men, the Admiral's Prince Henry's Men and the recently established Worcester's the Queen's Men. The number of productions presented at court greatly increased, as did royal payments. The sharers in the King's Men became Grooms of the Chamber, a sharp rise in social rank, though it could involve standing around at court to swell the numbers when foreign ambassadors needed impressing. Shakespeare's company was now recognised both at home and abroad as the finest in the land.

In 1608 the company finally got hold of the Blackfriars Theatre (the boys' company had put on a politically contentious play that had offended James I). And from the following year the King's Men began to perform at the Blackfriars in winter and the Globe in summer, thereby extending their season and becoming less dependent on touring. Blackfriars only seated 600, against the Globe's 2–3,000, but its price range was sixpence to two shillings and sixpence, while most of the Globe's audience only paid one penny standing and up to sixpence seated (at a time when an artisan might earn a shilling a week and a schoolmaster eight shillings). Blackfriars therefore had a potentially bigger take (in 1612 it took £1,000 more a season than the Globe); it was not dependent on the weather; and the acting could be subtler, so that it gradually became the company's preferred venue. Shakespeare's final plays were probably written for this smaller stage. High society certainly approved, as the prices made the venue more exclusive, women felt safer, and, unlike the Globe, the more you paid, the closer you were to the stage. In the 1630s Queen Henrietta Maria paid four private visits – *pace* the film *Shakespeare in Love*, Queen Elizabeth wouldn't have been seen dead in a common playhouse.[6]

By 1610 Shakespeare was a rich man. His share of the rents and box office of the two theatres must have yielded him over £150 p.a. With payment for the two plays a year, which he wrote on average for the company, and rents and tithes round Stratford worth £80, his total income was not far short of £300 p.a. This was not wealth to compare with an aristocrat at £3,000 p.a., or even Edward Alleyn (1566–1626), star of the Admiral's Men and shrewd property investor, who eventually bought the manor of Dulwich for £10,000. But in modern terms it certainly put Shakespeare's income into six figures.

REPERTOIRE, CASTING AND TOURING

In the 1590s a company might put on thirty to forty plays in a season (late summer till spring, with a six-week break during Lent), of which over half would be new. This is a huge number, and the majority haven't survived. Even if we have the name of a lost play we rarely know its author: it's only by one chance reference that we know Thomas Kyd wrote *The Spanish Tragedy*, perhaps the most interesting pre-Shakespearean work. £6 seems to have been the going rate a playwright could expect for a new play in the 1590s, and, though not princely, it was enough to attract many hard-up, university-trained writers. Some new plays only got one performance, most only three to five, and few plays stayed in the repertoire for more than a year or two. *Richard II*, probably written in 1595, was described in 1601 as 'so old and so long out of use that they should have small or no company at it'. By the early 1600s the King's Men were giving plays longer runs (*Henry VIII* was on its third consecutive per-formance when the Globe burnt down in 1613), and this would reflect the growing popularity of Shakespeare, Jonson, Beaumont and Fletcher. By the 1630s the company was only buying three or four new plays a year, though the price had risen to £20.

It seems from cast lists that all company members were in every play, performing a different one almost every afternoon of the week. Typecasting must have been common; Hamlet, talking to the Players, lists the king, the adventurous knight, the lover, the humorous man, the clown and the lady as typical characters in a play. Although he may be poking fun at an old-fashioned minor troupe, in the printed texts Claudius and Gertrude are always referred to as 'King' and 'Queen', and the Gravediggers are 'Clowns'. Some characters never even acquired a personal name – Lady Macbeth (she is simply called 'Lady' in the folio), the Jailer's Daughter in *The Two Noble Kinsmen*, and the Duke in *Measure for Measure* ('Vincentio' is only found in the folio cast list). Some actors were praised for their versatility – Burbage could easily have played Hamlet and Malvolio on successive afternoons – but in those plays frequently revived actors probably stuck with an agreed line of roles, and handed them on at death or retirement. We know that when Burbage died in 1619, Joseph Taylor joined the company and took over many of his parts – and probably his interpretations.

Touring took place in the summer, or when, as in 1592–4 and 1608–9, the London playhouses were closed due to plague. The King's Men concentrated on aristocratic country houses and areas not too far from London – Cambridge and Ipswich; Dover and Rye; Bristol and Bath – though at times they went as far west as Devon and as far north as Shropshire.[7] It is unlikely that all the sharers went on these tours, and sometimes they must have expanded to two companies. Then, as later, there were dozens of out-of-work actors hanging round London waiting for ill-paid summer tours.

REHEARSAL

Rehearsal took place in the morning (probably 9 a.m. to noon), performance in the afternoon (2 to 5 p.m.), and visits to the tavern most evenings. New plays entered the repertoire roughly every fortnight, but the demands of reviving old shows made it unlikely that they got twelve mornings' rehearsal.[8] The best-case scenario was that an author gave a reading of the substance of a play to the sharers, who then paid him to finish it. The author might then give a reading to the whole company of his finished draft (as Chekhov and Shaw later did), which was his chance to give line-readings and a general indication of how he wanted it performed. The actors themselves might then read through the play, before taking their parts home to learn. Sometimes none of these stages took place, and the actors learnt their parts before they had any idea what the play was about.

The 'part' was what we now call a cue-script and contained only the words to be spoken by an individual character, with a few cue-words preceding each speech. This was to save on paper and copying – a hugely expensive and time-consuming task – and also to prevent a complete script falling into the hands of a rival company or an unscrupulous printer (there were of course no copyright laws). The one 'part' that survives gives only one, two or three words of cue, and no indication of the cue speaker or to whom the speech is directed. There are a few property and action notes, viz: 'begins to weep'. Cue-scripts in fact survived into the 1950s, and were regularly used by the Aldwych farceurs, presumably adding a teasing element of surprise and improvisation to the rehearsals.

Learning ('studying') a part must have been done in the evenings – before, during or after the tavern – or when not called to rehearsal. Actors needed to be 'quick studies': Quince tells his cast, 'Here are your parts, and I am to entreat you, request you, and desire you, to con [learn] them by tomorrow night.' It seems that only one group rehearsal took place, but this would have concentrated on entrances and exits, the blocking of large group scenes, and on costumes and props. There was no run-through or dress rehearsal as we would understand it. There must have been rehearsals of songs, dances and fights, and it seems likely that actors who needed to work closely with one another – Othello and Iago, Belch and Aguecheek – would have gone through their scenes together, perhaps in the small tiring rooms. Boy players might be instructed by their masters; and schools, universities and the court might call in playwrights or players to instruct their actors. Little analytical discussion took place, actors were simply told how to 'speak their parts emphatically and to the life'. Hamlet instructs his players to 'speak the speech . . . as I pronounced it to you'.

If Quince's direction of the Mechanicals is anything to go by, Shakespeare or Burbage might have given some of the actors line-readings and moves, and would have made arrangements about rehearsals, costumes, props and music. Shakespeare very likely wrote his later plays with certain actors in mind, but much of his direction was already written into the text (see pp. 94–6). Authors weren't the play's principal selling point: deaths, madness, royalty and comedy held greater attraction for customers. Authors' names rarely appear in the printed quartos, though it's a measure of Shakespeare's fame that his name features more after 1600, and that unscrupulous printers attached his name to plays clearly not his. A key figure was the book-keeper (prompter), who seems to have cast the small parts, made revisions to the text (suggested by actors, authors, or even the Master of the Revels who licensed each play), and may have given further instruction during performance. At rehearsals and/or performance, a 'platt', or plot, about two feet wide and three feet long, was hung in the wings to inform or remind the cast of entrances and give some outline of the plot.

The first performance must have been quite a happening. No one may have seen a complete run-through of the play, so it was tried out cold on an audience. If they disapproved ('damned' it), the play was probably never seen again, and it is possible therefore that the cast didn't invest too much time and effort in it – though it would seem likely that they took a new play by Shakespeare, their house dramatist, very seriously indeed. If the play succeeded, it is likely that author and cast set about rewriting and re-rehearsing it in the light of what they had learned for a second presentation a week or two later. Productions must have markedly improved as they settled in, however much adrenalin had been generated at the first performance through not being sure when to speak or what happens next. Some of Shakespeare's more difficult plays, like *Timon of Athens*, seem to have received very few performances. *Troilus and Cressida* was never presented at the Globe: the 1609 quarto says it was not 'sullied with the smoky breath of the multitude'. What is clear is that actors needed a fabulous memory, since they couldn't rely on the constant repetition of rehearsal to learn a part, and yet they needed to keep twenty or thirty plays in their head at a time (I've carried 1,800 lines round with me during a Stratford season; 6,000 would be mind-blowing). Several texts show how playwrights scorned the actor 'who is out of his part', but a lot of extemporising must have gone on. Sometimes improvisation was written into the part: *Greene's Tu Quoque* offers the stage direction, 'Here they two talk and rail [jest or rally] what they list', just as they do in pantomime to this day.[9] Shakespeare disapproved of ad-libbing, if Hamlet is any indication: 'Let those that play your clowns speak no more than is set down for them.'

In the absence of elaborate scenery the most lavish visual attraction were the costumes. Theatres carried a certain amount of stock, and their loss in a fire could be a catastrophe, but they relied mainly on actors providing their own. An actor playing several parts had a basic costume, to which he added a tunic, cloak or helmet to distinguish the role for the audience. A rare contemporary drawing of a play in performance, *Titus Andronicus*, suggests that even in Roman plays the basic costume was Elizabethan, and a toga or a wreath was added to give a period feel. Leading actors had ornate and probably very fashionable costumes, particularly when playing royalty. Thomas Heywood was paid £6 13s for a black velvet gown for his play *A Woman Killed with Kindness*, when he had only been paid £6 for writing it. The most valuable possession that one actor could bequeath to another was his stock of costumes, swords and musical instruments. Theatres had fines for lateness, drunkenness and missing rehearsals, but at the Rose the fine for removing a costume from the playhouse was forty times greater than that for missing a performance.[10]

VOICE, GESTURE AND ACCENT

The Elizabethans had a strong belief in truthful acting; 'lively and naturally' were the watchwords. The player who 'affects grossly' is 'so far forced from life' that he betrays himself 'to be altogether artificial'. If the actor is not moved himself he cannot move his audience; 'the passion which is in our breast is the fountain and origin of all external actions'. The key was 'vox, vultus, vita': voice, facial expression, and life/animation.

Voice was key, particularly in the open air. Actors learnt to 'speak their parts emphatically and to the life'. Men and boys who had been taught 'every trope, every figure, as well of words as of sentence' would be able to handle the verse. The inflection of the voice was vital not merely for sense but to do justice to the language, for 'without this change of voice neither any irony, nor lively metaphor can well be discerned'. Heywood, who wrote or contributed to some 220 plays, says in his *Apology for Actors* (1612) that 'actors should either know how to speak as scholars, or possess a natural volubility' which enables them to speak well even when they don't understand the text [never trust that an actor knows what he's saying]. But through training, the scholar could be taught to speak well, and the natural actor to appreciate the 'ingeniousness' of the lines, 'but where a good tongue and a good conceit [witty understanding] both fail, there can never be a good actor'.[11] So, no change there.

Equal importance was attached to 'external action'; movement, facial expression, gesture. It is difficult to reconstruct how broad this 'action' was. In *Henry VIII* Norfolk describes Wolsey thus:

> Some strange commotion
> Is in his brain. He bites his lip, and starts,
> Stops on a sudden, looks upon the ground,
> Then lays his finger on his temple, straight
> Springs out into fast gait, then stops again,
> Strikes his breast hard, and anon he casts
> His eye against the moon. In most strange postures
> We have seen him set himself.   (3.2.113–9)

How strange is this posture? Is Norfolk exaggerating, parodying, or faithfully reporting? We know that 'wringing of the hands' was an accepted expression of grief. Did men strike their breast hard to express passion or remorse? One spectator claimed actors 'would revoke and bow back their whole body, and wind and wrest about their very sides'.

The whole matter is complicated by seventeenth-century manuals of gesture. They were intended for use in schools and universities, and for anyone who practised 'oratory' or public speaking. John Bulwer writes in his *Natural Language of the Hand* (1644) that 'the art was first formed by rhetoricians . . . but most strangely enlarged by actors, the ingenious counterfeitors of men's manners'. Bulwer gives 120 illustrations of hand gestures, denoting triumph, indignation, scorn, despair, supplication, etc., forms of mime we now associate with classical ballet. We don't know if actors routinely used these. It seems likely that young actors and boys were taught some of these gestures as a shorthand, an agreed external expression of inward passion: 'in a sorrowful part the head must hang down; in a proud, the head must be lofty; in an amorous, closed eyes, hanging down looks, & crossed arms; in a hasty, fuming & scratching the head &c.'[12] It may have been necessary at the Globe, where the actor's face and front were never visible to the entire audience and he may therefore during long speeches have turned through 180 degrees. The new replica Globe on the South Bank has shown, however, that quite small gestures and expressions, skilfully placed, can register even at the extremities of the theatre.

The Elizabethans rightly attached great importance to the eyes. Shakespeare is full of references to them; angry, rolling, terrible, subdued, cloyed, still-gazing. The 'throwing of the eye' was an essential part of the actor's equipment.[13] Cymbeline comments at the end of the play:

> See,
> Posthumus anchors upon Imogen,
> And she, like harmless lightning, throws her eye
> On him, her brothers, me, her master, hitting
> Each object with a joy. The counterchange
> Is severally in all.   (5.5.393–8)

Every generation, every decade even, proclaims a new naturalism. This was certainly true in the 1590s. As early as 1592 Shakespeare has Buckingham comment on the current mode of tragic acting, though we can't be certain whether he is recording or making fun of it:

> Tut, I can counterfeit the deep tragedian,
> Tremble and start at wagging of a straw,
> Speak, and look back, and pry on every side,
> Intending deep suspicion; ghastly looks
> Are at my service, like enforced smiles . . .
>   (*Richard III*; 3.5.5–9)

Pistol's bombast in *Henry IV* and *V*, however, we can take to be a parody of the old 'pantomimick' speech and manner. By 1600 the departure of the ad-libbing clown Will Kemp, the move to the Globe, and the great cycle of tragedies starting with *Hamlet* seem to mark the point where Shakespeare's company was identified with truthful naturalism. 'Overdoing' is the most consistent criticism of actors brought by contemporaries, but they also emphasise that each actor must develop his own individual style: 'no man can put off his own and put on another's nature'.[14] It seems agreed that actors, however flamboyant, were much better at natural gesture than orators. 'Take care,' Bulwer warns, 'that variety of gesture may answer the variety of voice and words.' In other words, 'suit the action to the word, the word to the action'.

We will never be certain how Elizabethan actors pronounced Shakespeare's text, but certain deductions have been made from spellings in folio and quartos, rhymes, and the number of feet and the rhythms of the iambic pentameter. The general tendency was towards speed and economy, and experiments at the new Globe have shown that verbal contractions can help actors to deliver the text significantly faster. Syllables were often missed out, as in 'murd'rous', 'wat'ry', and 'nat'ral'. It would seem the 'h' was often dropped from 'him' and 'her', and 'he' was often 'a'. Nature and torture have no 'ch' in the middle, nor pleasure its 'zh'. The final 'g' of words ending in '-ing' was often dropped. The 'r' after vowels was strongly rolled, giving it a West Country sound, and for words beginning with 'wh' the 'w' was strongly aspirated. Vowels are more difficult to pin down, as there seems little consistency. When 'haste' is spelt 'hast' in the folio, is that how it was pronounced? 'Love' sometimes rhymes with 'prove', 'feast' with 'best', 'one' with 'alone' – but sometimes not. The 'ee' in 'see' and 'peace' was pronounced 'ay', yet the 'ay' in 'say' is quite short and staccato.[15]

It is clear that regional accents were very varied. Plays often poke fun at northern, Welsh, Irish and Scottish accents – witness Fluellen, MacMorris and Jamy in *Henry V* – and Raleigh was mocked at court for his broad Devon. There was also a lower-class London accent, much used by Ben Jonson in his comedies, but also by Shakespeare for Bardolph and Nym. By process of elimination there would seem to be a recognised south-eastern accent used at court, and aped by the emergent middle classes. It may have had the flavour of West Country, Irish or even modern American, but it is hard not to conclude that there was an accepted upper-class southern accent which would have been used on stage in posh parts and contrasted with lower-class characters. George Puttenham advised writers in 1589 to:

take the usual speech of the Court, and that of London and the shires lying about London within sixty miles, and not much above. I say not this but that in every shire of England there be gentlemen and others that speak . . . as good Southern as we of Middlesex or Surrey do, but not the common people of every shire, to whom the gentlemen and also their learned clerks do for the most part condescend.[16]

CHARACTER AND PERSONATION

It is often said that the idea of 'character', the study of a person's complex and varied psychology, didn't emerge till the birth of the novel in the mid-eighteenth century. It is true that to the Elizabethans 'character' meant simply handwriting or a distinctive mark, but it would be hard to argue that Hamlet or Cleopatra are not 'character studies' in our modern sense. Elizabethan science had a theory of 'humours', that a person's health was determined by the balance of the elements of water, air and heat within the body, and that this controlled the production of blood, phlegm and bile which might result in anger or melancholy. The 'comedy of humours' therefore was based on a cast of 'types', whose actions were determined by an unwavering disposition to lust, jealousy, anger, etc. Ben Jonson's plays are usually cited as examples of this approach – as in *Every Man out of His Humour* (1598) – though his characters often have more range and complexity. Shakespeare's studies of jealousy in *Othello* and *The Winter's Tale*, or melancholia in Jacques and Don Armado, owe something to the concept of humours.

By 1600 a new term appears – 'personation' – to describe the way the actor behaves as if he were the imagined person come to life. Heywood wrote that good actors should 'qualify everything according to the nature of the person personated . . . and they should appear to you to be the self-same men' they represented. It was 'as if the personator were the man personated, so bewitching a thing is lively and well-spirited action, that it hath power to new-mould the hearts of the spectators'. When Hamlet speaks of the Player King's 'whole function suiting with forms', he means that everything – pace, tone, rhythm, stress, volume, gesture and movement – was adjusted to the character he personated. Hamlet also calls for 'a passionate speech' and describes the player being 'in a dream of passion'. 'Passionating' was the other key word the Elizabethans used to describe the art of acting. They loved to see actors passing rapidly from one emotion to another, and this Hamlet's quicksilver imagination supplied in plenty. A spectator at *Macbeth* in 1611 described how, at the sight of Banquo's ghost, Burbage 'fell into a great passion of fear and fury'. The fluidity of passion, of life itself, was the touchstone of great acting.[17]

Shakespeare's tragic heroes have a far greater complexity of characterisation than had ever been attempted before. It may be that Burbage was the inspiration for this. For his generation he *was* Richard III, in the way that Olivier was in the 1950s. In James I's reign, when Edward Alleyn had retired, Burbage's name was synonymous with great acting – as were Betterton, Garrick, Kean and Irving in later centuries. Richard Flecknoe wrote of him 'so wholly transforming himself into his part, and putting off himself with his clothes, as he never (not so much as in the tiring house) assumed himself again until the play was done'. It is the quality we now associate with film actors like Robert de Niro and Daniel Day-Lewis. Flecknoe was writing in 1664 and had never seen Burbage in life, so perhaps we should look elsewhere for confirmation. The only real evidence we have lies in the plays themselves. After 1594 Shakespeare wrote most, if not all, of his great leading parts for Burbage, and these may therefore reflect the qualities Burbage had as an actor. He must have had a good voice, strong and flexible, and he must have possessed the authority to convince as Othello and Lear. Great outbursts of energy and violence are symptomatic of tragic heroes from Romeo to Coriolanus and Leontes. Allied to these is a quality of danger, vital to any leading actor and much needed for Macbeth and Antony. All great actors excel at comedy, and Shakespeare must have known that he could trust Burbage with Hamlet's sense of humour, and perhaps with Benedick and Malvolio. In contrast to violent energy, Burbage must have had a sense of introspection, an ability to handle Macbeth's and Brutus' soliloquies.[18] Shakespeare may have been making Burbage give himself notes when, as Hamlet, he instructs 'in the very torrent, tempest, as I may say the whirlwind of your passion, you must acquire and beget a temperance that may give it smoothness'. (3.2.5–7).

BOY PLAYERS

Boy players had to be apprenticed to their actor masters as if they were training to become grocers or goldsmiths: there was no guild of actors.[19] The apprentice was housed, fed and clothed in his master's house, but was paid no regular wage. If he proved to be a good actor and his treble voice lasted five years or more, he was an excellent investment. Voices often broke quite late in the teens, though this and growth spurts were unpredictable and may explain why Celia is called 'the taller' by Le Beau, while in the next scene Rosalind declares that she is herself 'more than common tall' (of course it may just be Shakespeare's carelessness). Masters probably rehearsed their own apprentices, teaching them enunciation, gesture and movement. Very few plays have more than four female parts, and some of these could have been doubled. Several plays make it easy for boys to be rehearsed in pairs – Rosalind and Celia, Viola and Olivia, Mistresses Ford and Page. Others enabled most of a boy's part to be rehearsed with a very few other actors – Desdemona and Emilia with Othello, Iago and Cassio; Isabella with Angelo and the Duke.[20] This would not have been possible with women who dominate the play – Portia and Cleopatra – which makes it all the more likely that Shakespeare wrote these parts only when he knew he had an exceptional boy player. Between 1604 and 1610 such a boy would have had a very heavy workload – the Countess of Roussillon, Lady Macbeth, Goneril, Marina, Cleopatra, Volumnia and Queen Katherine. The term 'boy', however, needs qualification. There is increasing evidence that female parts were played by males no younger than twelve and no older than twenty-two, with a median of around sixteen. It makes sense to imagine Volumnia played by a very experienced twenty-year-old, whose voice had long broken.

Why did Elizabethan audiences, half of whom may well have been female, accept boys as women? It was a convention of course, which women seemed unable to challenge despite the fact that actresses played on many European stages. The boys must have had talent: Burbage and other leading actors would have demanded a very high standard in their Lady Macbeths and Cleopatras. In size, movement and voice they must have been sufficient contrast to adult males. They also had a status in society not dissimilar to most women, as rich Portia makes clear in her submission to Bassanio, 'her lord, her governor, her king'. Dramatists must have known just how much boys could achieve and written accordingly: Rosalind may dominate *As You Like It*, but her part is shorter than most of the great male leads. It is significant that most contemporary accounts speak of the female characters as if they were women: they make little or no reference to the boys playing them. Illustrations of scenes from plays clearly show female characters as women, sometimes with breasts fully exposed. It is not too big a leap to infer that dramatists also thought of their characters *as* women and wrote accordingly (see pp. 123–7).

Theatres and audiences may have been content with the situation, but commentators and the clergy were often critical. There was much heated debate. Did it transgress the primary boundary between men and women, offend against decorum and degree, disobey biblical injunctions against cross-dressing? Was homosexual attraction one of the pleasures of both actor and theatregoer? No specific charges of homosexuality were ever brought against an actor or boy player, though their total absence may suggest that it was an accepted covert practice. Puritan opposition to cross-dressing gathered steam after Shakespeare's death, and it was one of the reasons the theatres were closed from 1642 to 1660. When they reopened, actresses almost immediately took their rightful place.

Nevertheless, the role of cross-dressing seems to have added to the Elizabethan audience's sense of the comic, if Rosalind's epilogue is anything to go by. The signification of 'woman' didn't seem dependent on the gender of the actor. Symbol is everything. Flute can play Thisbe, even though he claims to have a beard 'coming', as Quince says he can 'play it in a mask'. Bottom too wants a go at Thisbe, by hiding his face and speaking 'in a monstrous little voice'. Viola as Cesario remains female even though played by a male. Orsino's attraction to a boy, being played by a boy pretending to be a woman pretending to be a boy, presumably added to the complexity and the fun. Once again it depended on the audience's acceptance that the stage was a stage and not real life.

PERFORMANCE

Star actors had their personal followings. In the 1590s Will Kemp was probably a bigger draw than Burbage, certainly than Shakespeare. Kemp was essentially a clown, and the clown's relationship has always been firstly with the audience, and only secondly with his character or the play. Richard Tarlton had only to stick his head through a curtain (like Eric Morecambe) for the audience to fall about. A certain amount of improvisation undoubtedly went on, and some actors may have rewritten, or misremembered, lines. Jonson condemned actors for changing things, but it was hard for a writer outside the company to control an actor who had 2,000 people in the palm of his hand. Shakespeare as a sharer/actor may have had better luck. Entrance and exit rounds were common. As one critic noted, 'When [the actor] doth hold conference upon the stage; and should look directly in his fellow's face; he turnes about his voice into the assembly for applause-sake.'[21] So, no change there either.

The theatre's licence dictated that the plays had to be performed between 2 and 5 p.m. The 'two-hour traffic of our stage' was possible for *Macbeth* (2,100 lines) and *A Midsummer Night's Dream* (2,120 lines), and even perhaps for a cut *Romeo and Juliet* (3,000 lines uncut: I've been in a production that did it in 2 hours 20 minutes). The quarto of *Henry V* (1,620 lines as against the folio's 3,380) suggests how the company may have routinely cut Shakespeare's plays – in this case leaving out much of Acts 1 and 5, and shortening or even omitting Henry's big speeches; though it's possible this was a touring version. It is a sobering thought that Shakespeare may never have seen the full text of *Hamlet* performed (though there is some evidence that performances at court could go on for four or five hours). The action at the Globe was probably without intervals, as food and drink were served during the performance, though some act breaks were marked by music.

It was normal practice, certainly before 1600, to end the performance of both comedy and tragedy with a jig, played by the company clown and a few assistants. This was usually a bawdy tale told in song and dance, accompanied by the clown's tabor or side-drum and pipe. Will Kemp was a jig specialist, and the theatre often filled at the end of the play to catch his latest bawdy satire. When Kemp left (or was dismissed) in 1599 – to dance his way to Norwich – the jig may have been dropped. In *Hamlet*, written the same year, the prince sneers at Polonius' liking for 'a jig or a tale of bawdry'. It is possible that Feste's song at the end of *Twelfth Night*, or the dance at the end of *As You Like It*, were attempts to supply a different musical ending. But it is also possible that the jig was too great a crowd-pleaser to be abandoned. In 1612 the Middlesex Sessions tried to ban jigs altogether, but they were still common twenty years later.[22]

The Globe was set in the bad, bold world of Southwark, amid the brothels, bear pits and pleasure gardens, much frequented by law students, freethinkers and gallants, but also by any artisan who could afford a penny to stand in the yard. The make-up of the Globe audience is still much disputed, but of the four social classes – nobles and gentlemen; citizens and burgesses; yeomen; artisans and labourers – it is likely the citizens dominated. They, after all, could take afternoons off, sometimes several times a week, since the demand for new plays suggests that some people went to the theatre very frequently.[23] It may seem remarkable that so many large theatres could thrive, but London with a population approaching 200,000 was one of the largest cities in Europe. Many plays assume an audience familiar with in-jokes and cross-references to other plays, and one that could follow quite complex thought and language. The tragedies of the period made greater demands on the audience than anything produced in the next three hundred years. It may be that the actors were broad and generalised by our standards, but there is no doubt that their intentions speak directly to us. The advice Jonson gave his boy players is thoroughly modern: 'Practise language and behaviours, and not with a dead limitation: act freely, carelessly and capriciously, as if our veins ran with quicksilver'.[24]

2

SHAKESPEARE'S LANGUAGE

The life of the plays is in the language.
Richard Eyre

INTRODUCTION

All we have of Shakespeare the dramatist are the playtexts. For all the educated guesses we don't know for sure when or where he wrote the plays, how long they took him, how much they were revised, and above all we have not a line to show what he thought of any of this. Ben Jonson wrote that Shakespeare 'flowed with that facility, that sometime it was necessary he should be stopped',[1] but there is some contrary evidence that he experimented with many different versions of a speech and that he was a great reviser and reworker of material. We don't know whether the texts that have come down to us are accurate representations of what he wrote or what his company performed. Are there missing scenes in *Macbeth*? Would he prefer us to play the quarto or the folio version of *King Lear*? We don't know whether a plot was chosen because it reflected something in Shakespeare's own life or in contemporary society. Did he want to impress James I, or keep Burbage happy? Was he affected by the 1608 corn riots? Was he suffering from syphilis? The absence of firm answers might seem like a catalogue of obstacles. In fact I find it a huge release. All we have are the words. We are free.

Well, not quite free. Shakespeare's language is a great enabler. But it is also at times a problem. A little help is needed to overcome this. First, and most obviously, the language is sometimes archaic, and occasionally impenetrable. Words like 'biggin', 'fardel', 'jennet', 'mobled', 'skirr', and 'wappered' have to be translated. Goneril's 'May all the building on my fancy pluck / Upon my hateful life', or Coriolanus' 'They are no less / When, both your voices blended, the great'st taste / Most palates theirs' are almost impossible to decipher. Good footnotes are a vital aid.

Second, some words have changed their meaning. Though Polonius' and Hamlet's 'What's the matter?' often gets a laugh today, Shakespeare meant by 'matter' something being read or discussed. There's nothing to be done about this, just accept the laugh (gratefully). Some slight changes of usage are deeply frustrating to the actor. 'Anon' and 'presently' both meant 'at once' not 'soon'. When Kent is trying to take Lear out of the storm, Lear repulses him with 'When the mind's free / The body's delicate'. I longed to say 'sensitive' rather than 'delicate', to make the meaning more obvious. Modern productions (particularly on film) do sometimes change a few words. In decades to come, since language is changing more rapidly than ever before, substitutions may become the norm.

Third, and most commonly, the language can be multi-layered, overblown or compact to a point where it can seem difficult and remote. Shakespeare at times seems almost perversely to obscure his meaning, to hold things back, to raise questions that he's not prepared to answer. Leontes' unbalanced mental state causes him to skip almost unintelligibly from thought to thought in this wonderful passage:

> Ha' not you seen, Camillo –
> But that's past doubt; you have, or your eye-glass
> Is thicker than a cuckold's horn – or heard –
> For, to a vision so apparent, rumour
> Cannot be mute – or thought – for cogitation
> Resides not in that man that does not think –
> My wife is slippery? If thou wilt confess –
> Or else be impudently negative
> To have nor eyes, nor ears, nor thought – then say
> My wife's a hobby-horse. . .
> (*The Winter's Tale*, 1.2.269–278)

Shakespeare can also be terse to the point of obscurity. Macbeth ends his disastrous dinner party with the lines:

> Come, we'll to sleep. My strange and self-abuse
> Is the initiate fear that wants hard use.
> We are yet but young in deed.   (3.4.141–3)

To be immediately understood today we would need to say: 'My strange self-delusion is the fear of the novice that lacks experience'. The terrible implications of those final seven syllables (there is no attempt at a verse line) are enormous, but you need to understand that 'deed' implies enterprise, or even murder.

Such obscurities can be serious problems, but take heart on two counts. First, it isn't just our generation that is puzzled: Elizabethan audiences must have found such writing difficult. Compared with nearly all his contemporaries Shakespeare took language on a gargantuan spree. John Heminges and Henry Condell, his two actor colleagues who compiled the First Folio in 1623, seemed aware of this in their introduction. They ask their readers:

> We hope . . . you will find enough both to draw and hold you . . . Read him therefore; and again and again: and if then you do not like him, surely you are in some manifest danger not to understand him.[2]

Even allowing for the fact they had an expensive book to sell, this reads as a heartfelt and uneasy plea. They had been acting in his plays for nearly thirty years, and presumably knew the popular ones backwards. They know they can be difficult, that they will require several readings, and if you are not held and engaged you won't understand him.

The second reason to feel confident is that Shakespeare wrote his plays to be heard, not read. He seems to have paid little attention during his lifetime to the publication of his plays in single quarto form and, since the First Folio was not published until seven years after his death, putting his collected plays in order was hardly the preoccupation of his final years. Without Heminges and Condell's perseverance eighteen of his plays would almost certainly have been lost, including *Macbeth*, *Antony and Cleopatra*, *Julius Caesar*, *Twelfth Night*, *As You Like It*, *Measure for Measure*, *The Winter's Tale* and *The Tempest*. Shakespeare wrote for an audience over half of whom were probably illiterate. Everyone was used to listening to stories and music from their earliest childhood. At school they learnt largely by rote, reciting and repeating information aurally. They developed their ability to listen and distinguish sounds to an acute pitch we have almost entirely lost today, obsessed as we are by the visual. Puns, antitheses, and plays-on-words were meat and drink to an Elizabethan audience, and the stage was where they heard words being most richly and eloquently used. Writers could afford to be wayward about punctuation and spelling, even where their own names were concerned (there were dozens of different spellings of 'Shakespeare'), because listening was everything, and the *sound* of words communicates at a deeper level than simple meaning – a theme we shall constantly return to. Viola's line 'How will this fadge?' may look difficult to us on the page: in the theatre it seems to be readily understood. I have been amazed how much foreign audiences, with only a partial knowledge of English, understand quite sophisticated wordplay simply by listening.

The actor's first job is of course to understand what is being said. For this we need the help of a text with good footnotes and glossary. This in turn should lead to an understanding of the more crucial question: what is the character thinking? The indications in Shakespeare's language as to rhythm, stress, intonation, pace and pauses will help us to a greater and subtler realisation of both meaning and emotion. Thought, feeling, and response to language exist as an organic whole. We can't regulate the process by prioritising one over the other. Everyone starts with the text, but some will respond first to meaning, others to sound and shape. But the final intention is the same – to be clear about what Shakespeare, and in turn your character, is doing. Once we are clear, then there's a good chance the audience will understand and appreciate a passage which might defeat them when read.

VERSE

The sight of VERSE on a page can be daunting, and might suggest that everyone speaks in the same formal idiom. But as soon as we start speaking the verse out loud, even if there are passages we don't understand, it comes to life. Individual character immediately starts to emerge. As the poet Seamus Heaney says, 'What was hypnotic read aloud had been perplexing when sight-read for meaning only.' Granville Barker memorably said that in one of Shakespeare's earliest plays, *Romeo and Juliet*, he had already solved 'at a stroke all the essential problems of the dramatic use of blank verse'.[3] He could easily have written Juliet's homely, chattering nurse in prose (and it's printed as such in both quartos and folio), but in fact it's in fairly regular verse:

> Even or odd, of all days in the year
> Come Lammas Eve at night shall she be fourteen.
> Susan and she – God rest all Christian souls! –
> Were of an age. Well, Susan is with God;
> She was too good for me. But, as I said,
> On Lammas Eve at night shall she be fourteen,
> That shall she, marry, I remember it well.
> 'Tis since the earthquake now eleven years,
> And she was weaned – I never shall forget it –
> Of all the days of the year upon that day,
> For I had then laid wormwood to my dug.
> Sitting in the sun under the dovehouse wall.
> My lord and you were then at Mantua.
> Nay, I do bear a brain! But, as I said,
> When it did taste the wormwood on the nipple
> Of my dug and felt it bitter, pretty fool,
> To see it tetchy and fall out wi'th' dug! (1.3.18–34)

This is a bravura display of reproducing the fits and starts of colloquial speech. It also contrasts with the verse of the other two women in the scene. Lady Capulet's language has a consciously wrought formality and is rich in metaphor and rhyme:

> Read o'er the volume of young Paris' face,
> And find delight writ there with beauty's pen.
> Examine every married lineament,
> And see how one another lends content;
> And what obscured in this fair volume lies
> Find written in the margin of his eyes. (1.3.83–8)

Juliet also uses metaphor, rhyme and alliteration, but her speech has the simple, dutiful gravity of a teenage daughter:

> I'll look to like, if looking liking move;
> But no more deep will I endart mine eye
> Than your consent gives strength to make it fly.
>   (1.3.99–101)

From quite early in his career Shakespeare understood how to make verse work for him and help to individualise character.

THE IAMBIC PENTAMETER

The IAMBIC is two syllables with the stress on the second, so that it scans 'de-DUM' or ' ˘ — ' (short long). Five such 'de-DUMs', or FEET, make up a PENTAMETER ('penta' is Greek for five). The Elizabethans adopted this form because it most closely approximates to the normal rhythms of English speech – for example, 'I want to go to bed and sleep till ten; don't wake me up for anything at all':

    ˘ —   ˘ — ˘ —   ˘ —   ˘ —

I want to go to bed and sleep till ten;

    ˘   —   ˘   ˘   ˘ —˘ —   ˘ —

Don't wake me up for anything at all.

Juliet's speech above is also a regular example:

    ˘   — ˘ — ˘ — ˘   —˘   —

I'll look to like, if looking liking move;

    ˘   —   ˘   — ˘ —˘   —   ˘   —

But no more deep will I endart mine eye

    ˘   —   ˘ —   ˘   —   ˘   ˘—

Than your consent gives strength to make it fly.

The syllables we would naturally stress – 'look', 'like', 'look . . . ', 'lik . . . ', 'move' – are all second syllables (DUM or —). There is no *rule* that says we *have* to stress those five syllables. In line 2, for example, we might want to stress 'But' rather than 'no'. This would make the first foot 'DUM-de' or ' — ˘ ', and is known as a TROCHEE. The line would still flow quite naturally. We might go further and want to stress both the 'But' and the 'no'. If we speak this out loud we'll hear that by calling attention to both the first two syllables we have seriously disrupted the flow of the line. We then have to decide if this is right for what Juliet is doing in the speech. Since her apparent intention is to be dutiful and submissive the jarring effect of 'BUT NO' is probably unhelpful. If there is a rule, it is: scan each line as if it is a regular iambic pentameter; see where we would naturally break with regularity because we feel the stress does not lie on the second half of the foot; and be aware of the effect this disruption makes. In fact Shakespeare frequently wants us to disrupt the line.

Shakespeare didn't invent the iambic pentameter or BLANK
VERSE ('blank' because it doesn't rhyme). Henry Howard, Earl
of Surrey seems to have originated both blank verse and the
English sonnet form in the 1540s. The French, whose Latinate
language usually takes more syllables to say anything, felt happier with a six-foot line (the ALEXANDRINE). Shakespeare
occasionally uses this for monumental effect. King Lear's opening line has six feet:

   ⌣ — ⌣   —   ⌣   —   ⌣   — ⌣ —   ⌣   —
Attend the lords of France and Burgundy, Gloucester.

In his early plays Shakespeare, like his contemporary Marlowe,
used fairly regular verse, each line ending with a slight break (END-
STOP). In *2 Henry VI* (1591?) Humphrey, Duke of Gloucester,
addresses the court:

> Brave peers of England, pillars of the state,
> To you Duke Humphrey must unload his grief,
> Your grief, the common grief of all the land.
> What – did my brother Henry spend his youth,
> His valour, coin, and people in the wars?
> Did he so often lodge in open field
> In winter's cold and summer's parching heat
> To conquer France, his true inheritance?   (1.1.71–8)

Each line has ten syllables and is end-stopped. Lines 2, 5, 6, 7
and 8 are regular iambics. Lines 1, 3 and 4 all start with syllables
that call out to be stressed – 'Brave', 'Your', and 'What'. We
might also want to stress the syllables that follow – 'peers',
'grief', and 'did'. This drawing attention to the start of a line is
a rhetorical trick Shakespeare used all his life. But despite this
slight irregularity, the speech can sound very monotonous
spoken out loud; and it continues in the same de-DUM, de-
DUM, end-stopped manner for another twenty lines.

Shakespeare was a quick learner, and an even braver experimenter. In *Romeo and Juliet*, written perhaps four years later,
Romeo starts in grandly emotional, if rather hackneyed, verse
that identifies a teenager in love with love. The irregular beat,
however, shows his perturbation:

   ⌣ — ⌣ —   ⌣   —⌣—   —⌣ ⌣
O heavy lightness, serious vanity,

   ⌣ — ⌣   — ⌣ ⌣   —   — ⌣   —
Misshapen chaos of well-seeming forms,

$$\overline{}\ \smile\ \smile\ \overline{}\quad\overline{}\quad\overline{}\quad\overline{}\quad\overline{}\quad\overline{}\quad\overline{}$$
Feather of lead, bright smoke, cold fire, sick health,

$$\overline{}\quad\overline{}\ \smile\ \overline{}\quad\smile\ \overline{}\ \smile\ \quad\overline{}\ \smile\ \overline{}$$
Still-waking sleep, that is not what it is!   (1.1.171–5)

By the end of the play, when real love has brought crisis, his verse has become terse and direct:

> Is it e'en so? Then I defy you, stars.
> Thou knowest my lodging. Get me ink and paper,
> And hire posthorses. I will hence tonight.   (5.1.24–6)

The cosmic enormity of 'Then I defy you, stars' is all the more eloquent for being so simply stated, surrounded by lines of such plainness. This is not to say that Shakespeare doesn't use highly wrought verse in his later plays, but only when there is an emotional necessity for it. Othello, convinced of Desdemona's guilt, declares in almost regular iambics:

> Arise, black vengeance, from the hollow hell.
> Yield up, O love, thy crown and hearted throne
> To tyrannous hate! Swell, bosom, with thy freight,
> For 'tis of aspics' tongues.   (3.3.451–4)

But when, at the end of the play, Othello realises suicide is his only viable option, he starts his final speech with great simplicity and understatement:

> Soft you, a word or two before you go.
> I have done the state some service, and they know't.
> No more of that.   (5.2.347–9)

These two speeches show the enormous flexibility of the iambic pentameter, that it can move from overblown bombast to prosaic statement, while still retaining its beat. By the end of his career Shakespeare stretched his verse almost beyond its limitations, throwing regularity to the winds in the character of Leontes in *The Winter's Tale*:

> It is a bawdy planet, that will strike
> Where 'tis predominant; and 'tis powerful. Think it:
> From east, west, north, and south, be it concluded,
> No barricado for a belly. Know't,
> It will let in and out the enemy

With bag and baggage. Many thousand on's
Have the disease and feel't not. – How now, boy?
                    (1.2.202–8)

Lines 1 and 5 scan regularly; lines 4, 6 and 7 can just about be fitted into a pentameter, but lines 2 and 3 are very irregular. Stresses vary enormously. In line 3, with four points of the compass, we might want six stresses; in line 6 only four; followed by six in line 7. Despite this, the structure of the iambic pentameter is still discernible; Shakespeare hasn't abandoned it, and neither should we. Try and make it scan regularly; depart from it knowingly.

The beat of the line can sometimes produce unfamiliar stresses; '-èd' being the commonest example. Count the number of syllables. If there are ten, as in Othello's 'I saw't not, thought it not, it harmed not me', then 'harmed' is one syllable, not 'harmèd'. A few lines later Othello declares, 'Farewell the plumed troops and the big wars'. There are only nine syllables here, unless we make it 'plumèd'. Normally maths isn't needed, your ear will tell you what to do naturally. Fortunately most editions mark the '-èds', and footnotes should also help you out in more esoteric exceptions. '-ion' sometimes has to be two syllables, as in

　　　˘ — ˘ —　　　˘ — —
'opin-ee-on', not 'opin-yun'.

Troilus is scanned sometimes as two, sometimes three syllables, as in 'Troy-lus' or 'Tro-ee-lus'.

　　—˘ ˘ — —　　　— —˘ — ˘
'Coriolanus' is on occasions 'Coriolanus',

with a stress on the long second syllable. Finally, Richard II's line will only scan,

　˘ — ˘ — ˘ — ˘ — ˘ —
My manors, rents, revenues, I forgo,

with the stress on the second syllable of 'revENues'. These oddities, however, are rare, and a good edition will nearly always guide you.

THE STRUCTURE OF THE VERSE

There are a number of other structural devices that help us to serve the verse. Where there are eleven syllables the final one is usually unstressed – now called a LIGHT ENDING. The most famous line in Shakespeare is an example of this:

    ˘ — ˘ — ˘ —   ˘ — ˘   — ˘
    To be or not to be; that is the quest/ion.

Sometimes Shakespeare preserves the scansion of the line by the ELISION of two syllables, as in Hamlet's 'That patient merit of th'unworthy takes'. Pronunciation of these can be tricky: best to make the slightest of breaks between 'th-' and 'un', rather than say 'thun'. One way to achieve this is to *suggest*, or at any rate *think*, the missing vowel. On no account say 'toot' in Horatio's line, 'So Guildenstern and Rosencrantz go to't'! Sometimes Shakespeare's elisions are simply a representation of ordinary speech; 'y'are' for 'you are', and 'give't' for 'give it'. When in doubt, go for what is most intelligible for a modern audience.

    The CAESURA is a break, or at least a check, in a verse line. It may be marked by a comma, a colon, or a full stop; for example: 'O heavy lightness, serious vanity'; 'Not so, not so; his life is paralleled'; or 'Thou knowest my lodging. Get me ink and paper'. It very rarely indicates a full pause, which might come at the end of the line if there is a full stop. The caesura may not necessarily come in the middle of the line:

    Soft you, / a word or two before you go.
    I have done the state some service, / and they know't.

But we can sense that virtually every verse line has some sort of caesura – often a break in the syntax after an adverbial clause, or between subject and verb; for example, Juliet's couplet:

    But no more deep / will I endart mine eye
    Than your consent / gives strength to make it fly.

The flow of the line need not be disrupted, but 'thinking' the caesura often means you can launch the second half of the line with greater emphasis: it forms a kind of springboard. Shakespeare moves the caesura around a great deal to vary the tempo and yet maintain the flow of the argument.

Where a speech ends on a HALF-LINE, and the next speaker completes the pentameter with another half-line, it is an indication that the cue should be taken up immediately. In the later plays whole scenes are written in this fashion. Without such direction Lear's reconciliation with Cordelia could be slow and sentimental:

> LEAR   Would I were assured
> Of my condition.
> CORDELIA   O look upon me, sir,
> And hold your hands in benediction o'er me.
> You must not kneel.
> LEAR   Pray do not mock me.   (4.6.49–52)

Cordelia immediately takes up her cue on 'condition', with the added charge of driving to the end of the line because she needs Lear to take in who she is. She might pause at the full stop after 'o'er me' to allow Lear to kneel, but Lear comes in immediately with 'Pray do not mock me'. This is a vital indication of their new relationship. Cordelia is horrified that her father should kneel to her, but Lear in turn is desperate not to be laughed at.

Where the sense of one line runs directly on into the next this is called ENJAMBMENT (from the French for 'stride over'). This raises the much debated question of END-STOPPING. Some maintain that the end of each line should be marked, not by stopping or necessarily taking a breath, but by a tiny sense break, an acknowledgement that the whole line has done its work before launching into the next. Take any speech of Shakespeare and we will find that we are marking this quite naturally most of the time. The bulk of the verse has the important meaning in the last words of the line. In his 'To be or not to be' soliloquy, Hamlet is driving towards the final words, 'question', 'suffer', 'fortune', 'troubles', 'sleep', 'end', 'shocks', 'consummation', etc.

> GERTRUDE   And for your part, Ophelia, I do wish
> That your good beauties be the happy cause
> Of Hamlet's wildness; so shall I hope your virtues
> Will bring him to his wonted way again,
> To both your honours.
> OPHELIA   Madam, I wish it may.   (3.1.40–44)

The first three lines are enjambments, though they drive towards 'wish', 'cause', and 'virtues'. 'To both your honours' could follow a slight hesitation (the preceding comma is in the folio), though Ophelia dutifully picks up her cue. In the first line Gertrude might take a tiny break after 'Ophelia', but the 'wish' carries naturally into the second line, just as 'happy cause' leads to 'of Hamlet's wildness'. Then comes the break at the caesura, which launches Gertrude into her second 'hope': that 'your virtues will bring him to his wonted way again'. How much should the ends of these lines be marked? Peter Hall argues that they are 'the herald of the next complex thought . . . a going-on point, an energetic hesitation that summons up the strength to proceed and define the next line'.[4] I am not fully persuaded. In any text an actor knows that to run a sentence together in one breath is the clearest way to deliver the thought, the one most easily understood by the audience, and in comedy often the best way to get the laugh (Shaw and Wilde are witness to that). Hesitation, however energetic, can be an impediment. Othello, in full flow, might not want to end-stop half the lines in:

> Never, Iago. Like to the Pontic Sea,
> Whose icy current and compulsive course
> Ne'er knows retiring ebb, but keeps due on
> To the Propontic and the Hellespont,
> Even so my bloody thoughts with violent pace
> Shall ne'er look back, ne'er ebb to humble love,
> Till that a capable and wide revenge
> Swallow them up.   (3.3.456–63)

Shakespeare would seem to have used enjambment as a way of escaping from the monotony of the heavily end-stopped line, but no handy Elizabethan manual exists to tell us how he wanted his verse spoken. It must finally be down to the actor's instinct. The words exist to communicate the character's thoughts to the audience. Each actor communicates in her own individual way. As Sheila Hancock remarked, 'If I let it flow, just happen, it seemed the most natural thing in the world.'[5]

Just as Shakespeare indicates where he wants a line to be taken up on cue, so he writes in PAUSES. We can take a pause at the end of a line if the sense and the emotion justify it. Pausing to search for a word or phrase is a commonplace of modern naturalism, but it should be used very sparingly in blank verse. Shakespeare sometimes writes in hesitations in the form of parentheses, as he does in the Nurse's speech quoted above. He often writes three images in succession to indicate the character striving to find the best phrase, but his verse always works best if you don't disrupt its natural beat. But there is no absolute rule. Macbeth's 'Tomorrow and tomorrow and tomorrow' works well as a complete statement, but taking slight pauses after the first two 'tomorrows' seem to me equally valid.

A pause is clearly indicated when Shakespeare leaves a verse line incomplete. Just before Lear goes out into the storm he says, 'No, I'll not weep.' As if in explanation of the missing three feet the folio adds a stage direction: 'Storm and tempest' (did the Globe soundman have to squeeze his thunder into the space of three iambics, or is that sanctity of the verse-line gone mad?). Sometimes the text is not so clear:

CAMILLO   Business, my lord? I think most understand
Bohemia stays here longer.
LEONTES   Ha?
CAMILLO   Stays here longer.
LEONTES   Ay, but why?
CAMILLO   To satisfy your highness, and the entreaties
Of our most gracious mistress.
LEONTES   Satisfy?
                    (*The Winter's Tale*, 1.2.229–35)

The folio prints 'Ha!', 'Stayes here longer' and 'I, but why?' as three separate lines (as does the Oxford/Norton text), and perhaps that was Shakespeare's intention. However the lines are laid out, there's an open invitation to choose one or even two pauses. Camillo might pause before repeating 'Stays here longer', or Leontes might then take a pause trying to gauge how much Camillo knows, or Camillo might pause after 'Ay, but why?' as he tries to phrase a diplomatic answer. Leontes picks up his cue immediately on 'Satisfy?'

At the end of *Love's Labour's Lost* Mercade enters with the terrible news:

MERCADE   The King your father –
PRINCESS   Dead, for my life.
MERCADE   Even so. My tale is told.
BIRON   Worthies, away. The scene begins to cloud.
                    (5.2.702–4)

A pause is possible after 'The King your father, or after 'My tale is told', but not between 'Dead for my life' and 'Even so.'

Mercade is so relieved that the Princess understands his message that he replies immediately. It is acute psychology – and one of my favourite moments on stage. The space between thoughts can be as valuable as thoughts expressed in words.

RHYME

The Elizabethan love of RHYME is something we find particularly hard to embrace. 66 per cent of the verse in *Love's Labour's Lost* is rhymed, and Shakespeare even jokes at his own expense:

> BIRON   When shall you see me write a thing in rhyme,
> Or groan for Joan, or spend a minute's time
> In pruning me? When shall you hear that I
> Will praise a hand, a foot, a face, an eye,
> A gait, a state, a brow, a breast, a waist,
> A leg, a limb?
> KING   Soft, whither away so fast?   (4.3.177–82)

The internal rhymes are groan-worthy, and the King can (and Richard Griffiths did in rehearsal) reduce the rest of the cast to helpless laughter by pronouncing his final 'fast' as 'faist'. Nevertheless, the rhyme is there for a purpose and the challenge has to be met. It is often associated, as above, with fantasy, love, magic and escapism. In *A Midsummer Night's Dream* when the lovers first enter the wood they use rhyme extensively:

> HELENA   Lysander, if you live, good sir, awake.
> LYSANDER   And run through fire I will for thy sweet sake.
> Transparent Helena, nature shows art
> That through thy bosom makes me see thy heart.
> (2.2.108–111)

But as the quarrels thicken and the wood loses its charm, so rhyme disappears. Rhyme can have a witty, epigrammatic quality:

> ROSALINE   I dare not call them fools, but this I think:
> When they are thirsty, fools would fain have drink.
> (*Love's Labours Lost*, 5.2.371–2)

It can act as a trailer for a forthcoming scene:

> MACBETH   It is concluded. Banquo, thy soul's flight,
> If it find heaven, must find it out tonight.   (3.1.142–3)

Shakespeare sometimes uses it to suggest an ancient incantation, as in the Duke's strange four-beat verse that ends Act 3 of *Measure for Measure:*

> Twice treble shame on Angelo,
> To weed my vice, and let his grow!
> O, what may man within him hide,
> Though angel on the outward side!   (3.1.489–92)

And of course it is used extensively to close a scene or a play:

> ORSINO   But when in other habits you are seen,
> Orsino's mistress, and his fancy's queen.
> *(Twelfth Night,* 5.1.374–5)

In none of these examples should we try to avoid the rhyme or hide it as if we're ashamed of it. We need to find out why the character feels the need to use rhyme and then incorporate it into our concept. Biron and Rosaline are compulsive talkers who delight in expressing themselves rhythmically. Macbeth has come to a decision and is ironically aware of its terrible implication. He uses rhyme *knowingly,* as does Orsino in lighter vein, and the rhyme can be hit quite hard. The lovers in the *Dream* are partly conscious of role-playing in their protestations, though the rhyme should be touched on quite lightly or it will seem too artificial. Experiment in rehearsal is needed. It is surprising what different effects rhyme can produce, from joyous to chilling.

MONOSYLLABLES AND STICHOMYTHIA

Shakespeare uses MONOSYLLABLES to enormous effect. Sometimes they contrast with a passage of bombast or grandiloquence. Hamlet, confronted by Ophelia's grave, shouts:

> And if thou prate of mountains, let them throw
> Millions of acres on us, till our ground,
> Singeing his pate against the burning zone,
> Make Ossa like a wart.

And then adds ironically:

> Nay, and thou'lt mouth,
> I'll rant as well as thou.   (5.1.265–9)

Monosyllables always have a simplicity and a directness, which slows the verse down. Shakespeare experiments with them in his sonnets, as in the great opening of Number 94:

> They that have power to hurt and will do none,
> That do not do the thing they most do show.

If we rattle through these lines fast they sound trite. They demand to be taken slowly, to be given air. Characters almost always use monosyllables at moments of stress or solemnity, whether Othello's approaching murder:

> It is the cause, it is the cause, my soul

or Prospero's renunciation of his magic arts:

> Ye elves of hills, brooks, standing lakes, and groves.

Taken at the right tempo, they have an extraordinary poetic resonance. It is left to Edgar to conclude *King Lear*:

> The weight of this sad time we must obey,
> Speak what we feel, not what we ought to say.
> The oldest hath borne most. We that are young
> Shall never see so much, nor live so long.   (5.3.298–301)

STICHOMYTHIA, much used in Greek drama, was a favourite device of Shakespeare's, particularly in his early plays. The dialogue unfolds in alternate lines, usually in sharp dispute, and characterised by antithesis and repetition of the opponent's words – in this case with bawdy intent, if 'dance' is taken to imply sex.

> BIRON   Did not I dance with you in Brabant once?
> ROSALINE   Did not I dance with you in Brabant once?
> BIRON   I know you did.
> ROSALINE   How needless was it then
> To ask the question!
> BIRON   You must not be so quick.
> ROSALINE   'Tis 'long of you, that spur me with such
>   questions.
> BIRON   Your wit's too hot, it speeds too fast, 'twill tire.
> ROSALINE   Not till it leave the rider in the mire.
> BIRON   What time o' day?
> ROSALINE   The hour that fools should ask.
> BIRON   Now fair befall your mask.
> ROSALINE   Fair fall the face it covers.
> BIRON   And send you many lovers.

ROSALINE   Amen, so you be none.
BIRON   Nay, then will I be gone.
                    (*Love's Labour's Lost*, 2.1.113–26)

It's verbal tennis. It requires great concentration, pace and wit, as we whack the ball back over the net. Though much used in comedy, it is also effective in confrontations between Richard III and Lady Anne, and between Brutus and Cassius.

PROSE

Over a quarter of Shakespeare's text is in PROSE, though the balance varies from play to play. He never repeated his early experiments with writing entirely in verse in *King John* and *Richard II*. In a later play the Gardeners' scene in *Richard II* (3.4), for example, would almost certainly have been in prose. The comedies have most prose; *As You Like It* 40 per cent, *Twelfth Night* 60 per cent, and the very domestic *Merry Wives of Windsor* 87 per cent. The tragedies average 25 per cent, with *Macbeth* and *Antony and Cleopatra* having only 10 per cent.

Shakespeare found prose useful in several broad areas; firstly, in highly structured, almost Ciceronian rhetoric, whether of Brutus' carefully prepared oration:

As Caesar loved me, I weep for him. As he was fortunate,
I rejoice at it. As he was valiant, I honour him. But as he
was ambitious, I slew him. There is tears for his love, joy
for his fortune, honour for his valour, and death for his
ambition.   (*Julius Caesar*, 3.2.23–6)

or of Falstaff's outrageous excuses:

I would be sorry, my lord, but it should be thus. I never
knew yet but rebuke and check was the reward of valour.
Do you think me a swallow, an arrow, or a bullet? Have I
in my poor and old motion the expedition of thought? I
have speeded hither with the very extremest inch of
possibility.   (*2 Henry IV*, 4.2.28–32)

Both these speeches are extremely rhythmical and clearly stressed. The argument is developed with a sense of rational balance and antithesis, and set out with a lawyer-like seriousness and formality. A lot of breath is required: sentences need to be carried through right to their end, and words and phrases relished. The ill-judged nature of Brutus' formal rhetoric is contrasted with the much freer and apparently spontaneous verse of Antony:

> I speak not to disprove what Brutus spoke,
> But here I am to speak what I do know.
> You all did love him once, not without cause.
> What cause withholds you then to mourn for him?
> O judgement, thou art fled to brutish beasts,
> And men have lost their reason! (*He weeps.*) Bear with me,
> My heart is in the coffin there with Caesar,
> And I must pause till it come back to me.   (3.2.97–104)

On occasions Shakespeare's prose is so close to verse that it's difficult to decide which he intended. In *Romeo and Juliet* the first, so-called 'bad', quarto (1597) prints Mercutio's Queen Mab speech in verse, while the second, so-called 'good', quarto (1599) and the folio both print it in prose. When the demented Lear meets the blind Gloucester near Dover, his savage reflections on society are so fractured that no two editors can agree what is verse and what prose. Macbeth is so distraught at Banquo's ghost that he throws the iambic to the winds:

> If trembling I inhabit then, protest me
> The baby of a girl. Hence, horrible shadow,
> Unreal mock'ry, hence!   (3.4.104–6)

Conversely, prose is sometimes only a beat away from blank verse. Duke Vincentio counsels Isabella:

> The hand that hath made you fair hath made you good.
> The goodness that is cheap in beauty makes beauty brief
> in goodness; but grace, being the soul of your complexion,
> shall keep the body of it ever fair.
> (*Measure for Measure*, 3.1.181–4)

There can be no confusion, however, when Shakespeare uses prose with colloquial (if bawdy) naturalism. In *The Merry Wives of Windsor* Hugh Evans quizzes Mistress Page's son, William:

> EVANS   Come hither, William. Hold up your head. Come.
> MRS PAGE   Come on, sirrah. Hold up your head. Answer your master; be not afraid.
> EVANS   William, how many numbers is in nouns?
> WILLIAM   Two.
> MRS QUICKLY   Truly, I thought there had been one

number more, because they say "Od's nouns'.
EVANS   Peace your tattlings! – What is 'fair', William?
WILLIAM   'Pulcher'.
MRS QUICKLY   Polecats? There are fairer things than
polecats, sure.
EVANS   You are a very simplicity 'oman. I pray you peace.
(4.1.14–25)

Lady Macbeth sleepwalks in startled, fitful prose:

> Out, damned spot; out, I say. One, two, – why, then 'tis
> time to do't. Hell is murky. Fie, my lord, fie, a soldier and
> afeard?   (5.1.30–2)

Both these passages allow great licence in tempo and pauses, stemming perhaps from Shakespeare's recognition of the need to give his actors space. But still the potency of repeated words and the sense of rhythm are never far distant. Many of the comic characters, like Touchstone and Toby Belch, speak entirely in prose, though always sharply characterised and laced with verbal wit. Often there is the same structured rhetoric we saw in Falstaff, whether in Dogberry's malapropisms or Bottom's dream. But there's no mistaking the earthiness of Macbeth's porter:

> Knock, knock, knock. Who's there, i'th' name of
> Beelzebub? Here's a farmer that hanged himself on
> th'expectation of plenty! Come in time! Have napkins
> enough about you; here you'll sweat for't.   (2.3.3–6)

PROSE INTO VERSE

There are no fixed rules about this movement, but there's always a reason, and we have to be alive to the development. Some instances are very clear. Beatrice and Benedick speak in prose to one another until Claudio accuses Hero of infidelity, then they move into verse as tragedy looms and revert to prose when left alone. Troilus and Cressida declare their love for one another in verse, while their prosaic pander, Pandarus, speaks in prose; it's romance versus reality. In *As You Like It* Corin and Silvius, though peasants, speak of pastoral love in verse, while Rosalind, Celia and Touchstone, from the court, complain about their weariness in prose. Some shifts are more subtle. Viola woos Olivia in prose, until Olivia unveils her face. Viola is so struck by her beauty that she moves into verse, Olivia continues to tease her in prose, but then she too goes into verse as she becomes more interested in him/her (see pp. 201–2). After 'To be or not to be' Ophelia starts her scene with Hamlet in verse, but Hamlet's sudden attack on 'Ha, ha! Are you honest?' moves them into prose. On Hamlet's exit Ophelia moves back into verse for her distraught but strangely formal 'O, what a noble mind is here o'erthrown'.

When Menenius goes to persuade Coriolanus not to lay siege to Rome, he is stopped by two guards and they begin by talking in verse. As the guards become more eloquent and sarcastic they move the scene into prose. When Coriolanus enters, Menenius makes his plea in prose, but Coriolanus answers in verse. The contrast here is important. Menenius' speech is full of high-flown, artificial rhetoric:

> The glorious gods sit in hourly synod about thy particular prosperity, and love thee no worse than thy old father Menenius does! (5.2.66–8)

Coriolanus' verse is highly compressed and to the point:

> Wife, mother, child, I know not. My affairs
> Are servanted to others.   (5.2.78–9)

Shakespeare may also have intended a contrast with Volumnia's subsequent plea, which remains entirely in verse. Shakespeare seems to have had no set pattern in his head; he moved between prose and verse by instinct. The audience needn't necessarily be aware of the shift, but the help to the actor can be incalculable.

WORDS

At the Globe there was no scenery or lighting. The actors' physical appearance differed little from character to character, play to play, though costumes gave a guide to rank and status and many props are indicated in the text (swords, skulls, hand-kerchiefs, etc.). A great deal therefore was down to the language. The audience depended on WORDS to visualise and understand the rapidly changing dramatic worlds. Shakespeare's scene-setting could be brazenly direct, as in Macbeth's opening line, 'So foul and fair a day I have not seen', or Rosalind's 'Well, this

is the forest of Arden'. On occasions the setting can be much
elaborated, as in the Gentleman's twelve-line description of Lear
'contending with the fretful elements'.

Words are central to the communication of plot and character. Shakespeare alternates between the direct and the complex,
sometimes in the same speech. Hamlet, after his banishment,
questions:

> Now, whether it be
> Bestial oblivion, or some craven scruple
> Of thinking too precisely on th'event –
> A thought which, quartered, hath but one part wisdom
> And ever three parts coward – I do not know
> Why yet I live to say 'This thing's to do',
> Sith I have cause, and will, and strength, and means,
> To do't.   (4.4.39–46)

The sentence begins with a jumble of thoughts and parentheses
which, however interesting, make us wonder if he will ever get to
a clear conclusion. When it comes it could hardly be more direct,
26 monosyllables of apparent frankness. The first part of the sentence is loaded with rich and ambiguous expressions – 'bestial
oblivion', 'craven scruple', 'too precisely'. But the simplicity of
his conclusion is also open to question. Hamlet has 'cause', he
may have 'will', but exiled as he is he has no 'means' and little
'strength'. These seven lines are a revelation of Hamlet's restless,
probing uncertainty. Character in Shakespeare lies in the words.

Shakespeare always relishes the ambiguity and many-layered
sense of words. 'Opinion' in *Troilus and Cressida*, and 'become'
in *Antony and Cleopatra* recur again and again, and take on many
shades of meaning. Thersites exposes verbal disguise: 'love' is
lust, 'fame' and 'honour' merely anger and craftiness. Cicely
Berry (for many years Head of Voice at the RSC) teaches that
meaning isn't just literal translation, 'but lies in the rhythm, the
physical sensation, the multifarious associations and echoes set
up by a word which happens somewhere in our gut'.[6] As
Shakespeare prepared his tragedies he seems possessed by
certain words and motifs which form a network of sense and
allusion. They act as a kind of verbal ground-base to the whole
action. 'Time' is his most constant preoccupation and chimes
through comedy, tragedy and romance. It occurs 44 times in
Macbeth, but 'night', 'darkness', 'blood', 'man', 'done', and

'trust' also form a claustrophobic web. *Othello* examines 'thought', 'sight' and, in particular, 'honesty'; *King Lear* 'sight', 'nature' and 'nothing'. 'Honest' Iago doubts Desdemona's 'honesty'; Lear declares 'nothing will come of nothing' – and in both cases the tragedy is thereby triggered.

METAPHOR AND SIMILE

Shakespeare is rich in imagery – mental pictures, representations in the imagination. His images are most often METAPHORS – words or phrases substituted for the object or action meant. Thus tears are 'the melting mood', the Roman crowd is the serpent 'Hydra', Henry V's yeomen have 'pasture' rather than breeding, and Romeo announces dawn by noting that 'night's candles are burnt out'. The aim is always that the literal will be illuminated and enriched by the transference, and that the mental picture created will stimulate and excite the audience's imagination. Macbeth's own imagination is so great that it constantly stretches to take in the whole planet:

> What hands are here! Ha, they pluck out mine eyes.
> Will all great Neptune's ocean wash this blood
> Clean from my hand? No, this my hand will rather
> The multitudinous seas incarnadine,
> Making the green one red.   (2.2.57–61)

Metaphor does not always involve grandiloquence. It can be an economical way of expressing a complex idea. The mature Shakespeare knew how to describe world-shattering events in terse imagery. When Antony dies, Cleopatra exclaims:

> The crown o'th'earth doth melt. My lord!
> O, withered is the garland of the war.
> The soldier's pole is fall'n. Young boys and girls
> Are level now with men. The odds is gone,
> And there is nothing left remarkable
> Beneath the visiting moon.   (4.16.65–70)

Metaphor can also be used emblematically. In Elizabethan bawdy, 'rose' could denote genitalia, 'death' orgasm or, as above, 'pole' an erect penis. Metaphor can be passed from one character to another, as Juliet does by extending Romeo's image of lips as 'two blushing pilgrims'. The Elizabethans revelled in this 'artfulness' and technical virtuosity. Today we may find some of it overdone and even sentimental ('the melting mood'). But at its best it extends the boundaries of ideas and images, and opens up further possibilities. It is essentially experimental and suggests that language and imagination have limitless reserves to be tapped.

SIMILE compares two objects or ideas more directly, usually by means of 'like' or 'as'. Gloucester characterises human fate: 'As flies to wanton boys are we to the gods, / They kill us for their sport'. Salisbury sees Richard II's glory 'like a shooting star / Fall to the base earth from the firmament', and Macbeth sees pity 'like a naked new-born babe / Striding the blast'. When passion is high Shakespeare mixes metaphor and simile to great effect. Henry V rallies his troops before Harfleur:

> Then lend the eye a terrible aspect,
> Like the brass cannon, let the brow o'erwhelm it
> As fearfully as doth a gallèd rock
> O'erhang and jutty his confounded base,
> Swilled with the wild and wasteful ocean.   (3.1.9–14)

Simile is in a sense a clumsier and more obvious way to create an image. It would weaken Coriolanus' reference to the crowd as 'Hydra' (the many-headed monster) to say '*like* Hydra'. At times, however, the comparison Shakespeare is attempting is too remote and unexpected to be understood without a 'like'. Henry V's 'eye' couldn't suddenly become a 'brass cannon' without some link. Metaphor is usually more compressed and full of energy: it has enormous muscle. For the actor there is no greater challenge than 'new-minting' such imagery within the structure of the verse.

ASSONANCE, ONOMATOPOEIA AND ALLITERATION

There are a large number of terms given to the many patterns of sounds and word order, but these three are probably the most important. ASSONANCE is a rhyming of vowels, or a correspondence in sound. Repeated 'o's were a Shakespeare favourite, as in Ophelia's '*O*, what a n*o*ble mind is here *o*'erthr*o*wn'. But he was alive to all the vowels, as in Henry IV's Machiavellian advocacy of foreign expeditions, 'Be it thy course to b*u*sy g*i*ddy

minds / With foreign quarrels'. An early piece of advice given me
was never let Viola's Sea Captain get drunk. His opening words
are a disaster when slurred: 'This is Illyria, lady'.

ONOMATOPOEIA is a word which imitates its meaning in
sound, as in 'roar', 'coo', and 'murmur'. Shakespeare often uses
words in repetition: 'Knock, knock, knock' grumbles Macbeth's
porter (three gets a laugh where two won't). 'Howl, howl, howl,
howl' cries Lear, who in the earlier storm has employed a whole
armoury of sound: 'Rumble thy bellyful; spit, fire; spout, rain.'
We need to be aware of these devices and use them, without
leaning on them too heavily.

ALLITERATION, the repetition of the sound of a consonant,
will usually do its work without comment, or the effect can be
too calculated or comic. Hamlet doesn't need to hit the 'h's in
'And shall I couple hell? O, fie! Hold, hold, my heart', but where
he intends humour or irony stressing the consonant may help:
'Marry, this is miching malicho. It means mischief.' Alliteration
is sometimes used for outright comic effect as in the
Mechanicals' play in the *Dream*: 'For by thy gracious, golden,
glittering gleams / I trust to take of truest Thisbe sight.'

Alliteration, like rhyme, can be a great aid to memorising a
part. Lear follows three 'd's with four 'p's:

> With my two daughters' dowers digest the third.
> Let pride, which she calls plainness, marry her.
> I do invest you jointly with my power,
> Pre-eminence, and all the large effects
> That troop with majesty.   (1.1.126–30)

Twenty lines later Kent picks up 'plainness', but he contrasts
Lear's concept of majesty that 'troops' with his concept which
'stoops', and then manages to get 'doom' into the same line. They
may be separated by twenty lines, but at some level an attentive
listener will register this. Shakespeare had an ear worthy of Bach
or Mozart.

WORDPLAY AND PUNS

This Mozartian ear led him into continual WORDPLAY. It's a preoccupation that can pass by or even annoy modern audiences.
Ben Jonson made fun of Shakespeare's love of PUNS, but his

isn't an isolated passion – they're common in classical literature and Chaucer, and in contemporaries like Spenser and Donne.[7] They have great comic potential. Beatrice and Benedick wallow in them:

> DON PEDRO   You have put him [Benedick] down, lady,
> you have put him down.
> BEATRICE   So I would not he should do me, my lord, lest
> I should prove the mother of fools.
> (*Much Ado About Nothing*, 2.1.247–9)

The pun here, as so often, is sexual, but it is also central to Beatrice's avowed indifference. Mercutio's very identity is in his wit. He lures Romeo into his web of conceits on 'pumps', 'geese' and 'cheverils', and then rejoices, 'Now art thou sociable, now art thou Romeo, now art thou what thou art by art as well as by nature.' But even in comedies puns are not always intended to be funny. In *As You Like It* Orlando first encounters his elder brother Oliver:

> OLIVER   Now, sir, what make [do] you here?
> ORLANDO   Nothing. I am not taught to make [produce]
> anything.   (1.1.25–6)

The pun on 'make' is full of bitter irony, and the actor can probably afford to put the word in heavy inverted commas. The dying Mercutio refers to himself as 'a grave man', and the Merchant of Venice, about to have a pound of flesh cut out of his breast, says he'll pay his debt 'with all my heart'. Hamlet is so full of linguistic improvisation that he cannot stop himself punning at Polonius' expense:

> POLONIUS   I did enact Julius Caesar. I was killed i'th'
> Capitol. Brutus killed me.
> HAMLET   It was a brute part of him to kill so capital a
> calf there.   (3.2.93–5)

It is possible that the joke here was enhanced for cast and audience by the fact that the actors playing Polonius and Hamlet had played Julius Caesar and Brutus the previous year (1599). When Guildenstern refuses to play upon the pipe he is handed, Hamlet upbraids him, 'You would play upon me. You would seem to know my stops.' These puns go to the heart of a scheming, manipulative court.

The pun is an overt, sometimes crude, way of demonstrating that words rarely have single meanings. Shakespeare's characters no sooner conjure up a word or phrase than they are struck by other possible interpretations. This expands the whole world of the play, and puns are therefore central to Shakespeare's exploration of the possibilities of language and character. They can be a form of code, an image perhaps of a secret agenda that operates in many of the plays, where contemporary questions of politics, religion and sexuality could not be openly discussed for fear of the censor. The actor can't afford to ignore them; they have to be made part of the character and relished.

DOUBLES AND REPETITIONS

Another Shakespeare fixation were DOUBLES or HENDIADYS: meaning two words, usually nouns or adjectives of similar sense, joined by 'and'. The words reinforce and define one another, but almost always suggest a comparison or a movement in different directions. Othello's 'the head and front of my offending' may sound like synonyms, but both words are so many-layered that they enrich one another. Cassius has a 'lean and hungry look': he may be lean because he's hungry, but the hunger may be ambition. *Hamlet* is steeped in such doubles. Hamlet talks of 'honour and dignity', 'the whips and scorns of time', and 'things rank and gross'. Polonius' advice to his children includes 'rank and station', 'select and generous', 'sanctified and pious', and even 'words and talk'. Ophelia catches her father's habit with 'steep and thorny', 'expectancy and rose', and 'form and feature'.[8] They are so frequent that they set up a rhythm and a tune that characterises the whole play. It is as if one word or image is never sufficient. Shakespeare no sooner chooses a word than he wants to set it off against another and observe the contrast. The actor has to be aware of this constant need to redefine, to describe more exactly, or sometimes more ambiguously, what she is thinking.

REPETITION is another key element. It is used most obviously to make sure the audience understands the importance of a particular theme, but, as always, it illuminates the character who is speaking. Hamlet feels the need to repeat 'O villain, villain, smiling, damned villain' and then to write it down to make doubly sure. Richard II wants to make it clear that no one else can un-anoint his divinity:

> With mine own tears I wash away my balm,
> With mine own hands I give away my crown,
> With mine own tongue deny my sacred state,
> With mine own breath release all duteous oaths.
>
> (4.1.197–200)

The repetition of a word or phrase always sets up other resonances. How clear is the word, how reliable? Lear's five 'never's, Hamlet's three 'words', Macbeth's three 'tomorrow's make us question and re-evaluate. Sometimes the actor tries to play one or more repetition differently, sometimes the bald monotony is more telling. Repetition also brings out double meanings. When Othello says 'Put out the light and then put out the light', he sets the extinguishing of a candle against the extinguishing of Desdemona's life. 'If it were done when 'tis done, then 'twere well / It were done quickly' is central to Macbeth's doubts of salvation. Shakespeare often chooses to repeat the simplest of words – 'do', 'be', 'see' – to test their many connections. 'Nature', 'seeming', 'time' he returns to again and again for the actor to probe.

IRONY, PARADOX, AMBIGUITY AND ANTITHESIS

There is no more fraught question in Shakespeare than how much IRONY is intended, moment to moment, scene to scene. A French professor once floored me, when I gave a paper in Paris, by asking if I thought the entire play of *Coriolanus* was an irony. In 1756 irony was defined as 'a figure of speech by which one indicates the opposite of what one says' – a useful definition for an actor, though much lies in the degree of 'indication' (see pp. 115–16). Edmund in *King Lear* will leave the audience in no doubt how much he despises Edgar when he calls him 'a brother noble' – the inversion gives an added sneer.

A broader definition of irony is 'an outcome of events that mocks their promise', a disparity between appearance and reality that lies at the heart of so many of the plays. Claudius and Lear's courts appear to be settled and united, Macbeth seems to be a loyal and admired subject, Othello and Desdemona have a loving and understanding relationship guarded by a watchful Iago. The plays explore the realities of these appearances. Tragic irony also explores the contrast between individual hopes and actions, and the unyielding power of fate. Lear hopes by dividing up his kingdom to enjoy a peaceful retirement. Is it Goneril and Regan or fate that has other plans?

The actor, however, is more concerned with the immediate demands of the text. Some irony is clearly placed, as when Mercutio remarks of his mortal wound,

> No, 'tis not so deep as a well, nor so wide as a church door; but 'tis enough, 'twill serve.   (3.1.92–3)

Richard II mocks kingship when he imagines the antic death

> Allowing him a breath, a little scene,
> To monarchise, be feared, and kill with looks.   (3.2.160–1)

Lear in his madness discovers ironic truths that he had ignored his whole life:

> Plate sin with gold,
> And the strong lance of justice hurtless breaks;
> Arm it in rags, a pygmy's straw does pierce it.
> (4.5.155–7)

Hamlet investigates the ironies of his mother's remarriage in:

> Thrift, thrift, Horatio. The funeral baked meats
> Did coldly furnish forth the marriage tables.
> (1.2.179–80)

When Ophelia protests that his father's death was not two hours but 'twice two months' ago, Hamlet exclaims, 'So long? . . . O heavens, die two months ago and not forgotten yet!' Lightly touched this is ironic; heavily placed it is nearer to SARCASM, an important but not always identifiable distinction, since sarcasm leaves no one in doubt that the opposite is intended. Irony always has a certain ambiguity. Shakespeare's fools also love irony, from Feste's put-down of Olivia's mourning, 'The more fool, madonna, to mourn for your brother's soul being in heaven', to Touchstone's summary of Corin's rustic wisdom, 'Such a one is a natural philosopher' (one meaning of 'natural' being 'idiot').

In many passages the irony is more debatable: the apparent may be the whole meaning. Is Lear being ironic when he says,

'While we unburdened crawl toward death', and 'I will be the pattern of all patience'? Is Henry V sincere when he says that he will 'believe in heart' that what his archbishop speaks is 'in your conscience washed / As pure as sin with baptism'? When the murderers agree to kill Banquo, how ironic is Macbeth when he says, 'Your spirits shine through you'?

Irony is much connected with PARADOX, a union of contradictory words that yields an unexpected truth. Falstaff's wit feeds on paradox:

> LORD CHIEF JUSTICE   Your means are very slender, and your waste is great.
> FALSTAFF   I would it were otherwise; I would my means were greater and my waist slenderer.
> (*2 Henry IV*, 1.2.128–31)

Claudius' opening speech tackles the tricky question of his marriage to Gertrude with paradoxical rhetoric – his 'sometime sister',

> Have we as 'twere with a defeated joy
> With one auspicious and one dropping eye,
> With mirth in funeral and with dirge in marriage,
> In equal scale weighing delight and dole,
> Taken to wife.   (1.2.10–14)

The whole speech could be taken as ironic since Claudius in reality feels neither 'defeat' nor 'dole'. The speech is also rich in OXYMORON, a combination of two usually contradictory terms, of which 'defeated joy', 'mirth in funeral', and 'dirge in marriage' are perfect examples.

Shakespeare always delighted in AMBIGUITY, and this is another minefield for the actor (see pp. 115–8). Tullus Aufidius promises Coriolanus 'a noble memory', but the whole play has examined the ambiguity of 'nobility', 'name' and 'fame', just as *Troilus and Cressida* examines 'truth', 'worth' and 'value', or Falstaff deconstructs 'honour'. Words, motives and actions in Shakespeare are open to so many readings. How naive and innocent, or how pompous and self-regarding, is Othello; is 'One that loved not wisely but too well' an accurate summary? How manipulative is the Duke in *Measure for Measure* (see Appendix 1)? Would Macbeth have murdered Duncan without his wife's promptings? Is Prospero triumphant or defeated at the end of *The Tempest*? Their language ripples with alternative meanings and interpretations. Of course Shakespeare may have made it clear to his actors what *he* intended; but now we only have his words, and therefore the luxury and the responsibility of interpretation.

Shakespeare expresses much of his ambiguity and paradox through ANTITHESIS, the juxtaposition of contraries, and we need to be constantly aware of this. When Claudius summarises his attempts to pray, 'My words fly up, my thoughts remain below', 'words' is contrasted with 'thoughts', 'fly' with 'remain', and 'up' with 'below'. It would be almost impossible for the actor to highlight all three antitheses without mangling the flow of the line, so probably better to go for the nouns and prepositions and leave the verbs unstressed. Macbeth explains away the murder of the two grooms: 'Who can be wise, amazed, temperate and furious, / Loyal and neutral in a moment?' This combines antithesis, paradox and irony (since of course he's killed them deliberately). His fear of Banquo is fuelled by the Sisters' antitheses, 'Lesser than Macbeth and greater. / Not so happy, yet much happier.' I feel that when he wrote a key word, it actually hurt Shakespeare not to include its antithesis somewhere in the dialogue. When you see 'rich' you can be sure 'poor' is lurking – perhaps ten lines later.

QUARTO AND FOLIO, PUNCTUATION AND SPELLING

Once Shakespeare had sold a play to his company (or fulfilled his commission), it became their property. Both company and author may have been alert to its publication potential, or the initiative may have come primarily from printers. Nineteen of the plays were individually published in the small quarto format, ranging from *Titus Andronicus* in 1594 to *Othello* in 1622. About a dozen of these are reckoned 'good' quartos, most probably printed from Shakespeare's or the company's own manuscript. There are 'bad' quartos of some eight plays, some thought to be reconstructions from memory by actors in minor parts out to make an illegal buck, while others may reflect cut-down touring versions. Thus the 1603 quarto of *Hamlet* has 2,200 lines (including 'To be or not to be, I there's the point'), and was quickly followed by an authorised quarto of 3,800 lines. It is hard to fathom the choice of plays for quarto publication. *Titus*

Andronicus we know was popular and went into three editions, but why *Troilus and Cressida* but not *Macbeth*, why *Love's Labour's Lost* but not *Twelfth Night*?

The 1623 folio printed 36 plays in all (*Pericles, Two Noble Kinsmen* and *Edward III*, all co-written, were added to the canon later). Comparisons between quartos and folio are often revealing about cuts and rewrites, particularly in the case of *King Lear*, where the folio cuts some 300 lines that appear in the quarto, but adds a further 100. The folio texts may represent Shakespeare's second thoughts, or may simply be the versions the King's Men were playing in the 1620s. These texts seem to have been drawn from prompt-books, transcripts of theatre copies, printed quartos with emendations, and Shakespeare's own papers. Some plays can be ascribed to one or other of these sources, many cannot. So who authorised the text, its spelling and punctuation – Shakespeare, the keeper of the prompt-books, professional copyists, or the various compositors?

These problems can be very important to the actor. If a theatre practitioner notated the texts, this may point to Jacobean theatre practice; if a compositor, it may be to make the plays more readable or easier to fit on the printed page. In other words, are the plays being printed to be read or to be performed? Until the late nineteenth century some editions recorded current stage practice, but even to this day there is a sense that editors rearrange and repunctuate the texts primarily for their readership. The snag is that what makes the most logical sense on the page may not be what works best in the theatre. The actor therefore should never trust that the printed version she has in front of her is necessarily an 'accurate' or 'authorised' text.

The Greek director Karolos Koun told the RSC company in 1967 to learn *Romeo and Juliet* from any text they liked. The late Terence Spencer, editor of the play in the New Penguin Shakespeare, told me that on the first night he could tell which edition each actor had chosen simply from the words and phrasing their texts had indicated to them – it can make that much difference. This is especially true of PUNCTUATION. The only surviving example of what may be Shakespeare's textual handwriting is three pages of *Sir Thomas More*, and these suggest that, like most of his contemporaries, he paid little attention to punctuation. Its systemisation only began with the development of printing.

Joseph Moxon, author of the first English printing manual, advised that it was the compositor's 'task and duty to discern and amend the bad spelling and pointing [punctuation] of his copy'. Though different compositors had different habits, it seems that printers often used colons and semi-colons where we would use full stops. Interestingly, this may reflect the author's or actor's desire to present the speech as a fluid, sustained unit, and cut down on pauses and heavy sense-breaks. Commas, however, often occur at the ends of lines, where we would think the sense carried straight on. Question and exclamation marks sometimes seemed interchangeable.[9] This can create problems. In the folio for example, Macbeth's speech is printed ('u' replaces 'v'):

> She should haue dy'de heereafter;
> There would haue beene a time for such a word:
> To morrow, and to morrow, and to morrow,
> Creepes in this petty pace from day to day,
> To the last Syllable of Recorded time:
> And all our yesterdayes, haue lighted Fooles
> The way to dusty death.   (5.5.17–23)

What are we to make of these punctuations and capital letters? The semi-colon and colon at the ends of the first and second lines may suggest that the speaker should not interrupt the flow of thought as much as he would if there were full stops. Modern editors vary: New Penguin puts a full stop and a dash; Riverside a semi-colon and a full stop; Oxford/Norton two full stops. Each editor is altering the folio punctuation, the only text of *Macbeth* we have, to indicate how he thinks the speech should be phrased. Some actors and directors have reacted by claiming that the folio must be the ultimate authority, but this is clearly unworkable. If we accept that the Elizabethan colon equalled a full stop, then the colon after 'Recorded time' seems very odd. Claims have been made that commas mark places to take breath, but why then a comma after 'yesterdayes'? We certainly wouldn't need to take a breath there, so soon after the colon at 'Recorded time'. Some maintain capital letters mark heavy stresses, but their distribution here seems random. Why stress 'Recorded' but not 'time'; why not 'Dusty Death'? Some bizarre examples of the folio punctuation suggest that compositors used question marks when they'd run out of full stops, or simply reached into the wrong box of type.

Playing about with the punctuation can yield unexpected dividends. In *Much Ado About Nothing* (2.3.199), after Benedick has overheard his 'gulling' by Leonato, Don Pedro and Claudio, he declares in the folio: 'Loue me? why it must be requited.' Most modern editors change the '?' to '!' (already a major acting direction), and add a comma after 'why'. In 1982 at the RSC Derek Jacobi converted the line to: 'Love *me*! Why? It must be requited.'[10] As you can imagine, 'Why?' said expressively enough gets a big laugh. More significantly, it can make him seem less proud and self-assured. This reading caused some academic wrath, but it has been taken up by several subsequent Benedicks. Why look a gift-laugh in the mouth? How can we finally be sure what Shakespeare intended? Perhaps the safest, if most radical, solution is to write the text out without any punctuation at all, and start again from scratch (as most editors of new editions do).

Archaic SPELLING is another fraught area.[11] Some actors love the sound of 'dauncing' and 'burthen', but there is something rather arch about their use. Elizabethan language is difficult enough for some audiences without adding to their problems. What would they make of 'bankrout' [bankrupt] or 'fadom' [fathom]? Total modernisation may, however, rob the actor of useful ammunition. In *Henry V*, once the French ambassador has established that he comes from the Dauphin, Henry might delight in referring to his master as the 'Dolphin'. Some archaisms might help the comedy; Dogberry might like to keep 'vagrom' and 'lanthorn'. Scansion may demand that 'gainst' and 'stonish' are preserved. Rhymes should be observed unless they sound ridiculous. 'further' might justify keeping 'murther', but rhyming 'have' and 'cave' would produce bafflement. Contractions are another problem. 'Thou'rt i'th'right, girl; more o'that,' Lucio urges Isabella. No strict verse line is involved, so such a series of contractions may indicate how Shakespeare wanted it spoken, or it may be a scribe's usual shorthand which he intended the actor or printer to lengthen. If Lucio tries to say 'i'th'right' as one word it may flummox the audience. 'a made a finer end,' says Mistress Quickly of Falstaff. Does the hearer understand 'a' means 'he', or should it be pronounced 'ee' rather than 'ay' or 'ah'? Common sense and intelligibility must be the final guide.

3

PREPARATION

The preparation period is more like dreaming,
relevant dreaming.

Simon Callow

It's vital not to approach Shakespeare on our knees. True,
some writers have made daunting claims for him, whether it
be the critic Harold Bloom's view that Shakespeare's imaginative resources 'transcend those of Yahweh, Jesus and Allah' and
provide a grander alternative vision of human nature, or the
director Dominic Dromgoole's assertion that Shakespeare 'is
not just head and shoulders above the playwriting competition,
he's floating around in a hot-air balloon, waving benignly at
everyone from Aeschylus to Caryl Churchill'.[1] Don't be put off:
like all great playwrights Shakespeare was out to push the
boundaries, and our acting should reflect this. We should always
be looking for new ways to make the plays relevant to the
moment. We're not setting out just to please an audience, but to
provoke them and make them question. Shakespeare was a
master at combining the two: he was both a crowd-pleaser and
a disturbing, experimental provocateur.

THE TEXT

Start by reading the play. If a particular edition hasn't been
specified, choose one that has good footnotes. Of the many
individual editions the New Penguin is compact, cheap and easy
to read, as the notes are at the back; the Arden has the fullest
introduction and notes, on the same page as the text, though the
notes are sometimes abstruse; and both the Oxford and the New
Cambridge have excellent introductions and notes. Many individual folio editions are published by Nick Hern Books. Of the

editions that present the complete works in one volume neither the Oxford nor the Arden have notes; the Riverside hardback has excellent introductions and notes but is expensive; and the Norton is reasonably priced, with one column text and marginal glossary and footnotes.

We will need help to work out what difficult passages mean, but we can't rely on the notes to explain everything. Editors have a habit of assuming a sentence is clear when it baffles many readers, or of providing a complicated interpretation that leaves you little the wiser. Many theatres present actors with a newly typed A4 text, which is easy to read and has room to write on (since there will be no notes it's best to have a printed edition to hand). This 'director's text' will usually contain cuts. This is a mixed blessing. It can forestall argument and later disappointment (as an uncut part may be hacked a week before opening), but it will mean that the director has already made important choices and begun to shape a concept. Check what cuts have been made, and prepare any objections sooner rather than later. There is little chance of lines being restored in the second half of the rehearsal period.

Editions vary because there is no definitive text of a Shakespeare play. Whether it's a quarto or folio text, or a combination of the two, we don't know what stage of production it represents. Are these Shakespeare's first or last thoughts, is it the King's Men's acting edition, has it been cut or added to (Middleton inserted verses and a song of his own into Act 4, sc.1 of the folio *Macbeth*)? This has encouraged directors to cut, alter the order of scenes and the position of speeches (particularly 'To be or not to be'), and even to rewrite. Productions in other languages have often felt no reservations about wholesale adaptation. Perhaps Shakespeare would have approved: his own cuts and revisions suggest that he saw no acting version as set in stone. At the same time the various printed texts that have come down to us are all we have to go on. Nothing else can claim to be authentic.

READING THE PLAY

Ideally, read the whole play out loud. If this seems too difficult, at least read 'your' scenes out loud. The only certain clues to your character are what he says and does: apart from a very few stage directions this is all Shakespeare has left us. Don't rush and don't perform – you're doing this for yourself. Actors vary in their approach to first readings. Some concentrate, above all, on clarity of thought: not just what the character is saying, but what he is thinking, with any emotional decisions left on hold (see p. 235). Others want to give their instinct and imagination full rein. They're aiming to let the text stir in them feelings and responses that will make them feel inside the character. In either case the words and images are inevitably invading our subconscious, because in the weeks ahead it's our subconscious that will be doing some of our best work. Hang on to your first gut instincts: they're invaluable (thought not necessarily infallible). The more you can trust your instinct, the more individual and inspired your performance will finally be.

One method is to take the text very slowly, phrase by phrase, pausing between each. Read the phrase and then speak it out loud in whatever way your instinct directs: whisper, shout, state flatly. Be as wild as you like; nothing is monitoring you. Take one of Hermia's speeches, for instance, when she attacks Helena for attracting Lysander's love:

> O me, you juggler, you canker blossom,
> You thief of love – what, have you come by night
> And stol'n my love's heart from him?
> *(A Midsummer Night's Dream*, 3.2.283–5)

'O me' (Flat: you've taken my breath away), 'You . . .' (what words are bad enough for Helena) 'juggler' (Shout: great tall sexy acrobat), 'you canker blossom' (Sarcastic: classy image, I'm the blossom and you're the canker), 'You thief of love' (Implacable: that's pinned it down, that's told her straight) – 'what, have you come by night' (Quiet: she's so stealthy, she wouldn't dare by day) 'And stol'n my love's heart from him?' (Sobbing: his heart was mine yesterday).

You know you won't finally do the speech so slowly and wildly, but the more you take your time and throw it about, the more each phrase and image will come to mean something to you personally. 'Juggler', 'canker blossom', 'thief of love', 'come by night', 'stolen my love's heart' are all powerful and varied word-pictures, and they need to be individualised if you are to make Hermia your own. Many actors would dispute this method:

much better to read the text quietly over and over again, con-
centrating above all on getting the thought clear. Peter Brook
perhaps best sums it up: 'To me the total words of Shakespeare
are a very, very complete set of codes, and these codes, cipher
for cipher, set off in us, stir in us, vibrations and impulses which
we immediately try to make coherent and understandable.'[2]

Reading the play slowly sets off all kinds of thoughts. We may
get an instant image of a character – that Richard III is a court
jester, Paulina is Germaine Greer, Wolsey is Richard Nixon. One
line may leap out as a clue to character – Aguecheek's 'I was
adored once too'; Sebastian on Viola, 'She bore a mind that envy
could not but call fair'; Emilia on Othello (and Iago), 'They are
not ever jealous for the cause, / But jealous for they're jealous.'
We may be struck by our character's function in the play – that
Queen Margaret and Viola are catalyst outsiders; Gloucester in
King Lear the Jacobean everyman; Thersites the cynical commentator. We may get a feeling for the play as a whole – that
Henry V is a debate about war; *Hamlet* a bitter farce; superstition
the key to *Macbeth*. We may find parts of the play obscure,
motives unclear, a character fails to develop, or the last act is
clumsily wrapped up. Hang on to these initial reactions. They
may not prove justified – you may find your Paulina turns out
nothing like Greer and the witches are not central to *Macbeth* –
but they have proved a way of opening up the questioning.
Above all, make sure you are clear about the story: that's what
you will finally be communicating to the audience.

LISTS AND STRUCTURE

I have always made a habit of making a LIST of what is said
about my character by others in the play. As we inevitably begin
to concentrate on our own scenes, it's easy to forget vital information and opinions being fed to the audience in our absence.
Some actors take this list-making to further extremes. The actor
Philip Voss, for example, follows director Mike Alfreds' system
and makes three further lists: the textual facts about his character (who he is, what he does and says, what happens to him);
what he says about himself; and what he says about everybody
else. It takes a few hours, but it's a very good way of getting to
know the play, and it often yields surprising results.[3]

What one character says about another in Shakespeare is usually their honest opinion, but it is not necessarily accurate, nor does it reflect Shakespeare's view. In *Coriolanus* the patrician Menenius disparages the two tribunes of the people, 'wearing out a good wholesome forenoon in hearing a cause between an orange-wife and a faucet-seller', as if they were incompetent Warwickshire JPs. In fact this dismissal of the tribunes proves to be a fatal underestimation of their abilities, since they succeed in having Coriolanus banished. As Terry Hands says, regard other characters' opinions of you as 'enemy propaganda'.

In addition to lists, I always like to break down the plot STRUCTURE. The five-act structure was a classical convention of Terence and Plautus and was introduced into all of Shakespeare's plays by the editors of the first folio. Though clearly marked in *Henry V* by the Chorus, no plays written for the Globe before 1609 have act divisions, just scene breaks. It's the indoor Blackfriars plays that have acts marked, providing four breaks for candle-trimming (the indoor stage, unlike the Globe, had to be lit). In fact most of the plays have an intrinsic three-act structure which has later become the norm for both plays and films: first act, a measured introduction; second act, a frenetic conflict; third act, an ordered resolution (Hamlet learns of his father's murder; he sets out to prove it and is banished; he returns and achieves his revenge). Of course you can then further break each act down into separate episodes. Shakespeare loved a complicated plot, witness *Cymbeline* and *All's Well That Ends Well*. Most dramatists would have been content to deal with Lear and his three daughters, without adding Gloucester and his two sons. If in a later age he had written novels, he would have been a Dickens rather than an Austen. Like Dickens his exploration of every byway led him into some very strange structuring, witness *Measure for Measure*. Academics can always make out a case for the brilliance of Shakespeare's structure, but don't be taken in. There is some terrible plotting in certain plays (*Macbeth, Cymbeline, Measure for Measure*), and it is vital for the actor to reduce any quirky ramblings to some sort of order in his mind.

BACKSTORY AND OMISSIONS

Arthur Miller wrote that 'the biggest single dramatic problem' is 'how to dramatise what has gone before'.[4] Shakespeare didn't see it that way. In many of his plays we have to accept a simple premise. The Capulets and Montagues feud – the cause doesn't matter. Oliver has mistreated Orlando, his younger brother – we are told no more. Viola and Sebastian are shipwrecked – we don't know why they were travelling, what their destination was, or why they don't take the next boat home. On the whole we and the audience accept these openings, as we would in a fairy story. The nature of the feud, Oliver's bullying, and Viola's travel plans don't really affect the story. In some plays, however, particularly the tragedies, the BACKSTORY is more crucial. The past relatioships of Hamlet and Ophelia, Macbeth and Lady Macbeth, Antonio and Bassanio, Beatrice and Benedick are central to the action but left tantalisingly vague. Why is Lear abdicating and why, being so old, does he have a daughter as young as Cordelia? Why have Prospero and Duke Senior been banished? Why does Don John hate Claudio? Why is Leontes so suddenly jealous? Shakespeare gives us the occasional clue. Shylock and Lear both make one reference to their wives, Lady Macbeth tells us she has had a child (or children), Beatrice makes two mentions of her past life. But these details seem random. If Shakespeare had thought it important, he would have told us something of Gertrude's feelings for Old Hamlet or Macbeth's attitude to his dead child/ren (one production of *Macbeth* opened with the funeral of his son). On occasions Shakespeare seems aware of the problem. Othello tells us why he thinks Desdemona was attracted to him. Prospero tells Miranda a lengthy history of how they came to be in exile – a tedious way of handling a backstory and one Shakespeare was usually wise to avoid.

The missing backstory is a problem for the modern, Stanislavsky-reared actor. The actor playing Gertrude will feel the need to work out her attitude to Claudius – have they fancied one another for years, or is it a hasty marriage of convenience that turns out sexually liberating? Is Lear abdicating because he feels some onset of dementia, or simply to enjoy his last few years free from the cares of state? Has Leontes suspected

Hermione's 'infidelity' for some time, or is it a sudden revelation? Making some decisions about our character's past can be an enormous help to our concept, but it has to be demonstrated with caution. The audience can't necessarily be party to it. Unless we put in a wordless scene showing the recent funeral of Macbeth's son, there's no way of showing when and how this happened. However much Claudius and Gertrude fondle one another, they can't indicate whether they've been doing this for weeks or years. We must be wary of playing something that will simply puzzle the audience. If we decide Hamlet and Ophelia, Beatrice and Benedick, or Antonio and Bassanio have slept together at least once in the past, this may feed our imaginations but we can't rely on its feeding the audience's. On the whole audiences accept Shakespeare's point of departure. The two cases that seem to have caused the most perplexity are Leontes' jealousy and Lear's treatment of Cordelia. I know of many people who can't get over these initial hurdles, which present near insoluble questions for any production.

If Shakespeare is economical with his backstories, he is at least honest with what he tells us. He very rarely misleads an audience or holds back vital information – the survival of Hermione and the revelation that the Abbess in *The Comedy of Errors* is the mother of the Antipholuses are rare exceptions. The problem lies more with what he doesn't tell us, with what he presumably thought no one needed to know. These OMISSIONS can cause actors great problems. Lady Macbeth has to jump from the Banquo ghost dinner to her sleepwalking scene without any further scenes to chart her disintegration. Angelo has no scene in which he can argue the pros and cons of executing Claudio despite Isabella/Mariana's agreement to sleep with him: he is left with a short soliloquy the following morning. Capulet and Lady Capulet are dealt with fully; Montague and Lady Montague are very cursorily sketched in. The Elizabethan audience must have felt cheated that a play about Henry V doesn't contain a re-enactment of the battle of Agincourt: the actual fighting is reduced to Pistol and M. le Fer, a knave and a fool. Characters sometimes disappear for no good reason, as the Fool does in *King Lear*; or reappear as someone else, as Fabian supplants Feste in the gulling of Malvolio. If there are missing scenes, there are far more missing motives. Does Bolingbroke return to gain his dukedom or the crown? Why does Gertrude agree to marry Claudius so rapidly, and does she suspect foul play? Why does Prince Hal tell us early on that he's only idling away his time in a tavern so that his 'reformation . . . shall show more goodly', and should we believe him? The list is endless, and we shall have to confront this sort of problem again and again.

FUNCTION IN THE PLAY

It is important at the outset to consider what FUNCTION a character has in a play, and for the actor to come to terms with it. With leading parts it is usually clear. Othello, Iago, Desdemona and Cassio are central to the plot, and their interaction is fundamentally what the play is about. But Shakespeare is more ambiguous, or liberal, or careless (depending on your point of view) about the hundreds of smaller parts. What are Emilia's and Roderigo's functions in the play? Emilia is partly there to give Desdemona someone to confide in, just as Hamlet has Horatio, Lear the Fool, or Antonio Salerio and Solanio. Roderigo is partly there as comic relief, just like Osric, Macbeth's porter or Cleopatra's clown. But both characters are also carefully threaded into the scheme of the play. Emilia is a commentator on humanity, a critical supporter of Iago, a speaker of home truths, and a vital part of the plot in her stealing of the handkerchief. Roderigo's attitudes cast light on both Iago and Desdemona, and he too becomes central to the plot in his botched attempt on Cassio's life. Montano and Gratiano, however, seem only to be authority figures introduced to help wind up the play. Their function is choric, rather like those comic commentators, Touchstone or Lavatch, in *As You Like It* and *All's Well That Ends Well*, whose precise part in the plot is hard to pin down. The actor Simon Russell Beale was much perplexed by this when he came to work on Thersites, and realised that 'Thersites is a movable feast, that his function in the play was determined as much by audience response and by my own state of mind at the time of playing as it was by the work I did in rehearsal. I also realise that, since Thersites' function is essentially choric – he plays no part in the admittedly slender plot-line of *Troilus and Cressida* – it is in his gift to push the audience's response in the direction he chooses.'[5]

RESEARCH

Robert de Niro and Michael Gambon differ on RESEARCH. De Niro does it to make him feel that when he gets in front of a camera no one in the world has more right to be that person at that moment than him. He needs the research to feel absolutely confident that he has the right to play the part.[6] Gambon's line is simpler: 'I don't do research.'[7]

Of course no amount of research on where our character went to school and what he had for breakfast will turn us *into* the character; we can never *be* him. And since we're dealing with societies four hundred and more years ago, knowing the strange food he may have had for breakfast will be of little help. At the same time many actors feel impelled to dig around the facts, and this can prove very rewarding. Research into historical figures and events helps us to understand the Wars of the Roses or the Roman civil wars. We will quickly learn more than Shakespeare knew about the historical Richard III and Cleopatra, and realise his versions are travesties of their historical selves. Shakespeare conflated characters, put them in places they never visited, altered their motives and actions, and generally reordered events. But a knowledge of the siege of Harfleur and the battle of Agincourt does help to clarify *Henry V*, just as a study of the position of the Venetian Jews does illuminate *The Merchant of Venice*. Most actors playing Cleopatra have felt enriched by research, however careful they have to be not to play things the text contradicts.

Shakespeare never bothered much with precise ages: Juliet's fourteen years and Lear's eighty plus are rare exceptions. How old is Hamlet? The Gravedigger takes him to be thirty, while the student we meet in Act I seems to be in his early twenties. How old are the Macbeths, and could Lady Macbeth have had more children (Macbeth doesn't seem to rule out future heirs)? Queen Margaret was actually fifteen at the start of *Henry VI* and only 53 in *Richard III* (though the director Adrian Noble suggested she should be played in the later play as 200).[8] Geographical research is of limited use, as Shakespeare seems to have been no traveller. A feeling of Italian heat can help a production of *Romeo and Juliet*, but a knowledge of the Dalmatian coast doesn't clarify *Twelfth Night*. The Elephant tavern is clearly not in the south suburbs of Dubrovnik, just as Quince doesn't belong in a Greek wood. Job research is more fruitful, particularly where church and state are concerned. Most Isabellas try to discover the nature of the convent she was entering, just as Friar Laurences wonder what boundaries a solitary friar is meant to observe (very few, judging by his actions). The various offices – general, lieutenant, ensign, chancellor, chamberlain, marshal – are all worth clarifying.

We now know a great deal more about the mental and psychological states that Shakespeare so acutely described. Antony Sher, for example, found it a great help when playing Leontes to discover a psychological condition known as 'morbid jealousy', which, some medics claim, attacks men in their forties with regard to their partners (special pleading, I think).[9] Lear has proved a field day for the medical profession. Is he suffering from dementia, Alzheimer's, manic depression, apoplexy, syphilis or merely an extreme sense of dislocation? Each diagnosis can offer a way into the part.

Finally, you can research how the part has been played in previous productions. Actors differ widely on this. David Suchet examined the Stratford archive and found it very helpful to know what labels had been attached to Iago in the past (ringmaster, devil, Machiavel, homosexual), and to test each one out against the text.[10] It can also be very helpful to know what pitfalls to avoid and ideas to filch: to discover that playing Gertrude as a drunken lush has proved limiting, but that playing Kate's 'submission' speech as a shared understanding with Petruchio has proved liberating. Many actors find such research abhorrent. They want to approach the play entirely afresh, and not feel cabined and confined by tradition or past experiment. As always, you must find what works best for you. If wearing Elizabethan underwear, knowing how Peggy Ashcroft did this speech, or adopting an authentic syphilitic walk helps you – go for it.

PRECONCEPTIONS AND LABELS

It is difficult to tackle the better-known plays without some foreknowledge, some baggage that we have to deal with. We may approach *Twelfth Night* with the impression that Olivia is a shallow lightweight and Toby Belch a loveable anarchist, only to find on a first careful reading that we thoroughly empathise with Olivia's quandaries and see Belch as a despicable manipulator. Take nothing for granted. LABELS in the text itself can be very insidious. Does Brutus have to be 'the noblest Roman' or Hermione 'the good queen'? It is a positive relief to be cast in *Henry VI* or *The Two Gentlemen of Verona* because we (probably) have no preconception of the play or the part. As Jonathan Miller says, 'I think there is a conspiracy in the theatre to perpetuate certain prototypes in the belief that they contain the secret truth of the characters in question.'[11]

The issue is not clear-cut. Elizabethan dramatists were in general concerned not so much with unique or unusual characters but with presenting convincing renditions of types, and Shakespeare is not entirely free of creating such archetypes. He clearly explored different aspects of the same character type in Iago, Don John and Edmund; Kate and Beatrice; Falstaff and Belch. You can find the seven deadly sins represented in his plays, with Iago as envy, Lear wrath, Coriolanus pride, Shylock avarice, Antony and Cleopatra lust, and Falstaff gluttony and sloth. These basic prototypes have to be observed; a thin Falstaff, a frigid Cleopatra, an even-tempered Lear won't serve the play. But Shakespeare is too good a writer not to subvert the archetype. Henry V is shown to be much more, or less, than a national hero; Shylock is not the comic villain of Marlowe's *Jew of Malta*; Falstaff is much more than the medieval Vice figure or the Lord of Misrule; Hamlet is not the classic avenger sweeping to his revenge.

At the same time actors can feel their character imprisoned by PRECONCEPTIONS, as Alan Rickman did with Jacques. 'I just wanted to let him out,' he declared, maintaining an improvised jack-in-the-box quality. Julian Glover was initially reluctant to play Friar Laurence, such was his reputation as a meddling bore, until he examined the text and found him altogether more interesting and intelligent.[12] Hero and villain labels are a particular problem. How much of a hero is Hamlet or Henry V; how much of a villain is Macbeth or Edmund? Actors have felt weighed down by laudatory descriptions of Viola, Portia and Imogen, and longed to find their weak spots, just as they look for redeeming features in the 'villainy' of Goneril, Regan and Cymbeline's Queen. Tradition has shackled characters like Lear, Cleopatra and Falstaff with a 'greatness' that can prejudice ruthless examination. Nigel Hawthorne could find no evidence in the text to call Lear a 'cruel tyrant', still less to justify Coleridge's Titan in the storm, 'a picture more terrific than any a Michelangelo inspired by a Dante could have conceived'. Sheer familiarity can also make some Shakespearean characters richer and more real than the text may warrant. I remember a friend's delight at being cast as Falstaff in *Merry Wives*, and his despair when he finally read the play: 'There are only two-and-a-half laughs in it,' he moaned.

It is not only actors and directors who are dogged by preconceptions. As Ian McDiarmid remarked when he approached Shylock, 'the central problem . . . was not so much to divest myself of the paranoias, echoes, concepts, traditions of previous productions and performances but rather . . . to persuade an audience to do this'.[13] The public can be hidebound in their demand for traditional readings to be upheld. Beware!

PHYSICAL IMAGE

One of the main preconceptions about certain parts is PHYSICAL IMAGE. Richard III, Caliban, Ariel and Puck are the most obvious examples, though there are many other parts where appearance can come to seem fundamental – Falstaff, Othello, Shylock, Cleopatra, Malvolio, Lear for example, not to mention the whole range of clowns and fools from the Dromios and Bottom through to Autolycus and Trinculo. It seems important that Richard III has some form of deformity, Falstaff is fat, Othello looks like a Moor and Cleopatra like an Egyptian (though her father was actually Greek), since these are all mentioned in the text. Some actors find inspiration from portraits. Thus Donald Sinden found his Malvolio in Graham Sutherland's portrait of Somerset Maugham, and Tony Church based his Polonius on Elizabeth I's minister, Lord Burghley. Settling on a physical image as a preliminary is one way of working from the outside in, and some actors prefer this kind of behaviourism. Once they have found the 'look' – the costume, the hair, the shoes, the walk – they feel they are some way to discovering the character. A Falstaff might want to wear padding from the start of rehearsals, a Richard III some form of scoliosis (or in Antony Sher's case travel on crutches). Other actors may want to leave these decisions as late as possible – though the wardrobe department will often object that they can't make a start on the costume without knowing the shape of the hump or the belly. When Olivier played Othello in 1964 he decided before the first read-through not only on his appearance (Afro-Caribbean), but on the voice (trained down an octave to bass-baritone). Simon Callow argues that the 'first physical aspect I need to explore is voice . . . to get a sense of how the character speaks'.[14]

This approach can yield very good results. In our increasingly visual age the first sight of a character can be vital to audience acceptance: a Shylock has to consider what signs of Jewishness he should adopt. At the same time this preoccupation can prove an impediment: it is sometimes a way of compensating for a feeling of being miscast. Romeo and Juliet don't have to be stunningly attractive just because they fall in love with each other. Achilles, Hector and Warwick the Kingmaker may be great warriors, but they don't have to be giants. Since nobody knows what a spirit or a fairy looks like, Ariel and Peaseblossom don't have to be radically dehumanised. All this has more to do with tradition and audience expectation than interpreting the part. When David Suchet researched Caliban he found that he had been played as a fish, a dog, a lizard, a monkey, a snake, a tortoise and an ape, despite clear indications in the text that he is a human.[15] Vocal image can also prove a major hang-up. Some female actors in 'breeches' parts have limited themselves by lowering their voice to a 'manly' tenor, just as Gielgud and Jacobi worried that as natural tenors they were odd casting for Macbeth (warriors are supposedly baritones). In reaction some recent productions have swung right against individualised appearance by dressing the entire cast identically. This certainly liberates cast and audience from their preconceptions, but I find creates more problems than it solves.

FAMILY RELATIONSHIPS

One of the first things to look for in any Shakespeare play is the FAMILY or domestic theme. Very few of his leading characters are isolated from family ties, whether as parent, spouse, sibling or child, and Shakespeare lavished attention on these bonds. As Jonathan Miller says, 'I think what is common to both Shakespeare and our time is simply the fact . . . that we have parents and siblings, and share a grammar of relationships . . . He seems to me to be the great chronicler of the family that survives, of a species that reproduces as we do.'[16] *Hamlet* and *King Lear* are each essentially the story of the destruction of two parallel families: twelve deaths in all, with Edgar the sole survivor. *Othello* examines two marriages: Othello and Desdemona, Iago and Emilia. Children lie at the heart of *Macbeth*: Duncan and Malcolm, Banquo and Fleance, Macduff and his 'pretty chickens', and the Macbeths and their (presumably) dead child.

Shakespeare was not equally at home with all family relationships. Fathers and sons are examined in some detail: Henry IV with Hal, Gloucester with Edmund and Edgar. In *Richard II* a contrast is made between Gaunt and Bolingbroke, York and Aumerle, Northumberland and Hotspur, Richard II and his lack of heir. But Shakespeare lavished his greatest attention on fathers and daughters: Polonius and Ophelia, Brabantio and Desdemona, Capulet and Juliet, Lear and his three daughters, Prospero and Miranda. Even dead fathers retain their influence in the case of Portia and Olivia. There is surely something autobiographical here. Shakespeare's only son Hamnet died in 1596, aged eleven, but his two daughters Susanna and Judith survived. The theme of daughters rebelling against their fathers runs through many of the later plays, beginning with Celia and Duke Frederick in 1599 (when Susanna would have been sixteen). Mothers and sons feature a little (Volumnia and Coriolanus, Gertrude and Hamlet), but mothers and daughters hardly at all (Juliet and Lady Capulet have little in common, Perdita says nothing when reunited with Hermione). In fact most daughters are left strikingly motherless: Rosalind, Celia, Helena, Hermia, Hero, Ophelia, Desdemona, Cordelia, Miranda – the list goes on. Shakespeare couldn't do mothers and daughters, and kept well clear.

Love and marriage are central to Shakespeare's interests, particularly in the comedies, where it is the prescribed ending. But it is in the tragedies that he takes his hardest look at marriage: the Macbeths, Claudius and Gertrude, Iago and Emilia,

Goneril and Albany. Apart from those that begin as the play ends (Beatrice and Benedick etc.), and we don't know how they will pan out, it is hard to find a happy, fulfilled marriage in the whole of the canon. Lady Percy and Hotspur, Portia and Brutus appear to have intimate, feisty relationships, though they are mostly seen quarrelling. Hymen makes clear at the end of *As You Like It* that Touchstone and Audrey, and perhaps Phoebe and Silvius, have squalls ahead of them; and we might well tremble for the futures of Angelo and Mariana, Leontes and Hermione, Camillo and Paulina. The importance of chastity and fidelity are always underlined: suspected unfaithfulness is a recurrent theme, clearly in the case of Othello and Leontes, but even in *Cymbeline* Imogen and Posthumus seem only too quick to believe the other deceitful. 'Too ready hearing' is a constant theme in Shakespeare.

As well as marriage and relationships, Shakespeare was also interested in households – more important to Elizabethans than to our own society. One of the first questions the actor Maggie Steed asked when approaching *Much Ado About Nothing* was how does Leonato's household operate and what is Beatrice's place in it. Shakespeare carefully examines the households of the Capulets, Shylock, Portia, the Merry Wives, Orsino, Olivia, the Countess of Roussillon, Cleopatra and Volumnia. Even the Mistresses Quickly and Overdone have households of sorts, with all their hierarchies and tensions, and it is one of the first things an actor needs to look at.

CLASS AND MONEY

Shakespeare, like any Elizabethan, was very aware of CLASS. Jealous rivals made him conscious that he was the son of a small-town glover, who had never been to university and had no income outside the theatre. The patronage, and possibly the friendship, of the Earl of Southampton, and his successful application for a coat of arms ('not without right') obviously meant a great deal to Shakespeare. He had achieved the status of 'gentleman'. This awareness of the minute gradations of class runs right through the plays, and it's important for the actor to establish early on where his character is in the social pecking order. What is the status of ladies-in-waiting like Nerissa and

Maria? How far can Wolsey's position and wealth compensate for his lack of breeding? Does Beatrice have class but no money? Is Duncan allowed to nominate his successor? See how the Windsor bourgeoisie coo over Falstaff's knighthood and relation to the court; how Olivia checks Cesario's parentage; how Polonius advises Ophelia that 'Lord Hamlet is a prince out of thy star'; how delighted Capulet is to have secured a count (Paris) as a son-in-law; and how Bertram objects to marrying Helena, 'a poor physician's daughter'.

MONEY rivalled class in importance, and Shakespeare, who had witnessed his father's declining fortunes and had a sharp eye for a good investment, introduces it at every opportunity. Iago fleeces Roderigo, Belch fleeces Aguecheek, Autolycus fleeces everyone. Celia urges Rosalind to escape with 'our jewels and our wealth', and together they buy a cottage in the forest (Shakespeare knew the harshness of Arden). The Athenian senators calculate Timon's credit rating with Wall Street precision. *The Merchant of Venice* revolves around the lending of money and its surety. Antonio in *Twelfth Night* lends Sebastian his entire purse, but only gets half Viola's purse in return. Falstaff arrives with an army of 'pitiful rascals' because he's made £300 by allowing 'likely' men to buy themselves out of having to do military service. The smallest details of money transactions are itemised. Falstaff claims he's had a seal-ring worth forty marks (£26; perhaps £3000 in modern money) picked from his pocket, but Hal says it's only worth eightpence (3p; perhaps £3). With this degree of precision in the writing it will repay the actor to look into his character's exact financial status.

CHARACTER

It is impossible to read and reread a play, knowing the part we've been given, without conceiving some idea of CHARACTER. However hard we try to remain objective, the language and situations will be sending out messages that we find ourselves converting into individual human behaviour. The first steps we take in building a character today may be heavily under Stanislavsky's influence, but I find it hard to believe that Shakespeare's actors didn't feel something of the same. No good actor has ever just said the lines and avoided the furniture – or the pillars. At the same time it's vital to put on hold any final character assessment. The rehearsal period, with the input of the director and the other actors and the continual re-examination of the text, should open up choices and avenues that no preliminary reading could anticipate.

Not everyone is agreed about this search for character. Willem Dafoe, of the Wooster Group, writes, 'I do not think an actor's job is to interpret; an actor's job is to do the story and be the story.' Others believe that the modern actor's subjective, introspective construction of character is alien to the Elizabethan dramatist's use of archetypes, humours, rhetoric and plot functionaries. As W.B. Worthen writes, 'Actorly reading is notably trained on questions of character, the integrated, self-present, internalised, psychologically motivated "character" of the dominant mode of modern theatrical representation, stage realism.' He goes on to argue that this approach can be inappropriate: 'Conceiving Shakespearean character as an organic whole, the actors stage a Shakespeare closer to Ibsen or O'Neill.'[18] On the other hand there seems general agreement, persuasively borne out in James Shapiro's *1599*, that the creation of Hamlet marks a turning point. As Granville Barker puts it:

> With Hamlet, character for the first time totally defeats plot. The discovery which turned Shakespeare from a good dramatist into a great one was that the outward clashing of character with character is poor material beside the ferment in the spirit of a man.[19]

Hamlet is in essence a typical revenge plot, but Hamlet is no typical avenger. As the academic Peter Thompson says, 'It is in behaviour inconsistent with personal impulse that the idea of character is contained.'[20] The critic Frank Kermode is categoric: 'The whole idea of dramatic character is changed for ever by this play . . . no one much like Hamlet ever existed before.'[21] This concentration on 1600 and *Hamlet* can be misleading. It would be ridiculous to claim that Falstaff and Brutus, Beatrice and Rosalind don't live as 'characters', or that after 1600 Shakespeare always created a complete, fully rounded gallery – witness Troilus or Cymbeline's Queen. But there's no argument that the great tragedies and late romances are more mature studies of spiritual ferment.

Two cautionary notes about approaching character. First, the Olivier syndrome: 'One thing that may lead an actor to be successful in a part . . . is to try to be unlike someone else in it.'[22] This has led to some terrible misrepresentations. Frances Barber puts it more subtly: 'In an attempt to make the character your own there is a great temptation to invent an entirely new characteristic "hidden" in the text.'[23] The text just won't allow you to turn Ophelia into a militant feminist, though the attempt will probably continue. Remember that you don't have to strive to be 'original', your own personality will ensure your performance is unique. Second, a reminder that the 'character' is only lines in a play. As Simon Russell Beale points out, 'the person called Hamlet doesn't exist. There is only a series of actors' responses to, and reactions with, the part.'[24]

THE DIRECTOR

Actors, of course, think that the DIRECTOR has too much power. We often see ourselves as the last to be hired, first to be fired, and occupying the front line only in performance. Out there before an audience, the actor is at last in control: up to that point power lies with the director. This has been largely true for centuries. Shakespeare's company may have operated as a shareholder collective, but I doubt if it was an egalitarian democracy – we know that Burbage took most of the leading parts. After 1660 theatre managers, usually actor-managers, took over. Betterton, Garrick, Kemble, Macready, Irving, Beerbohm Tree and their like dominated London theatre for 250 years. They picked the plays, cast them, handled the finances, and played many of the leading parts. Laurence Olivier, first director of the National Theatre (1963–73), may prove to be the last of that breed. The modern artistic director is mainly a director, often with no professional acting experience, but with vastly increased administrative, public and programme planning responsibilities.

Actors are vitally concerned with choice of play and casting but, unless they are major stars, have no say in either. We are therefore wholly dependent on the director to pick plays suitable to the available talent, the box office, and the temper of the times; and then to cast them appropriately. Much lies in the casting: some claim 80 per cent of the production's potential has been decided by the first day of rehearsal, and that casting is the most important part of the director's job. Sometimes their choices can seem recklessly bizarre. Interplay between actors is so important in Shakespeare that miscasting can fatally undermine a production's balance. However good you are as Roderigo, you won't be able to fulfil yourself if you can't relate to your Iago. Feeling *yourself* to be miscast is a different problem. I have found it best to be positive, and concentrate on what I can uniquely bring to the role rather than try to fit into some conventional mould for which I'm clearly unsuited. Shakespeare may have intended Friar Laurence to be elderly, but a young friar opens up other possibilities.

Some directors approach Shakespeare with an overarching concept, and it's important to discover this as early as possible. If you are playing Hamlet you should have discussed this before rehearsals begin; if you are Voltimand it may not be of vital concern. It's when you are Ophelia or Laertes, and you haven't been taken into the director's confidence, that it can be very frustrating. You may not want to play Ophelia as an adolescent hysteric, or Laertes as a myopic guards officer. Some directors are anti-conceptual, and declare that they have no idea what the play is about and that everyone will be going on a journey of discovery together. This can be liberating, or may just betoken laziness. This book deliberately tries to avoid discussing how to direct Shakespeare (there's plenty of literature on that), but at the same time we must deal with the influence a director may have on how you play the part.

Twentieth-century directors of Shakespeare have differed significantly in their approaches. With the return from nineteenth-century excesses to a form of textual 'authenticity', Granville Barker could write optimistically, 'Set the play in motion and all the hidden things *should* come to light and life.' Peter Brook takes a slightly tougher line, 'The director is there to attack and yield, provoke and withdraw, until the indefinable stuff begins to flow', until 'the secret play' surfaces. Tyrone Guthrie wanted to strike a balance between the freedom the text gives the actor and the responsibility of recharging the play's first meaning, but Brook argues that the director is not 'serving Shakespeare . . . There is only one service, which is to the reality which Shakespeare is serving.' Bill Gaskill would agree: the director 'is not creating something new', but is instead 'on the quest of creating an experience for an audience of something that had already existed in the writer's mind'.

Not every director, however, has thought it possible to determine what was in Shakespeare's mind. Jonathan Miller argues success is 'rated not by the degree to which the performance approximates to an entirely unknowable state of Shakespeare's mind, but by the extent to which the text now speaks with more or less coherent vitality . . . The job of the artist in the theatre is illumination and reconstruction.' Charles Marowitz, who reordered *Macbeth* and *Hamlet* into provocative collages in the 1970s, goes a stage further: 'The modern director is . . . someone who challenges the assumption of a work of art and uses *mise-en-scène* actively to pit his or her beliefs against those of the play . . . The only fidelity that cuts any ice in the theatre is a director's fidelity to his personal perceptions about a classic; how well and how truly he can put on stage the visions the play has evoked in his imagination.' Marowitz has moved therefore from reinterpreting Shakespeare's ideas to presenting ideas which the text evokes in his mind. He's coming close to the Hollywood practice of the director not directing the script but what the script reminds him of. The logical extension of this is to rewrite the play, which is in effect what many translated adaptations do. The German director Peter Zadek, for example, claims, 'All I'm interested in is trying to find out what is *behind* what the author wanted, what was at the back of his mind . . . Shakespeare is a machine to make theatre, to reveal other cultures.' Zadek decided that *Hamlet* was, at the back of Shakespeare's mind, a surrealistic comedy, in which Hamlet was an elderly clown, Polonius a young woman, Rosencrantz and Guildenstern transvestite females, and Gertrude had red bull's eyes painted on her bare breasts.[25] The Spanish director Calixto Bieito goes to similar extremes. In 2004 he cheerfully told a RSC open day:

> *Macbeth* has to be a new piece by a new writer. We
> changed the text all the time. The fifth act is my favourite –
> it's like the last days in the bunker. Macbeth did not die
> at the end. He stays with all his ghosts. Death, we know,
> is for heroes. Always with Shakespeare you can do
> whatever you want. All you must do is surprise the
> audience. The text is not the limit. This is theatre. There
> is no limit.

All this provokes the kind of questions which the actor has to ask as much as the director. Do we play the text as truthfully as possible, and hope the hidden things come to life, the indefinable stuff begins to flow? Are we trying to recharge the play's first meaning, or are we reinterpreting what we think Shakespeare had at the back of his mind? Are we trying to realise the visions which the text has invoked in our imagination, or are we simply out to surprise the audience by the novelty of our ideas? Did Shakespeare intend Henry V to be a national hero, or did he secretly see him as a manipulative warmonger? If Shakespeare is Prospero, is he a magician who has finally found peace, or an embittered fantasist? Does it matter what was at the front or back of Shakespeare's mind – aren't we out to surprise and delight the audience with our personal take? Since the texts are always there, constantly being faithfully reproduced, may we sometimes do what we like, rewriting and reimagining them as we please? There is no doubt that the idea of Shakespeare as 'our contemporary' has changed production concepts. As the scholar Russell Jackson notes, 'It is more probable now than fifty years ago that the company will have treated Shakespeare more as a collaborator than an authority, and that they want to help audiences find the means and arguments to change society for the better.'[26]

PERIOD AND DESIGN

Most of the decisions about period and design will have been taken prior to rehearsals, so it's important for the actor to discover as early as possible, and hopefully discuss, what is planned. No good thinking of *Antony and Cleopatra* as Ancient Egyptian if it's going to be a Los Angeles swimming pool, or of *King Lear* as modern if it's to be Bronze Age. It's helpful to find out as soon as possible if Friar Laurence is to have his cell, Rosalind her forest, or Timon his cave. Designers sometimes have very set ideas about costume, which you need to grapple with at once. Sinead Cusack found as Lady Macbeth she was to have a black dress against a black set, and had to fight for some redeeming colour. Take nothing for granted where designers are concerned.

There is no wholly satisfactory solution to the problem of PERIOD. Each play exists in three time schemes: the period in which the action is set (usually pre-1550), the year it was written in, and any subsequent period. *Coriolanus* can be set in 491 BC Rome, 1608 England, or any recent state experiencing revolution. But whether Shakespeare is writing about Rome, Athens or Verona there is always a feeling of Tudor society, so Elizabethan settings are a safe bet. Peter Hall is a great advocate of Tudor productions, feeling 'unless what's on the stage looks like the language, I simply don't believe it'.[27] On the other hand, I find the Roman plays and many of the tragedies like *Macbeth* and *King Lear* sit oddly in Elizabethan England. The one surviving drawing of a production in Shakespeare's lifetime shows Titus Andronicus wearing a toga over his armour. A toga-less *Julius Caesar*, set at the time of the Gunpowder Plot, seems to me – and apparently to them – a reduction of the play. Accurate Roman settings, beloved of the nineteenth century, have gone out of fashion; for me, a mere suggestion of the original period is enough.

Modern settings solve certain problems and create others. They can make a play seem relevant and immediate, but they can also throw up political, religious and social questions which Shakespeare was in no position to answer. A modern setting which eschews modern technology throws up distorting questions: why isn't Macbeth using a gun with a silencer to murder Duncan, why doesn't Friar Laurence get on his mobile phone? Many recent productions have got round the gun/phone problem by setting the plays in the period 1850–1920; so that *Othello's* Cyprus becomes a study in Victorian colonialism. I was once in an Edwardian *Much Ado*, but, though cucumber sandwiches on the lawn worked well for the comedy, the background war sat uneasily with the trenches of the Somme. Peter Brook thinks for plays like *King Lear* no period is suitable, and the only solution is eclecticism: don't tie design down to any particular period. The danger here is that Shakespeare usually creates a solid, coherent society, which an indeterminate, pick-and-mix setting can undermine.

What then is good DESIGN? Actor Paola Dionisotti believes 'it enables the audience to understand the terms on which the action of the play is happening'. Bad design, Ian McDiarmid thinks, tries 'to do the work of the text and the actors, rather than provide an architecture or a way of using the stage-space, in which the text and the actors could work'.[28] The actor wants the design to support him and provide a useable and resonant space in which to work, not to dictate to him or tell the audience what to think. This is not easy to achieve. The gap between helping the audience to understand the play and signalling a concept that overwhelms the action is a narrow one. The plays are not easy to design for the obvious reason that Shakespeare didn't have to take that into account. He switched the action from battlements to bedroom to forest in the knowledge that this could be achieved at the Globe with the simplest of effects – or none at all, relying solely on the words of the text. This is one of the reasons that chamber or in-the-round productions, with the barest of sets, work so well for Shakespeare. *Romeo and Juliet*, for example, set on a proscenium stage presents great problems for the designer. Juliet has to have a balcony, a bedroom and a tomb, Friar Laurence would like a cell, and yet there has to be a large open space for the fights. Some plays, like *Pericles, Cymbeline, Antony and Cleopatra* and the histories, have a multitude of locations. Actors need to be aware of these problems if they are to make the designer's solutions work.

MEMORISING

This is another area where actors differ. Some believe learning their lines before rehearsal starts – 'no decisions, no inflections', as Derek Jacobi said when he prepared *Macbeth* – is a positive gain.[29] Not having constantly to refer to the text can give you a greater freedom to chuck the lines about from the start, and it doesn't hold everyone else up during long speeches. The actor William H. Macy writes: 'You cannot act when you are memorising the lines. If you try to act while memorising lines, you inculcate line-readings into yourself, so it is better to learn lines by rote in monotone. Treat them as though they are gibberish, ascribe no meaning to them and memorise them as a technical exercise.'[30] But other actors fear that, however hard they try, they *will* settle into line-readings which they won't be able to alter later. Actor/director Richard Wilson is horrified at the idea: 'How can you possibly learn the lines before you know the first thing about your character, his relationship to the other characters, the situation of each scene? It's unthinkable!'[31]

Perhaps the ideal is the Anthony Hopkins method: you keep reading the script, a hundred times if possible, and you find you know it. This works well for film, where you may only have to say a dozen lines a day, but less well for stage. Two hundred lines in the last act can't be accurately memorised simply by reading. There is a compromise position. The method outlined in 'Reading the Play' on p. 61 is a great aid to memory. Once Hermia has related to the images of 'juggler', 'canker-blossom', 'thief of love', 'come by night', and 'stol'n my love's heart', those three lines are more or less learnt. A heckler – a friend, the director, or yourself – can be a great help. 'What did you say?' 'Canker-blossom.' 'Sorry?' 'CANKER-BLOSSOM.' 'Why canker-blossom?' etc. Nearly always when you forget a word later on it's because you've never examined, questioned, related to it; it's never become a picture in your mind. Fortunately blank verse is comparatively easy to learn; the rhythm of the iambic carries you along. The vowel sounds, the assonance, the alliteration all provide a music that lodges in the imagination.

> The human mortals want their winter cheer.
> No night is now with hymn or carol blessed.
> (*A Midsummer Night's Dream*, 2.1.101–2)

'Human mortals' (as opposed to fairy mortals?) sticks easily; 'want their winter cheer' and 'no night is now' have a monosyllabic rhythm and helpful alliteration; 'with hymn or carol blessed' has similar rhythm and both 'carol' and 'blessed' relate to 'hymn'. There are other traditional methods: writing the lines out, going down the page covering your speeches with a postcard, or recording them on tape and playing them back. The important thing is accuracy. Shakespeare's choice of words is too precise, his language too dense and allusive, to allow you to substitute or paraphrase. The more embedded the words are, the greater your freedom to experiment and go with the moment.

Slow readings of the text and the interplay and repetition of rehearsal are usually sufficient to get most medium-sized parts learnt. Parts of under 200 lines probably don't need learning in advance, and with scenes of short speeches and rapid interchange with other characters it can be a positive disadvantage because you need to take so much from the other actors. It's with parts of over 300 lines that some memorising of long speeches can be a positive gain. Try experimenting: do you find that knowing the lines frees you to turn a scene abruptly on its head, or closes off your choices too early?

VOICE AND SONNETS

It's important to get the VOICE into shape. We may have to do seven hours' rehearsal in a day, going over and over long scenes, and the voice needs to be able to cope. So get used to warming the voice up each day and doing some breathing exercises. Breath is central to the actor's creativity, particularly in Shakespeare. Our whole being is dependent on breathing, as breathing is dependent on oxygen. Together they feed the brain and the voice. Breath is fundamental in giving energy to the thought, the moment, the word, the line. As Edward Bond says, 'How we think is how we breathe.' Breathing exercises are the most basic part of an actor's preparation, and fortunately the easiest. If I sound like a fanatic, then I am. Breath is freedom.

The best preparation for working on a Shakespeare text is undoubtedly his SONNETS (choose two or three from sonnets 18, 29, 30, 60, 64, 97, 116, 129, 130 and 144). They present in concentrated form all the textual, verbal, rhythmic and breathing problems of the play-texts. They're mini-dramas, posing a question, a discussion and some sort of resolution. They're dramatic in that they work either as soliloquies, or addressed to another person. Although we can characterise the speaker, exploration of character and situation is not central; sonnets are complete and self-contained. Sometimes, as in sonnet 29, they are a single sentence, so that we have to navigate all the highways and byways of thought without losing the one central thread – excellent preparation for long speeches. Basically, if we can balance thought, feeling, and language in a sonnet, nothing in the plays' speeches will hold terrors for us.

4

REHEARSAL

It all lies in the detail.
Peter Stein

Rehearsal is for me the most interesting part of the whole process, though not necessarily the most enjoyable – that can come in performance. Actors approach rehearsal in very different states. Some will have thought about the play for a long time, read books, watched videos, gone into monastic retreat, travelled to Verona, and learnt all their words. Others will have done nothing, not even read the whole play. Underpreparation can waste a lot of time in rehearsal, but overpreparation can also be an obstacle. It can induce complacency: you may have made too many decisions too early. If you think you're ready, you're probably not ready.

Directors usually start with a read-through, because it's traditional, it breaks the ice, and it ensures everyone has read the play. The director is often the most frightened person in the room, so a read-through at least fills up the dreaded first day. Actors tend to divide into three groups: those who give a performance, those who read intelligently but non-committally, and those who seem to have first looked at it on the bus that morning. A way of varying the traditional read-through is for everyone to read other people's parts, perhaps swapping roles every act. I enjoy this method, particularly if we read the play two or three times: it helps both to see how the play works as a whole and to have an objective look at the part you're eventually going to play. A further method is to read the play with everyone taking a speech at a time, though I find this disrupts any sense of flow and continuity.

Some directors dispense with a read-through: as Tyrone Guthrie said, 'it bores those with little parts and embarrasses those with big ones'. If the play has an enormous leading part the director may spend several days alone with his Hamlet. Or he may meet with groups of characters: Claudius and Gertrude; Polonius, Laertes and Ophelia; Hamlet, Horatio, Rosencrantz and Guildenstern, etc. This can save a lot of time, but as a member of a company I find it frustrating: I long to know what has been discussed, and often have a feeling I've missed something and will never quite catch up. Adherents of the Mike Leigh method would disagree: much better the actor playing Hamlet never knows what the actors playing Claudius and Gertrude have decided about their past relationship.

It is also traditional on day one to look at the set model and costume designs. This can come as a shock. The director may have told you at the audition that he or she comes with an open mind, only for you to discover that he or she and the designer have decided that the play is set in a surrealist world with *Commedia dell'Arte* costumes, and the whole thing is already being made. Some immediate negotiation may be necessary. On rare occasions the setting is minimal and the costumes to be decided (but that usually assumes at least a six-week rehearsal period). Some directors start with improvisations and playing games; some think it best to get the cast on their feet as soon as possible; but most choose to sit round as a company for several days and go slowly through the text. This involves teasing out the meaning, seeing how the language works, and perhaps discussing how the verse might scan. Paraphrasing each speech into a modern idiom is useful and sometimes funny – 'Shuffled off this mortal coil' becomes 'Staggered down cemetery lane', and 'Go your gait', 'Get lost'. Questions of backstory and missing scenes, and of the politics and hierarchy of the play, usually need discussing, and inevitably questions of character and relationships will arise, though it's important to leave these open at this stage. This slow trawl through the text is a chance to take in what is said about our character throughout the play, what is our function in the play overall, what is the development of the story, and what ambiguities and inconsistencies arise: above all it's an important stage in clarifying our character's thought. Much time can be spent in working out objectives within scenes, often through ACTIONING – what one character wants to *do* to another with each successive thought. We speak in order to *change* the person we're addressing; that is our major impulse. As the director Max Stafford-Clark explains:

> An action has to be expressed by a transitive verb and gives the character's intention or tactic for that particular thought, [for example] 'to interest', 'to grip', ' to instruct', 'to fascinate' . . . Working with agreed actions means that each actor knows and subscribes to a particular shape to the scene . . . It's not a rigid plaster cast that will encapsulate the scene forever, but rather a first-stage rocket to fall away once the scene has been launched into orbit.[1]

Eventually you will have to get to your feet. The director will probably have worked out entrances and exits, but hopefully not detailed blocking – plenty of time for that. Some directors want immediate results, but don't allow yourself to be pushed on too fast. At a later stage it's easier to speed things up, than to slow them down. Other directors work extremely slowly, but don't think you've got to 'solve' every moment first time round. Actors work in very different ways: some put off making choices and wait for something to emerge organically; others make rapid choices, discard them and try others. Some actors write down every move and idea, but I find myself doing this less and less: if they seem right we will have automatically digested them. All the time the language should be working on us in a very physical way. We must be prepared to experiment, be vulnerable, and if necessary make a fool of ourselves. In the process we may discover things about ourselves we don't much like. This requires an atmosphere of trust, which the director should be nurturing. The important thing is to free the subconscious and let it have full rein, but at the same time to start shaping and taking responsibility for what is emerging. This may seem a paradox, but I'm convinced the balancing of freedom and control is central to the rehearsal process. Ben Kingsley talks of 'the meticulous making of a mould, the creation through the text and one's body of a silhouette into which, in performance, one pours the white hot-molten metal of the character'.

There will inevitably come moments when we feel stuck. Tell the director, and don't be put off by comforting assurances that everything seems fine. Try improvising the scene in your own words, or playing the complete opposite of what you've been doing – anything to free things up. It sometimes helps to remind ourselves how the part or the scene fits into the pattern of the play. We may have been overcomplicating things, and a return to a simple objective will help. It's important to discover what doesn't work: discarding unhelpful choices is a way of narrowing down the possibilities. It's also important to identify our strengths and weaknesses. My first director, Peter Dews, used to shout at me in rehearsal: 'Stop *thinking* it, just *do* it!' So if you find analysis comes easily, concentrate on instinct; and similarly with assertiveness and vulnerability, irony and emotional commitment, the verbal and the physical, and so on. Above all, don't worry at it remorselessly. It may seem less of a problem when you work through the play again, or it may become clear when you're away from the rehearsal room having a bath or feeding the ducks. Always remember that rehearsal is the time when you can make radical changes. Iris Murdoch puts it wonderfully:

> Any artist knows that the space between the stage where the work is too unformed to have committed itself, and the stage where it is too late to improve it, can be as thin as a needle. Genius perhaps consists in opening out this needle-like area until it covers almost the whole of the working time.[2]

The most fruitful period of rehearsal often lies in that state of near-completion which still allows for experiment and change – 'I know the words and the moves, I could go on and give an adequate performance, can I now improve it out of all recognition?'

LANGUAGE

> Theatre is essentially an aural art. The sound is the important thing. It's not what you see on the page. It's what you hear.
>
> *Arthur Miller*[3]

In all great plays, whether by Miller or Pinter, Shaw or Lorca, Shakespeare or Euripides, the structures of the LANGUAGE reveal the essence of the work. The exchange of ideas and feelings through language is the central pivot of theatre, but in many ways theatre is fighting a rearguard action. Film has always placed dialogue a poor second to the visual, and often doesn't care if the words are even audible. Television follows in film's wake: scenes get shorter, dialogue sparser, and rehearsal of the lines is fast becoming non-existent. We now live in a world of such noise and dissonance that language is barely heard or, when it is, twenty-four-hour television and radio has devalued its expression. In the world of commercial enterprise such highly emotive words as 'love', 'grace', 'power' and 'beauty' have lost all stature through their constant application to cars, cosmetics and lager.

Shakespeare was a great poet. If he'd been able to make a regular income out of his early successes with *Venus and Adonis* and *The Rape of Lucrece,* he might have left the daily grind of acting and concentrated on writing verse. He was drunk with the power of words (all 27,000 of his estimated vocabulary) and many argue that it is in his language that he reveals his most coherent attitude to life, and that it is language rather than plot which provides the real structure of his plays. Poetic drama works on the hearer in ways that are difficult to pin down. The combination of verbal music with heightened imagery and metaphor communicates to an audience at a level both conscious and subconscious. At his best Shakespeare has the power to get under the skin of his audience and tap into areas of feeling and experience that they are barely aware of. In this the actor is the go-between and the enabler. If the actor commits to the language with passion, it has a transforming effect both on the actor and the hearer. It's hard work. It won't happen just by speaking the words. Heightened language has to be marked, without becoming overladen. As the voice teacher Patsy Rodenburg writes:

> Actors have to engage fully with language before it can engage an audience. They must be able to connect to, experience and internalise the physical operation of certain structures in rhythm and form, and work to realise them. The language must penetrate them, filling them with its power.[4]

Harold Pinter told the cast of his play *The Dwarfs*:

> It isn't a question frequently of this doesn't mean this – it means that – but of emphasising the word and the meaning will become clear. If you hit a line with particular emphasis – within the rhythm – its meaning will become

> apparent. Listen to the sound first and the meaning will
> become clear through that. A half-hour debate can be more
> confusing than one clearly put sentence. Music and rhythm:
> they must be your guides.[5]

Shakespeare's characters exist in the moment they speak. The
actor has to be alive to their need to talk. It's often more than a
need, it's a desperation to express themselves and be understood. His characters are rarely incoherent; they mostly speak in
a very clear and structured way, not just because Shakespeare
wants to communicate the story to the audience, but because his
characters themselves take a pride in expressing ideas passionately and intelligently – clarity is everything. Ophelia may have
just been rejected by Hamlet, but she feels the need to express
her feelings. Gertrude has just seen the dead Ophelia, but she is
eloquent in her description of her drowning. This isn't Shakespeare being 'poetic' for the sake of it. Ophelia and Gertrude
need the richness and formality of this language to convey their
grief and distress. The instant coining of such images as 'that
sucked the honey of his music vows' or 'mermaid-like awhile
they bore her up' is a challenge to the actor that has to be met.
The two speeches can also be a guide to character: Ophelia
passionate and naive, Gertrude world-weary and despairing.
Shakespeare is so much inside his characters that he finds a way
for them spontaneously to express their feelings in entirely
individual language. It's an extraordinary gift, and one the actor
needs to seize on hungrily.

The iambic pentameter provides a pattern (see pp. 30–3).
Shakespeare, like a great jazz player, then varies the pattern,
sometimes wildly but without ever losing contact with the basic
beat. The pattern takes hold of the audience, perhaps because
the alternation of stressed and unstressed sounds approximates
to the rhythm of the human heart. If this is true then actor and
spectator are joined at the very core. In moments of crisis and
extreme emotion the pattern can almost disappear:

> Rumble thy bellyful; spit, fire; spout, rain.
> Nor rain, wind, thunder, fire are my daughters.
> *(King Lear, 3.2.13–4)*

But it's important not to confuse stressed syllables with emphases. Lear in his pain and anger might emphasise five or six

words in each of these two lines, but this can't be maintained for long. The audience would wilt under the barrage. A useful guide is that, if in doubt, only strongly emphasise one word in the line, and this may well be the first stress (e.g. 'To BE or not to be: that is the question'). Sometimes there is a wide choice. In Orsino's opening line – 'If music be the food of love, play on' – 'music', 'be', 'food', 'love', 'play on' are all possible emphases. 'Music' and 'play on' would seem the natural choices, since 'music' is the subject and 'play on' the verb of command. Whatever you do, don't stress them all, or the audience will feel hectored and, more important, won't be able to understand what point you are making. An elderly actor at Stratford once told me he could go through the plays and mark the correct emphases in every line. If he was right then the plays are set in aspic and there's no point in reviving them. Fortunately he was wrong: there are few 'correct' emphases. The language is not a blueprint; it's not there to box you in but to liberate you.

The greatest influences on my sense of speaking Shakespeare were John Barton and Cicely Berry, and a good start would be to read their respective books, *Playing Shakespeare* and *The Actor and the Text*. Cicely Berry's major concern is that the actor should connect with the physical energies of the language. She writes:

> There is in Shakespeare an energy which runs through the text which is not a naturalistic one; an energy which impels one word to the next, one line to the next, one thought to the next, one speech to the next, and one scene to the next. I would say there is really not a full stop until the end of the play; only places where the thought and action pause and change direction. [6]

The actor has a cardinal need to *be* in the moment, to inhabit but not dwell on it, and then respond to the way that moment impels him to the next. Hamlet is the supreme example of the way thought and word are so vitally energised. He finds Claudius kneeling in prayer:

> Now might I do it pat, now a is praying,
> And now I'll do't, and so a goes to heaven.
> And so am I revenged. That would be scanned.
> I, his sole son, do this same villain send
> To heaven.
> O, this hire and salary, not revenge!   (3.3.73–9)

Ten years earlier Shakespeare might have taken twenty lines to express this thought pattern. Now he cuts to the quick, and the key words – 'do', 'heaven', 'revenge' – tumble starkly out and are repeated. In six lines (the fifth contains a considerable pause) he decides to kill Claudius, senses a flaw, and decides against it. The speech is also full of changes of direction that give the language great impulse. These changes come here at the caesura, since the new thought is often more energised by starting mid-line than it would be at the line-end. A favourite rehearsal technique for marking each new direction is for the actor to move about the room, turning abruptly at each new thought.

Isabella pleads to Angelo for her brother's life with desperate improvisation:

> Because authority, though it err like others,
> Hath yet a kind of medicine in itself
> That skins the vice o'th' top. Go to your bosom;
> Knock there, and ask your heart what it doth know
> That's like my brother's fault. If it confess
> A natural guiltiness, such as is his,
> Let it not sound a thought upon your tongue
> Against my brother's life.
>
> (*Measure for Measure*, 2.2.137–44)

Isabella has grown in confidence during the scene, and now the ideas pour out: that authority can be fallible and has a self-remedy; that we may all have experienced the same impulse; and that this recognition may lead us to be merciful. The language and the sense are comparatively straightforward, but the chosen words have such resonance and energy: 'authority', 'err', 'medicine', 'vice', 'bosom', 'knock', 'heart', 'fault', 'confess', 'guiltiness'. The actor needs to respond not only to the rhythm of the speech but to the length of the vowels: the short vowels of 'that skins the vice o'th' top. Go to your bosom; / Knock there, and ask' are followed by the long vowels of 'your heart what it doth know / That's like my brother's fault'. This change in cadence and rhythm shows the actor how to pitch the sentence and underline the depth of her feeling. Shakespeare has also given Isabella language, however guileless, that contains a great irony. Angelo's bosom is already heaving with the natural guiltiness of unlawful desire.

'Knocking at your bosom' and 'asking your heart' are very potent images. The actor has to make them real and personal. Unless the image means something to us it won't convey itself to the audience. I was once in a production of *Twelfth Night*, in which Roger Rees, as Fabian, had the line to Aguecheek, 'Awake your dormouse valour'. Roger and I conceived the idea of writing a children's book (alas never finished) about a theatre mouse who longed to go on the stage and took the name of 'Dormouse Valour'. As we worked on the idea, so each evening the line began to get a bigger laugh from the audience, not because Roger was highlighting or colouring the line but because the image was growing increasingly rich to him. The actor Stephen Boxer told me how Robert Lepage workshopped his production of the *Dream* by asking his actors to remember all their dreams:

> Every morning we came in and drew our dreams on a huge area of paper on the floor. I remember water being a recurrent theme, obviously sex, buildings, strange animals, people from the past, sky, clouds, forests, colour – the list was pretty comprehensive. *Then* we read the play and, lo and behold, all these images revealed themselves in the text, thus making us (a) marvel at Shakespeare's imagination; and (b) begin to take collective ownership of the play – these images were not just Shakespeare's, they were *ours*.

Sometimes, however, Shakespeare gives us several images in a row and we have to make choices: we can't play every single one. Macbeth says:

> Come, seeling night,
> Scarf up the tender eye of pitiful day,
> And with thy bloody and invisible hand
> Cancel and tear to pieces that great bond
> Which keeps me pale.   (3.2.47–51)

We are presented with images that night is eye-closing, that it blindfolds day which is pitiful and has an eye that is tender, and that it has a hand which is bloody and invisible and not only cancels but tears to pieces the moral law that keeps us fenced in. If we try to respond to and communicate every single idea there, the audience would be punch-drunk and the play would last four hours.

At the same time the verse should sound natural. We would all like to earn Al Pacino's commendation of Mark Rylance, that he 'plays Shakespeare like Shakespeare wrote it for him the night before'. Rylance in turn praises his colleague, the director Giles Block, who 'believes that Shakespeare is trying to capture – more in verse than in prose – the way that people speak, the way that they suspend a sentence only when there's a question hanging in the air'.[7] When rehearsing, don't try to make 'naturalness' your first priority. There's a lot we need to attend to first in following all the clues in the verse. As we become confident in those, so the naturalness will begin to flow – but don't force it, or we will jettison all the help that Shakespeare is giving us. In my experience most actors respond to language quite easily: very few are tone-deaf to verse (fortunately different parts of the brain are used for music and speech). Our ear, informed and practised, will tell us what to do. As Gielgud said, 'Good verse-speaking is rather like swimming. If you surrender to the water it keeps you up, but if you fight, you drown.'[8] The more we run the scenes the more we will bring everything together: play the rhythmic structure of the lines, respond to the imagery, make the meaning clear – and sound spontaneous.

Two cautionary notes. First, it's not finally *how* we say the lines; it's why, to whom, and with what intention. Second, Shakespeare in translation is so popular in other countries it must follow that his power does not lie only in his language – think how *we* relish Chekhov and Ibsen in translation. Nor does it lie in his mostly borrowed plots. It rests surely in Shakespeare's perception of life and his understanding of human aspirations and failings. Never become so obsessed with form that you forget content.

DIRECTIONS IN THE TEXT

Shakespeare built a number of DIRECTIONS into the spoken text, either to save time in rehearsal or to ensure that revivals and touring versions stuck to his intentions. In *Romeo and Juliet*, for instance, we learn that Romeo kisses Juliet twice on first meeting, the Nurse enters looking 'sad' and 'out of breath', and in the final scene Capulet asks Montague to 'give me thy hand'. Othello and Iago both kneel to swear revenge on Cassio. Edgar tells us how he plans to appear 'grimed with filth' as Poor Tom. Cordelia tells us when Lear awakes. Moves are sometimes indicated: with the Ghost in the first scene of *Hamlet*, and the robbing of the travellers at Gadshill in *1 Henry IV*. Groupings are suggested, as in the *Hamlet* play scene, or Puck's squeezing of the juice on Lysander's eyelids. When Prospero, Othello and Polonius each conceals himself to eavesdrop, this is clearly indicated. Soliloquies are sometimes noted, as when Hamlet declares, 'Now I am alone' or 'Go a little before'. Exits are often marked with a blunt 'Come away'.

Changing methods of address can clarify relationships. In *1 Henry IV* Worcester starts by calling Henry IV 'liege' and 'majesty', but swiftly changes to 'my lord' when reminding him 'We were the first and dearest of your friends'. Celia calls Duke Frederick 'liege', 'sovereign', 'the duke', but after Rosalind's banishment boasts 'let my father seek another heir'. 'Thou' generally implies intimacy, while 'you' is more distancing. Superiors could 'thou' inferiors, but expected 'you' in return. Toby Belch advises Aguecheek that he can put his rival Cesario down by calling him 'thou'. As Polonius warms to his instructions to Laertes he switches from 'you' to 'thou', but with Ophelia he maintains the more distant 'you'. Angelo uses 'you' to Isabella until he declares his love, when he shifts to 'Who will believe thee, Isabel?' Lady Capulet addresses Juliet as 'thee' and 'thou' when she proposes the marriage to Paris, but switches to 'your' when Juliet rejects the idea. As Lady Macbeth is increasingly shunned by her husband, she calls him 'you', 'sir', 'my royal lord', rather than her previous 'thee'; while Macbeth continues to call her 'thee' and 'love'.[9]

Shakespeare also indicates changes of pace and tone. He first experiments with this in the comic patter of Launce, Costard and Lancelot Gobbo, and then applies it more generally. Richard II alternates between rage and calm at Flint Castle, Leontes' speech is extraordinarily broken in the first act of *The Winter's Tale*, and Lear declares in the storm:

> But I will punish home.
> No, I will weep no more. – In such a night
> To shut me out? Pour on, I will endure.
> In such a night as this! O Regan, Goneril,
> Your old kind father, whose frank heart gave all –

> O, that way madness lies. Let me shun that.
> No more of that.   (3.4.16–22)

Shakespeare has built into the speech anger and temperance, changes of direction and pace. This is a particularly clear example, but, certainly in the later plays, his whole construction of language and verse is steering us towards mood, tempo and volume. At the same time don't feel that the text is a complete score that you have to decipher with expert help. I think more and more that Shakespeare deliberately left major decisions to his actors. He wants us to seize the text and make it our own.

VOICE AND MOVEMENT

The actor's instrument is his VOICE and body, and these have to be kept in shape during rehearsal. In most Shakespeare rehearsals some attention is given to voice and movement sessions. If they're not provided, then there are excellent exercises to be found in books by Cicely Berry and Patsy Rodenburg. Berry is a great believer that words have a physical root and are an active force in themselves, freed from their literal meaning. The very act of speaking words out loud can shift their meaning and our understanding of them. We need to be aware of their physical movement and make them part of our own physical self. Once we're behind each word as we say it, giving it space without pushing or overexplaining it, then language becomes active and interesting. For this we need a lot of breath. The ideal is, as Peter Hall says, that the lungs are a kind of bagpipe, always full of air and always being replenished. Take this sentence of Hamlet's:

> How stand I, then,
> That have a father killed, a mother stained,
> Excitements of my reason and my blood,
> And let all sleep while, to my shame, I see
> The imminent death of twenty thousand men
> That, for a fantasy and trick of fame,
> Go to their graves like beds, fight for a plot
> Whereon the numbers cannot try the cause,
> Which is not tomb enough and continent
> To hide the slain.   (4.4.56–65)

His thoughts are tumbling out, and this has to be honoured. Can we do these lines on two breaths, or at the most three? Take heart: Shakespeare isn't deliberately setting us Herculean tasks. The root of our energy always lies with the breath. Once we are on top of the thought and its energy, the breath will follow. In real life we nearly always have enough breath for what we want to say – just listen to any animated conversation. As Kenneth Branagh said, 'If I was continually running out of breath at the end of a particular line, it was more to do with not having the character's thought and intention clear than insufficient intake of breath. If I could find out *why* I was saying something then they could help me with *how* I should serve it vocally'.[10] That said, in my own experience, with a large Shakespeare part there are usually half a dozen moments when you have consciously to take a breath to help you through a particularly taxing passage. For economic reasons many professional Shakespeare productions take place in large theatres. It's no good thinking that the *intention* to communicate the thoughts will automatically fill a large space. Language must be followed through to the end of the word, the line, and the sentence. Final consonants are vital. In Hamlet's speech above, the 'd' of 'stained', the 'm' of 'fame', and the 'n' of 'slain' must be articulated. 'V's are especially tricky: 'grave', too lightly touched, come over as 'grey', and, too heavily touched, as 'graver'. Talking about 'projection' is often unhelpful and can lead to shouting: better to think in terms of a lot of breath, vocal muscularity, response to the heightened language, and a *need* to communicate and penetrate the consciousness of a thousand people.

The plays demand a good deal of MOVEMENT. British actors used to have a terrible reputation for acting from the neck upwards, and Shakespeare productions were either rather static or full of self-conscious posturing. Things have improved a good deal thanks to drama schools' attention to movement and the general trend towards physical theatre. Television, however, has got actors into bad habits, because the static camera doesn't like too much movement and gesture, and close-ups can so easily disguise any bodily awkwardness. One of the most difficult things for television-bred actors, their hands used to pockets and props, is to stand still on stage, relaxed, with the arms by the side. Here the Alexander Technique can help, as it seeks to establish a resting position in which all the joints – shoulders, elbows, hands, hips, knees, ankles and feet – are lengthening away from each other. This lessens muscle tension in the neck and lower back, and therefore gives greater freedom and flexibility to both voice and movement.

Visual excitement has always been important on stage, and Shakespeare fully recognised this. The plays are full of battles, group arrivals and departures, processions, chases and conceal-ments. Think of the two parts of *Henry IV*, where there are robberies, fights, battles, tavern games and comic recruiting scenes with rifle drill. If Coriolanus, Hamlet and Tybalt have reputations as swordsmen then this has to be demonstrated. Gesture was very important to the Elizabethans and is often written into the text or the stage directions: Lady Macbeth washes her hands and Gertrude wrings them; Hermione leans cheek to cheek, meets noses and hangs about Polixenes' neck (or so Leontes claims). Gesture, even in a large theatre, doesn't need to be exaggerated: surprisingly subtle movements can register, as when Coriolanus holds Volumnia 'by the hand, silent'. As Mark Rylance says:

> Actors [at the new Globe] are learning again about
> gesture, but it's more about the antithesis and contrast in
> a good gesture rather than just hand signals for things or
> just largeness for largeness's sake. It's the marrying of
> contrast and the enjoyment of changes and rhythm.[11]

SHAPE

Each play, scene and speech contains a story, and the actor needs to find the SHAPE of that story. Most speeches have a headline prompted by the previous speaker (Portia's 'The quality of mercy is not strained'; Lear's 'O, reason not the need!'), then one thought leads to another, often in conflict, and there is some sort of resolution, which is then presented to the next speaker. The baton has always to be passed. In *The Winter's Tale* Leontes accuses his wife Hermione of adultery, without any grounds or evidence beyond his own paranoid jealousy. He brings her to trial, having sent her newly born daughter to be exposed in some 'desert place', and wildly rails against her,

ending with the half-line, 'Look for no less than death'.
Hermione replies:

> Sir, spare your threats.
> The bug that you would fright me with, I seek.
> To me can life be no commodity.
> The crown and comfort of my life, your favour,
> I do give lost, for I do feel it gone
> But know not how it went. My second joy,
> And first fruits of my body, from his presence
> I am barred, like one infectious. My third comfort,
> Starred most unluckily, is from my breast,
> The innocent milk in it most innocent mouth,
> Haled out to murder; myself on every post
> Proclaimed a strumpet, with immodest hatred
> The childbed privilege denied, which 'longs
> To women of all fashion; lastly, hurried
> Here, to this place, i'th' open air, before
> I have got strength of limit. Now, my liege,
> Tell me what blessings I have here alive,
> That I should fear to die. Therefore proceed.
> But yet hear this – mistake me not – no life,
> I prize it not a straw; but for mine honour,
> Which I would free: if I shall be condemned
> Upon surmises, all proofs sleeping else
> But what your jealousies awake, I tell you
> 'Tis rigour, and not law. Your honours all,
> I do refer me to the oracle.
> Apollo be my judge.   (3.2.89–114)

As you see, Hermione immediately takes up Leontes' half-line
with the simple, dismissive: 'Sir, spare your threats.' Her headline is clear: 'I seek death.' She further cuts Leontes down to size
by calling his threat a 'bug'. 'Commodity' (profit or comfort) is
a stingingly dismissive term to use in conjunction with 'life'.
Note the alliteration of 'can', 'commodity', 'crown' and
'comfort'. The line drives through to her key word 'favour', and
then follows the directness of two monosyllabic lines, dominated
by the antithesis of 'gone' and 'went'. She has five further points
to make, and nearly every line ends with a key word – 'joy',
'presence', 'comfort', 'breast', 'mouth', 'post', 'hatred', 'hurried'
– and every fresh point starts after the caesura. Her choice of

phrase is very charged: 'starred unluckily', the repetition of 'innocent', 'haled out to murder', 'proclaimed a strumpet', 'immodest hatred', 'privilege denied', and 'hurried here'. You feel a great emotional build, but each point is made quite succinctly, so that you sense her battling to stay reasoned and in control. There are always two energies at work in Shakespeare's speeches: the energy of the whole thought, and the energy of the individual phrases. If passion and temperance, phrase and sentence, have to be kept in balance, her summation is very simple and direct: 'Tell me what blessings I have here alive, / That I should fear to die. Therefore proceed.' 'Alive' and 'die' stand in antithesis, and her direction to 'proceed' finally brings a full stop at the end of a line.

This could be the intended end of her speech, and it presents the actor with an interesting choice. Had she always intended to continue, or are her next eight lines a spur-of-the-moment afterthought? Does the notion that to be 'condemned upon surmises' is 'rigour and not law' suddenly come to her? It's always more interesting if at least part of the speech is discovered by the character while speaking. Both actor and audience need to be open to the possibility of change. Hermione's language now seems less considered, departing from the regular iambic rhythm. The parenthesis, 'all proofs sleeping else / But what your jealousies awake' seems a sudden, spontaneous dig (note the antitheses of 'proof' and 'jealousies', 'sleeping' and 'awake'). She ends by appealing to the oracle. Was this always her intention, or is it a new thought? She has moved a long way from her headline, 'I seek death.' In any such speech there is a succession of arcs – the antithetical words, the caesura and the driving towards the end of the line; followed by the arc of the whole sentence; leading to the arc of the whole speech.

Scenes follow the same general pattern: introduction, conflict in discussion, a turning point, and some form of resolution whereby things will never be the same again. Ophelia wants to return Hamlet's 'remembrances', they argue about beauty and honesty, Hamlet realises they are being overheard, he rejects Ophelia and declares his intention of killing Claudius. Viola sets out in disguise to woo Olivia for Orsino, they argue to and fro until Viola demonstrates how she would declare her love, and Olivia realises that she is falling for 'him'. Of course in rehearsal you can pull the shape about. You might decide on different turning points, or that each scene has more than one turning point. The vital thing is to observe the conflict both between and within the characters. Ophelia doesn't want to return Hamlet's gifts, she wants his love. Hamlet may still feel love for Ophelia, but his father's murder and his mother's rapid marriage have changed everything. Viola doesn't want to woo Olivia for Orsino, she wants Orsino for herself. Olivia finds herself attracted to Viola/Cesario against her better judgement.

In turn the whole play has a shape and structure. Lear abdicates and is driven out into the open air, in his madness he realises truths about humanity and society, on his recovery he is reconciled with Cordelia and they die together. The turning point is perhaps his going out into the storm with 'O fool I shall go mad'. As Cicely Berry says, 'We should always be concerned with the predicament, and not the feeling: that will take care of itself.'[12] Story, situation, conflict between and within characters are the meat of drama, and it is essential to find a shape to them that feels right for you. Your biggest ally is the language. This is not unique to Shakespeare. As Sam Mendes says about Pinter: 'Each character has shape, each line has a shape, the words have shape. If an actor doesn't have an ear for it, it's like not having an ear for music.' Sometimes we only realise the shape of a part when we've finished rehearsing: it may even be the audience who finally teach us what the structure is.

Like all good writers, Shakespeare wrote to find out what he was thinking. He deliberately chose familiar subjects and characters and often borrowed his plots, so that the bare outline was provided for him. All his skill and passion was directed towards changing and shaping the stories in a way that would illuminate what it is to be human. These shapes are unpredictable, sometimes extraordinary, often rash (why does Cordelia have to die, or Celia fall in love with Oliver?). He is thinking intuitively, but also structurally, and the actor needs to respond both to his immediacy and to the pattern he is creating. If we can tap into the argument he is unfolding and find a shape to it, then we will be on course to understand both our character and the play.

SOLILOQUY

Shakespeare didn't invent the SOLILOQUY, but he pounced upon it and changed it almost out of recognition. It's a particular stage convention that a character is left alone and begins to speak out loud (film rarely allows characters to speak direct to camera). Who is the character alone on stage talking to? There are various possibilities. Shakespeare sometimes provides a person, Mark Antony talking to the murdered Caesar, Juliet to the absent Romeo, Malvolio to the imagined (though in fact hidden) Toby Belch; sometimes a prop, Hal to his father's crown, Macbeth to an imagined dagger; or sometimes to a force of nature, the sun, stars, storm, spirits or the heavens (God). These are useful partners, though soliloquies are rarely addressed solely to them as it can become monotonous if we persist in directing a whole speech at something inanimate or unseen. Where there is no partner or object supplied, the actor is left with three choices: talking directly to the audience, talking to herself, or talking with some acknowledgement that the audience are overhearers. The choice doesn't have to be absolute, it's possible to pass back and forth among them.

When it's clear that the audience are being addressed, then it's a form of public, even political, act. Richard III opens the play by taking the audience into his confidence as to his character, motives and intentions. Shakespeare never abandoned this direct address. Hamlet asks the audience, 'Am I a coward?' and calls on them to 'witness this army of such mass and charge'; Iago demands 'And what's he then that says I play the villain?' Clowns like Launce, Gobbo and Macbeth's Porter perform a kind of stand-up routine. Shakespeare always enjoyed challenging his audience, and he found that giving soliloquies to his villains – Richard III, Iago, Edmund – made them unsettlingly sympathetic. Falstaff never entirely loses our affection even when he confesses, 'I have led my ragamuffins where they are peppered.' I have always found the way to make a public soliloquy work is to treat the audience as your friend and confidant, and to assume that, however outrageous our proposals, they will understand and accept them, even connive in their morality. As

director Bill Alexander advised Antony Sher, Richard III should
assume he's addressing a convention of trainee Richards. It pays
great dividends, in terms of communication and reality, to
button-hole audience members individually, eyeball to eyeball.
It can be the best way of drawing the audience into our predicament (see pp. 220–1, 246).

Shakespeare realised early in his career that the soliloquy
needn't always be used for direct address. As the philosopher
Jerry Fodor writes: 'Language is not simply for communication,
it's also for the externalisation of thought – to speak out loud
what we're thinking. Thoughts inevitably seem different when
put into words. They often need to be edited, developed, re-
phrased. Shakespeare was a master at getting his characters to
speak their way through this thought-process.'[13] Richard III may
start by addressing the audience, but by the end of the play he
is gabbling to some alter ego:

> What do I fear? Myself? There's none else by.
> Richard loves Richard; that is, I am I.   (5.5.136–7)

It seems he's lost his buoyant assumption that the audience are
on his side, and believes they've become his critical conscience.
Shakespeare gradually explores the further possibilities of
characters' wrestling with their predicament. Richard II's prison
speech (5.5) demonstrates this transition. The thought-process
is not entirely clear, but the desire to hammer out existential
arguments is plain. It is used to better effect in the character of
Brutus, when, alone in his orchard, he argues out the case for
Caesar's assassination:

> It must be by his death. And for my part
> I know no personal cause to spurn at him,
> But for the general. He would be crowned.
> How that might change his nature, there's the question.
> It is the bright day that brings forth the adder,
> And that craves wary walking. Crown him: that!
> And then I grant we put a sting in him
> That at his will he may do danger with.
> Th'abuse of greatness is when it disjoins
> Remorse from power. And to speak truth of Caesar,
> I have not known when his affections swayed
> More than his reason. But 'tis a common proof
> That lowliness is young ambition's ladder,

> Whereto the climber-upward turns his face;
> But when he once attains the upmost round,
> He then unto the ladder turns his back,
> Looks in the clouds, scorning the base degrees
> By which he did ascend. So Caesar may.
> Then lest he may, prevent. And since the quarrel
> Will bear no colour for the thing he is,
> Fashion it thus: that what he is, augmented,
> Would run to these and these extremities;
> And therefore think him as a serpent's egg,
> Which, hatched, would as his kind grow mischievous,
> And kill him in the shell.   (2.1.10–34)

Brutus headlines his intention: Caesar has to die. He then tracks back and forth. It's nothing personal; it's just Caesar's determination to take the crown. A qualification: it's not the crown itself, it's how it might change his nature, since the powerful often lose any sense of conscience. A second qualification: it's true he hasn't let his emotions rule him in the past, but when the humble achieve their ambition they often turn their back on their former state. This may prove true of Caesar, and in case it does we'd better kill him. The snag is that he hasn't shown any sign of it yet, so we'd better argue that his nature is such that given the crown he will go to extremes, and best to kill him before he does.

In this instance the tortuous reasoning ends where it began, but it's not been a convincing argument, its flaws are plain to us, and perhaps plain to Brutus. Because it's not a logical, lawyer-like defence of assassination, the shape of the speech may not be clear at first sight, but there is a shape to be found. Shakespeare is inside the mind of the Brutus he has imagined, and is instinctively arguing the way his Brutus would. The actor in turn has to get inside this head and follow the argument point by point, weaknesses and all. Don't think of it as a long speech. It might have stopped after the six-word headline, after the first three lines, or after the first ten. He might have continued had Lucius not entered, though the missing two feet after 'And kill him in the shell' suggest a pause. The language will guide us at every turn, from the harsh monosyllabic opening through the powerful adder metaphor to the elongated ladder metaphor, as Brutus tries to bolster his case. The turning point of 'So Caesar may. / Then lest he may, prevent' returns to the monosyllabic, and Brutus then tries to make his political spin more persuasive with the simile of the serpent. Both the language and the structure of the argument will help us to separate the different beats, vary the tempo, and use different tones and colours. It's not a coherent statement, it's a living thought-process, jagged and wandering, and every twist and turn has to be marked in some way. At the same time it has to follow the speed of thought. Michael Gambon is very down-to-earth about this process:

> You have to make it interesting. That's what [the director] John Dexter used to say: if you had a long speech, you couldn't just do it, blah blah blah, you have to do the middle bit fast, then do the end a bit high and gradate it, do machinations with it, give it a bit of fireworks and then take it down, change the rhythm, and disobey the full stops and commas . . . It lives in you. It's intuition. That's technique, I suppose.[14]

The soliloquy achieves maturity in Hamlet's various debates with himself, though sometimes these are so far-reaching and consuming that the plot can hardly contain them. My favourite, 'How all occasions do inform against me' (4.4), is only in the second quarto and was cut in the folio, presumably because Hamlet's chance encounter with Fortinbras' army is almost incidental to the action. 'To be or not to be' is both simply expressed and tantalisingly unclear. Is Hamlet talking to himself or to the audience? If he has overheard any of Claudius' and Polonius' preparations (the first quarto and the folio have him entering at different places in the text), is he directing part or all of the speech at his eavesdroppers? Why is the speech placed there anyway (some productions move it)? Is there a specific reason why at this point in the action Hamlet should be contemplating suicide? Or is the speech about killing Claudius? Shakespeare seems to be experimenting (knowingly, mischievously, recklessly?) with the audience's uncertainty. Now that the speech has become so famous a further layer has been added: the audience are now complicit because they know it so well. It has become an anthem to mortality shared by everyone in the theatre. The problem for the actor is not to feel that he is conducting some verbal ritual, and most Hamlets have found the best solution is direct address and simplicity (see pp. 238–9, 248).

Shakespeare is careful not to overuse the soliloquy. Characters who have a deep interest in their natures, like Hamlet and
Macbeth, are given ample scope to explore their inner conflicts.
Othello, who has difficulty understanding his feelings, has only
two soliloquies; Lear, who disastrously lacks self-knowledge, has
none (while Edgar and Edmund have several). *King Lear* and
Macbeth, written close together, are like twin experiments in
self-understanding. Lear painfully acquires a little towards the
end of the play; Macbeth has it from the outset but is fatally
unable to profit by it. But when we say that Lear, King John and
Cleopatra have no soliloquies, because they are never alone on
stage, are we suggesting that they never address the audience?
John Barton believes that the Elizabethan actor addressed whole
speeches, or lines within speeches, to the audience as a matter of
course, and would have been surprised at our rigid definition of
'soliloquy'. Lear's 'Blow winds and crack your cheeks' and 'Poor
naked wretches' may be spoken with the Fool and Kent on stage,
but Lear seems oblivious to them. The presence of Charmian
and Iras doesn't prevent Cleopatra from debating her thoughts
out loud. Rehearsal is a good opportunity, and a safe place, to
explore this, though we need an audience to test it out. The
result can be very liberating, and I think most actors' experience
of the new Globe have borne out John Barton's point.

One final point: do characters ever lie in soliloquy? I think
they tell the truth as they see it at that moment, but we should
not rule out that they may be deceiving themselves. Hamlet may
claim that he can't kill Claudius because he's at prayer, but he
may simply be putting off the moment. Don't assume that
characters always know the truth about their inner selves: if they
did there would be no journey of discovery for them to make.

THE JOURNEY

It's natural for an actor to look for his character's JOURNEY
through the play – just as we try to make some sense of our own
passage through life. Journeying, literally or metaphorically, was
part of the medieval dramatic tradition, the progress through
hardship to redemption or death. As Peter Hall says, the
romances are all about 'journeys through purgatory, which meet
some resolution and forgiveness at the end'.[15] But while this is

certainly true of Imogen, Leontes or Helena, it is hard to determine what journey Autolycus or Lavatch go on, or to escape the conclusion that Shakespeare didn't give much thought to providing a journey for any but his central characters. What is the Fool's journey in *Lear* or Portia's in *Julius Caesar*? Even when playing a major character like Jacques, Alan Rickman came to the conclusion that he doesn't really move: he enters the play sitting under a tree and exits to sit in a cave. Paul Jesson couldn't find much of a journey as Henry VIII: the part seemed like eight separate scenes leading to no important conclusion.[16] Sometimes Shakespeare doesn't seem to chart a character's progress to maximum dramatic effect. It is arguable that Richard II and Titus Andronicus would have had more interesting journeys if more signs of self-discovery had come earlier in the play.

But despite these reservations, the actor's constant search for a shape, an architecture to the part, will often find the journey is central to the play. It can be a literal case of travel: Lear to Dover, Othello to Cyprus, Hamlet to England, Antony to Egypt and Rome. In many of the comedies the young women at the centre go to strange places: Viola to Illyria, Helena in *All's Well* to the French court, Imogen to Milford Haven, Rosalind to the Forest of Arden. These new environments free them from the trappings and constraints of their former lives. Their journey is also a psychological one. The forest proves a place of hardship and potential danger for Helena and Hermia, Rosalind and Celia, but it also has a transforming and liberating effect on them. The storm causes Lear great distress but the open countryside enables him to see clearly for the first time, just as Timon sees humanity in a harsher, more realistic light on his seashore. The physical journey, or in some cases the 'quest', often occupies the middle section of the play, allowing characters to return to familiar territory in Act 5, transformed by their experience.

STANISLAVSKY, OBJECTIVES AND SUBTEXT

The pure STANISLAVSKY 'system' is hardly taught any more, though a version of it, the 'Method', still flourishes in America, but we're all partly under his influence, and it's worth examining whether his teaching has any relevance to Shakespeare. It was a subject that engrossed Stanislavsky, witness his book on producing *Othello*, but I think it finally defeated him. The essential points of his 'system' are:

The construction of an 'inner life' and backstory for a character, and the use of 'emotional memory' techniques. Shakespeare's lack of interest in backstory and its importance to modern actors has already been discussed (see pp. 64–5). Stanislavsky has important things to say about the relationship between the construct of a character and the actor's own self, and this will arise throughout this book. The Elizabethans weren't much worried by which was character and which was actor. 'Emotional memory' – recalling a time when you had a similar emotion – is probably most useful in the comedies (love, jealousy, grief, joy). I find the histories and tragedies tend to deal with extremes (revenge, killing and death), for which most actors have no comparable experience. However hard we try, I doubt if we'll see Macbeth's dagger as he does, or know what it's like to order the killing of Lady Macduff and her children.

Breaking down the text into units and objectives, and settling on one super-objective. These have become the commonplace of modern acting, and it's important in Shakespeare, as in any dramatist, to divide scenes into units, to settle on whether a character enters a scene with an objective, whether that is achieved, and whether a new objective presents itself. This is in fact not so very different from Elizabethan teaching on rhetoric, which also saw language as a tool to secure specifiable goals: 'actioning' is a modern version of this process. In *Othello* (3.3) Iago sets out to persuade Othello of Cassio's dishonesty and, when this is established, to doubt Desdemona's faithfulness. Then Emilia hands him the handkerchief, and Iago sees a way to give Othello 'ocular proof', lead him to the murder of both Cassio and Desdemona, and gain the lieutenancy for himself. As Iago kindles and inflames Othello's jealousy he runs through a masterly gamut of actioning – questioning, probing, suggesting, warning, affirming, begging and reassuring. He speaks in order to *change* Othello.

Finding a super-objective for a Shakespeare character is a more debatable issue. You can argue that Hamlet's super-objective is to revenge his father's death, Viola to find Sebastian,

Friar Laurence to reconcile the Capulets and Montagues, and Henry V to defeat France. But you can see immediately that Shakespeare saw character in a much more fluid, many-faceted and inconsistent way. What is the super-objective of Lear, Falstaff, Timon or Antony? Is Prospero trying to bring Miranda and Ferdinand together, revenge himself on his usurping brother, or face up to a life without magic? It could almost be said of *Hamlet* that it is an essay on the absence of super-objectivity, of the way that humans are blown by chance and make up their lives as they go along.

Finding a through-line of action, and a psychological consistency for a character. Shakespeare's development as a dramatist saw him at war with consistent through-lines, while at the same time his interest in psychology continued to grow – witness Macbeth, Cleopatra and Leontes. As Jerry Fodor writes:

> What matters in Shakespeare's kind of tragedy is the characters' psychology: the motives and intentions out of which they act, and how their motives and intentions change as the fruits of their actions ripen . . . Contrast Greek theatre, in which the focus is more often on the dramatic situation itself than on the psychology of the protagonist's response to it . . . What do we know about Electra's psychology, except that she's angry and hell-bent on revenge?[17]

Physical preparation and the use of physical action to express the emotion. We've already seen the importance that Elizabethan actors attached to movement and gesture (see pp. 14–16), and the way that Shakespeare wrote physical action into the text. The tenor of much recent theatre has been to emphasise the physical, and this has been a welcome antidote to the tyranny of the text, but in Shakespeare it needs to be used with caution. His language is so rich and varied in emotion that physical action can hardly compete with, or be a substitute for, his verbal dexterity.

Discovery of a subtext that lies beneath the character's words. It's often stated that there is no subtext in Shakespeare – his characters say what they mean. In *Building a Character* Stanislavsky's own definition of subtext was: 'the manifest, the inwardly felt expression of a human being in a part, which flows uninterruptedly beneath the words of the text, giving them life and a basis for existence. The subtext is a web of innumerable, varied inner patterns inside a play and a part . . . It is the subtext that makes us say the words we do in a play.' This is a world away from the crude idea that subtext is simply a character saying one thing and meaning another. Shakespeare's plays certainly have a 'web of innumerable, varied inner patterns'. As Hamlet says to his mother in his first scene, it's not just his mourning clothes, his sighs and tears,

> Together with all forms, moods, shapes of grief
> That can denote me truly. These indeed 'seem',
> For they are actions that a man might play;
> But I have that within which passeth show –
> These but the trappings and the suits of woe.   (1.2.82–6)

Shakespeare alighted on a method of gradually revealing his characters' inner thoughts, often to maximum shock effect. Thus Claudius unexpectedly has the aside, 'How smart a lash that speech doth give my conscience', Othello reveals his doubts in 'Haply for I am black', and Henry V pours out his misgivings with 'What infinite heart's ease / Must kings neglect that private men enjoy?'. These revelations immediately make us question the confident front these rulers have presented. In the comedies especially, characters often disguise their feelings. Beatrice and Benedick do it constantly, and Viola speaks of her 'sister' sitting 'like Patience on a monument, / Smiling at grief'. If then we take 'subtext' to mean what is going on beneath the text that makes the characters speak, then Shakespeare is a master of it.

Stanislavsky does have much to offer the actor in Shakespeare, but always remember his dictum, 'this system is a companion along the way to creative achievement, but it is not a goal in itself. You cannot act the system.'

HAMLET'S ADVICE TO THE PLAYERS

This has often been taken to be Shakespeare's acting manifesto. There are doubters. Since Shakespeare appears so dedicated to making his characters speak in their own voice, why should he have obtruded himself in this one instance? Hamlet is not a professional actor, and the advice he gives contains points that had been familiar since Aristotle, and often repeated in books on rhetoric. The professionals are remarkably unforthcoming in response – the First Player simply says, 'We will, my lord' – and many productions have featured them listening in resigned boredom to this princely amateur mouthing advice which they either have practised all their working lives or have no intention of following.

But why then does Shakespeare make Hamlet go on at such length, some fifty prose lines, working himself up to a conclusion that clearly refers to the Elizabethan comedian's trade? It does *sound* like a professional dramatist/director speaking and, though we shall never be certain, it's worth breaking down what he says. The essential points are:

- Speak 'trippingly on the tongue'.
- 'Do not saw the air too much with your hand, thus; but use all gently.'
- 'In the very torrent, tempest, and, as I may say, whirlwind of your passion you must acquire and beget a temperance that may give it smoothness.'
- Don't 'tear a passion to tatters', and don't strut and bellow. Don't 'o'erstep the modesty of nature'.
- 'Be not too tame neither, but let your own discretion be your tutor.'
- 'Suit the action to the word, the word to the action.'
- The end purpose of playing is 'to hold as 'twere the mirror up to nature'.
- Clowns should 'speak no more than is set down for them'.

This is all good advice, but it's clearly not a complete acting blueprint à la Stanislavsky. It does, however, go to the heart of the balance between personal passion and technical skill. Passion runs high in all Shakespeare's plays, in the comedies as much as the tragedies: think of Petruchio and Kate, Angelo and Isabella, Ford's jealousy, and Malvolio's final line. 'Passionating' was a skill the Elizabethans revelled in. Emotion in Shakespeare has on occasions to be at full throttle to create and justify the language. When Isabella says of her brother –

That had he twenty heads to tender down
On twenty bloody blocks, he'd yield them up
Before his sister should her body stoop
To such abhorred pollution.
                    (*Measure for Measure*, 2.4.180–83)

– the actor has to *need* such extreme language to express the size of her experience. Audiences, however much they may appreciate the intellectual and literary qualities of the text, finally respond to its emotional impact, and this cannot be short-changed.

This can be a problem for the modern actor. Shakespeare preached temperance in reaction to the bombastic style of the 1580s, just as Brecht invented his so-called 'alienation effect' in response to the German bourgeois theatre of manners. Nowadays, partly through the influence of film, underplaying is the norm. Few actors are tearing any passion to tatters; they're more likely to be of the 'anything you can do, I can do less of' school. Control, Clint Eastwood-style, is at a premium, but then Clint has shown no desire to play Shakespeare. Shakespeare demands that his actors explore the extremes. Ben Kingsley knew that his Othello had to be a still being who, provoked at a primal level, would react with the violence of a psychopath. He had to find both the tranquil mind and the jealous violence, and the technique to convey both. That's not to say that the first had to be expressed with tranquillity and the second with violence. It's all to do with the inner dynamic: if the actor is responding with enough internal energy then the expression of it may be cool and temperate. As Kingsley says, 'the energy of the character and the predicament of the character are only available to the audience if the tension between the opposing forces is observed, relished and played'.[18]

Shakespeare often helps in this by showing the character standing a little outside the emotion, observing and even learning from it. When Macbeth is confronted for a second time by Banquo's ghost, he says:

Approach thou like the rugged Russian bear,
The armed rhinoceros, or th'Hyrcan tiger;
Take any shape but that, and my firm nerves
Shall never tremble. Or be alive again,
And dare me to the desert with thy sword.
If trembling I inhabit then, protest me

> The baby of a girl. Hence, horrible shadow,
> Unreal mock'ry, hence!   (3.4.99–106)

The 'rugged Russian bear' needs no histrionics, the image is doing the work. The important thing is the argument: I wouldn't tremble at a bear, a rhino or a tiger as I do at this ghost. Even in the final exclamations, when he calls the mockery 'unreal' he shows an understanding and a distancing of the experience. Wallow in too much emotion, and the story that lies at the centre of the speech is lost. The speech becomes just about us and our feelings, not what we're talking about. But be not too tame neither: if the character is not moved by this crisis in his life then the audience won't be either. As Peter Hall says:

> Here is the paradox: by hiding the feeling, you reveal it;
> by not indulging it, you express it. This is the contradiction
> in all great acting. Perhaps it is the ambiguity in all great
> art. The feeling may be a very torrent, a tempest, a
> whirlwind; but the audience needs an utterance which is
> controlled and considered in order to receive it.[19]

NATURALISM

Holding the mirror up to nature may sound uncontroversial, but the question of 'NATURALISM' in Shakespeare is a fraught subject. The Elizabethans thought Shakespeare had introduced a new realism, a 'counterfeit of life', 'as if the personator were the man personated'; but then this has been true of each generation in turn. Marlowe sounded more naturalistic than Sackville and Norton, Shakespeare more than Marlowe, Middleton more than Shakespeare, Wycherley more than Middleton, and so on. The 1820s thought Edmund Kean's acting reached new heights of naturalism, when subsequent generations might have found him ludicrously stagey.

Of course there is nothing 'real' about a stage. The actor walks on to a platform pretending to be alone in a vast palace. The audience knows she's an actor, the lines have been rehearsed, the blows are not real, and there is no palace beyond the wooden flats; yet despite this they suspend their disbelief (most of the time). So the actor knows that what she does won't be taken as 'true'; the most she can hope for is 'credibility'. In many modern plays, certainly from 1900 onwards, the life on stage does try to approximate reality – but not in Shakespeare. However much his blank verse may have the sound and immediacy of actual speech, it is an artificial form. No lovers parting after their first night together have ever spoken like Romeo and Juliet. As Ian McDiarmid argues, 'Naturalistic techniques are not appropriate to Shakespeare. The plays aim for a distillation of life, not an imitation of it.'[20]

Shakespeare wrote at a time when a presentational style of acting (Alleyn as Tamburlaine?) was giving way to a more representational (Burbage as Benedick?). Shakespeare ranges between the two, and so presumably did his actors. He could move in one scene from the cosmic verse of:

> Excellent wretch! Perdition catch my soul
> But I do love thee, and when I love thee not,
> Chaos is come again.

straight into this naturalistic-sounding exchange (albeit underpinned by iambic pentameters).

IAGO   My noble lord.
OTHELLO   What dost thou say, Iago?
IAGO   Did Michael Cassio, when you wooed my lady,
Know of your love?
OTHELLO   He did, from first to last. Why dost thou ask?
IAGO   But for a satisfaction of my thought,
No further harm.
OTHELLO   Why of thy thought, Iago?
IAGO   I did not think he had been acquainted with her.
OTHELLO   O yes, and went between us very oft.
IAGO   Indeed?
OTHELLO   Indeed? Ay, indeed. Discern'st thou aught in
    that?
Is he not honest?
IAGO   Honest, my lord?
OTHELLO   Honest? Ay, honest.
IAGO   My lord, for aught I know.
OTHELLO   What dost thou think?
IAGO   Think, my lord?

And by the end of the scene Othello is declaring:

> I had rather be a toad
> And live upon the vapour of a dungeon

Than keep a corner in the thing I love
For others' uses.   (3.3.91–109, 274–7)

Both language styles have to be honoured. Othello's exchange with Iago can be chatted almost as if it were an episode of a TV serial, but we can't chat through the image of a toad living upon the vapour of a dungeon. Of course the image must still have an internal, natural truthfulness: Othello means exactly what he says. But the delivery, whether forceful or contained, can't be prosaic. Playing Shakespeare in small studio spaces has had great success of late. It's striking how well the great tragedies, written for the Globe, work in an intimate dimension, and how much of the text can be delivered in a conversational tone. Our present generation's drive to make the language sound fresh, immediate and contemporary has made the plays much more accessible, but there is a limit to how far we can natur- alise the verse. If Othello says, 'Farewell the neighing steed and the shrill trump' as if he's reluctantly taking early retirement, then the delivery is at odds with the language. Like one of those tiny music-boxes that tinkle out Beethoven's Fifth, it sounds absurd.

AMBIGUITY, IRONY AND INCONSISTENCY

Ambiguity, irony and inconsistency are central to Shakespeare's art, but they present problems for the actor. The actor wants clarity about her intentions, to know what she is doing at any given moment. She can only play one thing at a time: trying to play every single variation results in a 'Variorum' performance, as Tynan said of Michael Redgrave's final Hamlet ('at times he seems to be giving us three different interpretations of the same line *simultaneously*').[21] Should the actor be aware of ambiguity and play that awareness, or should she leave it to the audience to observe and interpret it?

IRONY, saying one thing while meaning another, the actor certainly has to be aware of. It is intensely theatrical, and Shake- speare is full of it. Hamlet does not believe that his mother's sudden wedding was caused by 'Thrift, thrift, Horatio. The funeral baked meats / Did coldly furnish forth the marriage tables.' When Coriolanus submits to his mother, Tullus Aufidius means a great deal more than 'I was moved withal'. Disguised sexual ironies pepper the plays, as when Mercutio declares, 'If love be blind, love cannot hit the mark.' Once we look for irony in Shakespeare we begin to see it everywhere, discover hidden meanings beneath every line, and find appearance constantly contrasted with reality. We start to play against the text, send it up and indulge in self-mockery. We stand outside the character and comment on it, putting phrase after phrase in inverted commas. This can be interesting and liberating, but it can also be a trap. It can be a way of not committing ourself to the thought or the emotion of the moment, or even of declaring ourself superior to it. 'Playing God' is a temptation to an actor in any play, but in Shakespeare it is red-hot. The actor begins to hold up every line for ironic inspection, guiding the audience through the complexities of the part as if it were an illustrated lecture. The audience want us to inhabit the part, not stand outside it. Irony is a difficult quality to handle.

'Most great writers are two people, if not more: their art grows out of the splits in their personalities' (John Carey). This is as true of Shakespeare as it is of Chekhov or Dickens. What finally are we to make of Cleopatra or Othello; Konstantin or the three sisters; Lady Dedlock or Old Dorrit? What did their authors intend? AMBIGUITY lies at the heart of their genius, perhaps because they wrote so instinctively, allowing their inner psyche free play once they had fixed the outline of the story. T.S. Eliot wrote that in order to interpret Hamlet 'we should have to understand things [about Shakespeare] which Shakespeare did not understand himself'.[22] When Hamlet says, 'I do not know / Why yet I live to say "This thing's to do"', I always feel that Shakespeare doesn't know either. He might answer as Pinter did, 'I don't know *why* he says it, I just know he says it.' Writers don't always know what they have written. Frank Kermode says of *Hamlet* that Shakespeare's development 'is a mastery of the ambiguous, the unexpected, of conflicting evidence and semantic audacity . . . We are challenged to make sense, even mocked if we fail.'[23] Paul Scofield is more emphatic:

> We cannot pluck out the heart of his mystery . . . In the
> major roles of all the great plays there is a seeming
> contradiction of purpose or ambiguity of character; it is

only by the acceptance of paradox as being intrinsic to human behaviour that Lear or Hamlet, Othello or Macbeth can be more than objects of intellectual analysis.[24]

Ambiguity, however, is not a quality that can be actively played. The actor is concerned to find a coherent character who convincingly inhabits the text. The actor has to 'make sense' of what the character says and does. The audience are then 'challenged' to make sense of what may seem a welter of ambiguity. Shakespeare revelled in contradictions. He can be terse and long-winded, dense and repetitive, high-flown and bawdy, earnest and punning. He is sometimes clear and immediate, sometimes obscure and distanced. His characters share this confusion. Prospero is both a wise magician and an embittered manipulator, Polonius a shrewd politician and an old baby, Hal/Henry V a man of the people and a cold autocrat. Shylock in his five scenes can appear five different people. This is one of Shakespeare's great discoveries: that character lies in INCONSISTENCY. When in other Elizabethan plays characters stuck consistently to their 'humour' and appeared unremittingly choleric or melancholic, they remained two-dimensional. If Hamlet had simply swept to his revenge, like a Hollywood action hero, there would have been no character (and very little play). Shakespeare first experimented with inconsistency in Richard III and the Bastard in *King John*: Hamlet, Macbeth and Cleopatra were to build on this. Frances de la Tour relished Cleopatra's unpredictability, 'turning on a sixpence, charming and gracious, cruel and sharp, within a line, then sexy and involving in the next, and straight after simply annihilating'.[25]

The important thing is to learn how to play each moment, each scene, for what it's worth, how to turn on a sixpence and not try to iron out the inconsistencies. With Shakespeare we can't object that 'my character wouldn't do or say that', as actors in long-running TV series do. The contradictions are there, and we have to play them, because it's in their collision that the central dynamic is to be found. Macbeth is an opportunistic murderer with a great self-analytical intelligence. On the page the contradictions may seem unplayable, but be reassured – audiences take them in their stride. They see a living human being on a stage and are disposed to accept that whatever he does must have a unity and coherence. The plays that interest us most and are most often revived are those that have the greatest plurality of meaning. As Adrian Lester said of playing Henry V:

> Never before have I played a character when it is so essential to play every scene for all it's worth, without trying to make connexions with other scenes: the audience will make the links themselves and (if they can) make up their minds about Henry. The discussion of what kind of person Henry is must be continued, not answered, through my performance: if I try to answer it, it's dead; if I don't answer it, it remains alive and keeps moving.[26]

Shakespeare continues to be staged because there can never be a definitive production, a final statement of meaning. How much do Lear and Othello contribute to their downfall, does Hamlet's feigned madness turn his wits, is Prospero triumphant, resigned or defeated at the end? As Jonathan Miller says of directing Shakespeare, 'What I try to do is to create as much complexity and indeed, as it were, strategic ambiguity as I can . . . I think if you choose clear-cut, explicit lines, what you get is fairly boring, instructive theatre.'[27]

POLITICS AND POWER

Shakespeare was fascinated by POWER throughout his working life. His history cycle shows a complex grasp of the fifteenth-century power struggle, POLITICS are central to all the tragedies, and his final plays constantly probe the weakness of leaders (Cymbeline, Leontes, Prospero). The comedies too are much concerned with political clashes, whether by Oberon, Duke Frederick or Angelo. If Shakespeare was a covert Catholic, as many now argue, he would have been only too aware of conspiracies and state persecutions. He knew that Marlowe had been killed in 1593, probably assassinated by the state, and that Thomas Kyd had died the following year, probably from the effects of torture. It was therefore extremely dangerous for any writer to comment too directly on political matters. The deposition scene in *Richard II* was omitted from the published quarto, and the performance of the play on the eve of the 1601 Essex rebellion could have put Shakespeare in the Tower. It was around 1600, however, that Shakespeare wrote some of his most political plays, strategically set in the past but clearly redolent of contemporary themes.[28] *Henry V* (1599) examines the way Hal copes with the responsibilities of kingship, *Julius Caesar* (1599) questions whether monarchy is the best political system, and introduces the theme of political murder and the 'hideous dream' that lies 'between the acting of a dreadful thing / And the first motion'. This leads to the regicide in *Hamlet* (1600), and its most complete examination in *Macbeth* (1605/6), in both of which the protagonists are in a sense overwhelmed by the demands of power. *Troilus and Cressida* (1601/2) and *Measure for Measure* (1604) are both dominated by Shakespeare's political analysis.

Where does Shakespeare stand politically? The old truism was that he was a disengaged fence-sitter, yet his great interest in and understanding of politics would seem to belie this. It is clear that he had a horror of disorder, right through from his portrayals of the Jack Cade rebellion in *2 Henry VI* to the mob in *Coriolanus*. Yet at other times he seems to revel in freedom and anarchy, witness *A Midsummer Night's Dream* and *As You Like It*. Of course his plays end with a restoration of order – this formality seems to have been a requirement of the licence – but often you feel they are heading in quite another direction (*King Lear, Measure for Measure, Timon of Athens*), and are yanked into line only at the very last minute. This political ambiguity has proved rich material for modern interpretations. *Coriolanus*, for example, has been upheld by both right and left. The Americans banned the play in Germany in 1946 because Hitler's regime had promoted Coriolanus as an example of 'valour and heroism', De Gaulle took the play off the French school syllabus for being too left-wing, and Brecht reworked the play to strengthen the proletarian case. Many East European states under Soviet domination took inspiration from those plays that showed the overthrow of tyrants. As Jan Kott said, 'Shakespeare is like the world, or life itself. Every historical period finds in him what it is looking for and what it wants to see.'[29]

The actor is therefore picking his way through a political minefield. The dead Brutus, the symbolic political assassin that Elizabeth feared all her life, is lauded as 'the noblest Roman of them all', so what are we intended to make of his nobility? John Wood maintains that he made the right choices, but events turned out unexpectedly. John Nettles argues that 'there is no development of insight or understanding in him. He fails to acquire wisdom. He continues to make awful mistakes; he continues to change his mind from moment to moment; he continues to contradict himself despite his "great mind".'[30] Should the actor take a line on Brutus, showing him either wise but unlucky, or unworldly and vacillating, or should he play all the contradictions and let the audience take what they will from it? If we take Brutus to be sincere and earnest, as the text amply suggests, then I would opt for boldly playing the contradictions.

In 1979 I toured Germany with a RSC production of *Coriolanus*, directed by Terry Hands, in which I played Junius Brutus, one of the tribunes of the people. Terry's insistence was that each political interest – Coriolanus, Menenius, Volumnia, Aufidius, the tribunes and the citizens – should play their objectives as strongly as possible, and there should be no overt bias in the presentation. This was both a puzzle and a revelation to many Germans, who were used to Coriolanus being presented either as a crazed fascist or a bulwark of order, but I'm convinced that it was a Shakespearean approach. Just as Shakespeare had a gift for inhabiting character, so he had the ability to inhabit different political agendas. No one in the play holds the key to political wisdom, but everyone has a good case to make. The actor's job is to make that individual case as persuasively as possible.

Despite Shakespeare's even-handedness we sometimes feel there is a secret agenda at work The predominant conviction I have gained from acting in *Hamlet, King Lear, Coriolanus, Troilus and Cressida, Measure for Measure* and many of the history plays is that Shakespeare was mounting a many-sided attack on both the Elizabethan political system and its ruling class: hard to prove, but a fertile attitude for any actor approaching these plays. The many plays about the education of a ruler, a topic that so fascinated him, all contain covert political criticism. Direct criticism had to be presented in disguised form, usually by putting it in the mouths of villains, clowns and madmen. Only when Lear is demented is he allowed to lacerate society:

> The usurer hangs the cozener.
> Through tattered rags small vices do appear;
> Robes and furred gowns hides all. Get thee glass eyes,

> And, like a scurvy politician, seem
> To see the things thou dost not.   (Q1, sc.20.154–8)

The clearest example of the 'secret play' is *Henry V*, where the expected championing of a great English hero is undermined at every turn. Henry is given no convincing argument to counter Williams' assertion that 'there are few die well that die in a battle', and the irony of Gower's approval that 'the King most worthily hath caused every soldier to cut his prisoner's throat. O, 'tis a gallant king' would not be lost on a discerning spectator. It's a great anti-war play taking shelter within a conventional glorification of 'we happy few'. The St Crispin's Day speech may be a heart-warming rallying cry or a cynical piece of manipulation. I think it can be played as both: don't destroy its ambiguity.

SEX

SEX is everywhere in Elizabethan drama, though often fatally lacking in modern productions. As early as 1583, Philip Stubbes could write in his *Anatomy of Abuses* that the fundamental appeal of stage plays was to incite lust; audiences went home 'and in their secret conclaves they play the sodomites, or worse'. The popularity and sales of *Venus and Adonis* (1593) show how much the public lapped up Shakespeare's handling of eroticism. Sexual desire was the motor of his early romantic comedies, and one of his earliest tragedies, *Romeo and Juliet*. Confident young women like Juliet, Rosalind, Olivia and Helena pursued their men with sexual intent – Elizabethan women spoke very freely about sex in the presence of men – and this cannot be short-changed in performance. Nor should Shakespeare's use of bawdy, which Elizabethan audiences clearly relished. Farting ('break wind') and bums feature prominently, and Shakespeare's ingenuity in sexual euphemisms is supreme in our language. The male genitalia become the pike, lance, pen, pipe, weapon, carrot, stalk, bauble, organ, stump, pizzle, poll-axe, potato-finger, holy-thistle and dozens of others. The female genitalia stretches his imagination to the limit, and include the rose, lap, plumb, crack, treasure, mountain, velvet leaves, box unseen, bird's nest, Venus' glove, clack-dish, Netherlands and Pillock-hill. On the sexual act I am particularly fond of Benedick's 'hang one's bugle in an invisible baldric' and Beatrice's 'dance with your heels', though for obscurity the foul-mouthed Iago takes the prize with 'change the cod's head for the salmon's tail' (Pauline Kiernan claims that every single one of Iago's 1,070 lines contains a sexual pun). Shakespeare rarely went overtly beyond the bounds of contemporary taste, though Mercutio seems to have been at the limit when he declares, 'O Romeo, that she were, O that she were / An open-arse, and thou a popp'rin [pop her in] pear' (despite the fact 'open-arse' was the country name for the medlar fruit, the censor seems to have amended it to 'open et cetera'). Eric Partridge, the doyen of bawdy, concludes that Shakespeare believed 'the desire to write is at least as urgent and powerful, intellectually and spiritually, as the desire to make love (especially, to copulate) is on the physical plane'.[31]

If sex dominates the comedies, then it's a vital ingredient in the tragedies. Shakespeare is at his most sexually explicit in the period between *Hamlet* and *Antony and Cleopatra*: sex lies at the centre of *Othello*, *Troilus and Cressida* and *Measure for Measure*, and is significant in the relationship of Hamlet and Ophelia, and Goneril, Regan and Edmund. Hamlet's relationship with Gertrude was interpreted as early as 1910 as a classic Oedipal complex, Hamlet's unconscious desire being to kill his father and marry his mother. I find the Macbeths always work best if there is a strong sexual charge between them: the disintegration of their physical marriage is a key element in the play, as it is between Claudius and Gertrude. The hot rush of sexual desire was one that Othello is only too aware of, when he requests the Senate to allow Desdemona to accompany him to Cyprus:

> I therefore beg it not
> To please the palate of my appetite,
> Nor to comply with heat – the young affects
> In me defunct – and proper satisfaction,
> But to be free and bounteous to her mind. (1.3.260–4)

Basically, if there is no sexual rapport between Othello and Desdemona, Antony and Cleopatra, Rosalind and Orlando, Petruchio and Kate, then there is no play.

Shakespeare was interested in a wide range of sexual possibilities, and actors need to key into this. In *A Midsummer Night's*

Dream a night in the forest allows the four lovers to swap partners, a fairy king and queen to quarrel over a slave boy and the
queen to fall in love, and possibly have sex, with an ass. In
Twelfth Night Olivia and Orsino fall in love with Cesario, both
attracted by 'his' feminine boyish charm (whether Sebastian and
Viola later prove as alluring to them is left unexplored). Shakespeare was also fascinated by the grey area between friendship
and homosexuality. The merchant Antonio's feeling for Bassanio,
and the sea captain Antonio's devotion to Sebastian seem clearly
romantic, and Thersites, in a rare instance of overt labelling,
calls Patroclus the 'masculine whore' of Achilles (the classics
presumably gave Shakespeare licence to be more explicit).
Bolingbroke, rather confusingly, accuses Bushy and Green that
'you have, in manner, with your sinful hours / Made a divorce
betwixt his queen and him [Richard II]'. Sodomy was illegal,
but there were few prosecutions and the discreet were clearly
tolerated. Men and women, before marriage, nearly always
shared a bed with a relative or friend of the same sex, and open
physical intimacy was common. The homoerotic was everywhere but didn't automatically imply intercourse: Aufidius
could say to Coriolanus, 'That I see thee here, / Thou noble thing,
more dances my rapt heart / Than when I first my wedded
mistress saw / Bestride my threshold', without it necessarily
indicating homosexual desire. Just as Polixenes could say of
Leontes, 'We were as twinned lambs that did frisk i'th' sun', so
Helena could remind Hermia:

> So we grew together,
> Like to a double cherry: seeming parted,
> But yet an union in partition,
> Two lovely berries moulded on one stem.
> So, with two seeming bodies but one heart . . .
> (3.2.209–13)

WOMEN

In my experience of rehearsing and discussing Shakespeare
certain questions keep cropping up. How well does Shakespeare
write for WOMEN? How misogynistic is he? Did he subscribe to
contemporary ideas of the relation between the sexes? Was he

affected, or inhibited, by knowing that his female characters were to be played by young males?

The position of women in Elizabethan society was in a state of flux, and this is strongly reflected in drama. Greater social and economic possibilities were opening up for women, whether inheriting and running great estates or acting as shopkeepers, innkeepers or businesswomen in trades as traditionally male as blacksmiths and farriers. Puritan writings on marriage and the family argued for the spiritual equality of man and wife, for domestic comradeship, and for sexuality within marriage as a source of mutual joy. Drama both honoured these developments and detailed patriarchy's fear and resentment. Courtship, marriage, reproduction and inheritance were still the basic pillars of society. As maid, wife, widow or whore, women were placed in a sexual and economic relationship to men. The four female virtues were still held to be obedience, chastity, silence and piety. Women were also thought to be more lustful and less rational than men, and therefore in need of male protection and guidance.

Shakespeare subscribed to many of these views, both liberating and confining. He saw marriage as the 'natural' lot of both men and women, whether Beatrice and Benedick or Paulina and Camillo. His women are nearly all romantically attached and dominated by men, and the plays are full of the dangers of female 'wilfulness' – resisting arranged marriages, running off with the 'wrong' men, and committing adultery. Petruchio calls Kate 'my goods, my chattels. She is my house, / My household stuff, my field, my barn, / My house, my ox, my ass, my anything', and Kate enjoins other women that 'thy husband is thy lord, thy life, thy keeper, / Thy head, thy sovereign'. As always the words are open to interpretation. Is Petruchio exaggerating, even parodying, the traditional male position in his efforts to 'tame a shrew'? Is Kate's speech 'utter disillusion' (Paola Dionisotti), 'a choice that has dignity' (Fiona Shaw), ironic at Petruchio's expense, or a recognition of harmonious coexistence? Women are altogether more realistic about the pitfalls of marriage, as Rosalind tries to teach Orlando. Men on the other hand have exorbitant expectations of romance, and lose control when the possibility of a divided love appears. Is Othello a wronged innocent, or a selfishly jealous domestic tyrant? Time and again in the plays Shakespeare seems to suggest that marriage can be tyrannous and exploitative: certainly he dramatises few happy unions.

In the comedies Shakespeare presents a mostly liberated view of women, and they dominate the action. They are independent, assertive, resourceful, questioning, anxious to learn by experience and discover their true identities. In the histories and tragedies women are usually thrust into supporting roles and killed off by the end (Hamlet and Claudius have nearly 2,000 lines between them, Gertrude and Ophelia fewer than 400). Despite the fact that Cleopatra outlives Antony, Shakespeare had great difficulty in putting women at the tragic centre. What interested him in both comedy and tragedy were daughters in revolt: Juliet and Cordelia are as determined to defy their fathers as Imogen and Celia. He had little interest in female entrepreneurs: his lower classes are mostly servants, tavern-keepers and bawds, though he did celebrate middle-class women in *The Merry Wives of Windsor*. There's an undoubted strain of misogyny and sexual loathing in the plays, particularly *King Lear, Troilus and Cressida* and *Timon of Athens*. Hamlet declares of women, 'wise men know well enough what monsters you make of them . . . You jig, you amble, and you lisp, and nickname God's creatures, and make your wantonness your ignorance.' In *King Lear* women are shown as lustful and insubordinate, and Lear in his madness rants that below the woman's waist 'is all the fiend's: there's hell, there's darkness, there is the sulphurous pit, burning, scalding, stench, consumption [or 'consummation']'. In the later plays images of syphilis and venereal disease abound. Nevertheless for every Hamlet's 'frailty thy name is woman', there is Emilia's 'Have not we affections, / Desires for sport, and frailty, as men have?'. As feminist critic Marianne Ney says, 'For all the limitations on his feminism, Shakespeare is one of the few widely honoured culture heroes who can be claimed as a supporter of women at all.'[32]

How well does Shakespeare write for women? Here is an assortment of views from four writers and two actors:

MARGARET CAVENDISH (1664): 'One would think he had been metamorphosed from a man to a woman, for who could describe Cleopatra better than he had done and many other females of his own creating . . .'[33]

VIRGINIA WOOLF: 'Shakespeare's mind as the type of the androgynus [sic], of the man-womanly mind . . . it is one of the tokens of the fully developed mind that it does not think specially or separately of sex.'[34]

VALERIE TRAUB: 'To be a woman in Shakespearean drama means to embody a sexuality that often finds its ultimate expression in death . . . His representations of gender and sexuality are as complex, various, and fascinating as our own bodies and selves.'[35]

ANNE BARTON: 'No other writer challenges the aggressively limited feminist position, the intolerant and rigidly schematised view of human life . . . with such power. At the same time, disconcertingly, no other writer has created so many memorable and sensitively understood women characters.'[36]

HARRIET WALTER: 'Shakespeare's verse is as dense and as beautiful, the emotional depth as great, the wit even more brilliant, the psychology as complex in the female characters as in the male.'[37]

FRANCES DE LA TOUR: 'So many women who came to see [*Antony and Cleopatra*] told me how surprised they had been by the fact that Shakespeare should show us a woman behaving like that, how astounded they were by the wonderful outrageousness of the role. It isn't sympathy so much that the part demands; it's celebration.'[38]

What influence did the fact of boy players (see pp. 20–1) have on Shakespeare's view of women? He was obviously fascinated by the opportunities for gender ambiguity that all the 'breeches' parts gave him in the comedies. A boy acting a woman pretending to be a man gave him enormous scope. Tilda Swinton even argues that the breeches parts only work when played by boys, that Orlando being in love with a boy/girl/boy has a real frisson. It is true that Shakespeare couldn't show a boy and a man in too erotic a situation, but then the censor and public decorum wouldn't have allowed too graphic a representation of sexual desire even if the female characters had been played by women. Indeed there is an argument that Elizabethan audiences actually tolerated a display of women's sexual needs precisely because they were filtered through the medium of male actors. Modesty could thus be upheld through the raciest of female dialogue. In fact the more impersonal the actor, the greater the freedom of the dramatist to explore – as Greek masks have shown. Brecht too would have endorsed this approach: by 'presenting' rather than 'representing', the audience is encouraged to remain more alert. The boy player therefore becomes an emblem: the 'woman' has no connection with the actor playing her. If Shakespeare felt this, or something like it, it may explain why he wrote so well for women. In his mind, and perhaps in his audience's, they *were* women. The fact that they were to be played by boys not only freed him to explore femininity, but allowed him to show the similarities between the sexes and the way in which boyishness can be an integral feature of a teenage girl (which might explain, for example, Orsino's attraction to Viola/Cesario).

COMICAL-TRAGICAL

With Shakespeare of all writers we can't really corral comedy and tragedy into sub-sections: humour and grief keep rising to the surface, sometimes in the unlikeliest of places. Hamlet is often claimed as the first tragic hero who makes jokes, a revolutionary concept for the Elizabethans. And not just jokes – I was twice in productions of the play (as Horatio, and later the Player King) with Ian Charleson, who could get a laugh by throwing away 'By and by is easily said', not on the face of it a funny line. *Macbeth* is short on laughs, despite the Porter's efforts, but *Lear* has several. Lear himself has a confrontation with Kent that is pure pantomime repartee:

LEAR   What's he that hath so much thy place mistook
To set thee here?
KENT   It is both he and she:
Your son and daughter.
LEAR   No.
KENT   Yes.
LEAR   No, I say.
KENT   I say yea.
LEAR   By Jupiter, I swear no.
KENT   By Juno, I swear ay.   (2.2.187–93)

Though few would go as far as Jonathan Miller, who said, 'If you didn't approach it as a funny play about people going gaga you missed a dimension, and all you got at the end of the day was a rather depressing tragedy about madness and old age.'[39]

Just as it's important to look for comedy in the tragedies, it's vital to give weight to tragic passages in the comedies. Imogen, Helena, Portia, Viola and Rosalind don't have an obvious comic agenda: their predicament is at times very dangerous and the resolution serious. Think how laughter is banished at the end of *Love's Labour's Lost*, *The Tempest* and *The Winter's Tale*. At the same time actors who have set out to play Portia, Rosalind and Viola weighed down with problems have soon realised that the parts need to be infused with comic energy. Pace is crucial: actors find that the laughs come more surely when the text is taken at speed. Donald Sinden, who as Malvolio in 1969 worked out a scale of laughs from 1 to 9 and found ways of getting them every night, is perhaps an extreme example[40], though I well remember Emrys James in 1983 feeling he'd failed if he didn't get five rounds in the letter scene. There are a number of the great parts – Richard III, Falstaff, Malvolio – that veer between tragic and comic, and are often best played by 'straight' actors with a definite comic edge who can establish a strong relationship with the audience. In fact, though *Richard III* can be classed as a history or a tragedy, Simon Russell Beale thinks the part 'the best clown Shakespeare ever wrote'.

Tragedy presents the particular problem of who or what is responsible for the protagonist's downfall. The classical model was either the 'fatal flaw', some failing in judgement that leads to destruction, or Fate, in the shape of the gods, chance or accident. Shakespeare's early plays concentrated on these – Titus, Henry VI and Richard III have obvious flaws, Romeo and Juliet have terrible bad luck – but he soon moved on to a more complex view of humanity and the world. He examined the effect of human villainy in Claudius, Iago, Edmund, Goneril and Regan. He detached his protagonists from their position of leadership and created conditions in which they flounder – Hamlet, Lear, Timon, Antony and Cleopatra. He steadily made them more and more responsible for their own destruction: Lear's intemperance, Othello's jealousy, Antony's irresolution all propel them towards their downfall. With the Macbeths he experimented with how much the audience could identify with outright murderers, and with Coriolanus he created as unsympathetic a hero as he could muster. He never repeated himself: Leontes' jealousy is entirely self-induced and leads to a quite different conclusion from Othello's. Each individual and each set of circumstances is unique, and the actor faces a new challenge in every play. The flaw and fate, however, are always present. How should the actor steer a course between them? Should Othello, Lear and Coriolanus be made so insensitive, self-regarding and brutish that they deserve their fate, and should Hamlet and Timon be so virtuous that they fail only by accident? Or are Lear and Othello 'more sinned against than sinning', Coriolanus the victim of a militaristic upbringing, and Hamlet a destroyer of the Polonius family who deserves his comeuppance? Or is Shakespeare saying that all these are true, that humans are vulnerable, God/Fate is silent, and the world is unjust? Does the actor have to choose a particular path, or should every facet of the character be played to the hilt and the audience left to decide? I have no definitive answer to this. Every time I set out on a Shakespeare play these same questions arise. The purpose of this book is to identify some of the many choices open to the actor.

CLOWNS AND FOOLS

In the Elizabethan era clowns and fools belonged in a particular category. Tarlton and Kemp were in their day bigger names than the leading actors, Alleyn and Burbage: Kemp's name even appears in the quarto texts in place of Dogberry and *Romeo and Juliet's* Peter. The 'CLOWN' meant a type of role, rather than a jester: sometimes a servant, like Gobbo, Launce, the Dromios and the countryman who brings Cleopatra the asp; and sometimes a simpleton, a 'booby', like Peter Simple in *The Merry Wives*, William in *As You Like It* and the Young Shepherd in *The Winter's Tale*. The part usually went to the clown of the company, who was a one-man entertainment, singing, dancing, mimicking, and playing on the drum or pipe. The professional, 'wise' FOOL, Touchstone, Feste and Lear's Fool, often had a solo entrance, heralded in the text, and his first appearance probably got a huge cheer. Lear calls for his fool four times, alerting the audience to his arrival, and when he finally enters he takes over the scene for 100 lines.

Shakespeare's clowns present problems for the modern actor. What character should Touchstone, Feste, Lavatch, Cloten, Autolycus and Thersites have? As the text is not a great help, actors have been driven to constructing a character, trying to find clothes, accents, physical deformities – anything that will help them into the part. Feste might be Scots, Touchstone music-hall London, Cloten hooray-Henry, the Fool an old northern comic. There is also a clown tradition of stammers, silly walks and various physical oddities. Sometimes this offers a way into character that can be discarded as rehearsals progress; sometimes the accent or disability becomes central. Sometimes the quest for 'character' becomes an irrelevance, as text and situation become the only thing that matters. Simon Russell Beale found when playing Thersites that the audience reaction was such that 'I began to care less about why Thersites is the sort of man he is than about the fact that he is a brilliant performer – to care less about causes than symptoms, as it were.'[41] Is it then a matter not of character but of personality, the actor's own comedic presence? When comedians Max Wall and Frankie Howerd ventured into 'legit' theatre they usually relied on their own well-honed comic presence, not always with happy results. Perhaps Will Kemp gave much the same performance as Dogberry or Peter, and Shakespeare longed for a clown who would not only stick to the script, but find a credible character and integrate himself into the play?

The second problem is how to make the clown funny, since the modern audience is unlikely to greet Touchstone's arrival with a great whoop of joy. Actor Joe Melia recalls that as a comic you need a good gag to come on with, 'but Shakespeare gives him this heavy-handed elephantine joke about mustard and pancakes'. What you find in performance, however, is that sound and rhythm have a comic power independent of meaning – rather as in Oscar Wilde, where if the build-up suggests a witty epigram is imminent the audience will usually laugh however weak the final pay-off. Melia's advice is to 'adopt a confident vernacular tone, i.e. as long as I sounded as if I was saying something funny, so long as I used a recognisably comic rhythm, I would get a response regardless of whether the majority of the audience immediately understood the words'.[42] If the language seems impenetrably obscure, or if we get no response, it's best to cut the text and stick to the lines we know we can make work. Alec Guinness claimed that he cut Lear's Fool down to fourteen speeches, though spectators have disputed this.

The third problematic area is the clown as commentator. At a simple level the clown-servant endears himself to the groundlings by commenting on his master's follies, as Gobbo or the Dromios do. They are the voice of down-to-earth commonsense in a topsy-turvy world, and they can make villainy or cowardice acceptable. Richard McCabe found that Autolycus was 'on the surface a light-hearted, likeable rogue, always ready with a song. On closer examination of the text he reveals himself as arrogant, selfish, self-centred and mean . . . a thief, a liar, a pickpocket and all-round cheat.' But Autolycus shares certain characteristics with other clowns, 'he talks directly to the audience, offers an alternative view to the action of the play, and is almost completely in prose'.[43] Like Feste he's a loner, and blows in and out of the action almost at random, presenting a cynical, alienated view of human nature and society. The fool both questions the motives of the other characters and comments on the dangers and uncertainties of Jacobean England, as Lear's Fool probes his master's folly in dividing his kingdom (the only character in the play who does).

There's no model for how to play a Shakespearean clown; in fact the more individual, even anarchic, the better. Take heart from the fact that they always play better than they read. Don't worry too much about the character's psychology or his 'journey', as few clowns have either. With the professional fools concentrate on their job (by Shakespeare's time their whole existence was under threat). Feste and Lavatch are tolerated by Olivia and the Countess because they had been their fathers' fools, and they need to work hard to keep their place as their humour is now 'out of fashion' and 'grows old'. They need to be extra adept at playing by ear, picking up their employer's mood, and playing each moment as it comes. Though accents, props and business may help, remember language is the key, the tool of their trade: 'adopt a confident vernacular tone'. Above all, remember the basics: it's situation and interplay with others that counts.

SUPPORTING PARTS

Leading parts in Shakespeare are in many ways 'grateful' to play: Ralph Richardson likened them to lying on the floor with a machine gun and a ceiling covered with targets – you're bound to hit some. If Act Two has gone badly, Act Four may be better. Smaller/minor/supporting (there's no satisfactory word) parts present different problems.[44] If the first of our two scenes hasn't gone well, we can be in despair. But these two scenes may be vital to the play. In *Much Ado* Claudio and Hero are to be married and the officiant is Friar Francis: he's apparently the 'token vicar' of a thousand and one wedding scenes. Claudio denounces Hero for having known 'the heat of a luxurious bed', Hero faints, her father rejects her, all is chaos, Benedick 'knows not what to say', and then the friar takes over:

> Hear me a little,
> For I have only been silent so long
> And given way unto this course of fortune
> By noting of the lady. I have marked
> A thousand blushing apparitions
> To start into her face, a thousand innocent shames
> In angel whiteness beat away those blushes,
> And in her eye there hath appeared a fire
> To burn the errors that these princes hold
> Against her maiden truth. Call me a fool,
> Trust not my reading nor my observations,
> Which with experimental seal doth warrant
> The tenor of my book. Trust not my age,
> My reverence, calling, nor divinity,
> If this sweet lady lie not guiltless here
> Under some biting error.   (4.1.154–69)

Friar Francis then masterminds the plot that contrives a happy ending; and his reward is eight lines in the final scene. Any production of *Much Ado* needs a very good, experienced Friar Francis.

SUPPORTING PARTS can be very difficult for an actor to come to terms with. Are we a function, a cipher, a prop, a foil, a reactor, a sponge, a silent conspirator? Where do we stand in the structure of the play and the society it creates? How much are we allowed to express within this structure? Do we have to fall back on what I call the 'Michael Caine note' (he was given it by a director early in his career): 'You think of lots of things to say, but then decide not to say them.' I once worked with an actor who claimed that, however small the part, he always thought it the best in the play, because he saw the story entirely from *his* character's point of view. This explained why his performance was arresting, but also distracting. We have to be prepared to fit into the shape of the whole, not act out some private play in the corner of the stage. Much depends on how many colours Shakespeare has given us to play. Can we make something three-dimensional out of the part: can we make a brick with only odd bits of straw?

Supporting parts can be loosely divided into three categories:

ONE-SCENE PARTS. These are most often functions of the plot, and it's important to come to terms with this. Messengers are the epitome of this, and it's best to concentrate on delivering the message with clarity, energy and commitment. The balance lies in presenting a believable person with a pressing need to speak, without appearing, as Terry Hands used to warn, 'to audition for Hotspur'. Some one-scene parts have much greater scope. There are wonderful monologues, like the Porter in *Macbeth*; duologues, like William and Touchstone in *As You Like It*; and unforgettable climactic scenes, like the murder of Lady Macduff and her children. There are characters to whom Shakespeare has generously/carelessly/deliberately given great speeches. Philo introduces us to Antony, 'transformed into a strumpet's fool', with thirteen great lines and then never speaks again (though the actor probably does a great deal of standing around for the next three hours). Mistress Quickly has a spellbinding description of Falstaff's death in *Henry V*. The Welsh Captain in *Richard II* has one of my favourite speeches in the canon:

> The bay trees in our country are all withered,
> And meteors fright the fixed stars of heaven.
> The pale-faced moon looks bloody on the earth,
> And lean-looked prophets whisper fearful change.
> Rich men look sad, and ruffians dance and leap;
> The one in fear to lose what they enjoy,
> The other to enjoy by rage and war.
> These signs forerun the death or fall of kings.
>
> (2.4.8–15)

TWO- OR THREE-SCENE PARTS. Even with several scenes we can still feel ourselves a function of the plot. Our main task may appear to be reacting off the main protagonists, and both function and reaction have to be observed and delivered. At the same time there's usually some room for manoeuvre: Shakespeare has given us something extra to play. We may have a journey marked out for us, as Oswald does in *King Lear* or Titinius in *Julius Caesar*. They have a life, and especially a death, of their own. Oswald's clashes with Lear and Kent, and Titinius' friendship with Cassius and his subsequent suicide are rich in opportunities for the actor. Contrasting aspects of character can be played in different scenes. Sometimes a part that may not seem promising at first reading can emerge strongly in a production, as Ross can in *Macbeth* or Gardiner in *Henry VIII*. But some parts seem so undercharacterised that we may feel forced to impose one from outside. In *Love's Labour's Lost* can one do anything beyond making Longueville and Dumaine, Maria and Catherine a contrast to one another? What is one to make of the two Dukes in *As You Like It*, beyond the stereotype of nice and nasty (I've struggled with both more than once)? Leontes gets the full treatment, but who is Polixenes? In *1 & 2 Henry VI* Somerset starts promisingly with the scene where he and York pluck the red and white roses, but though he keeps appearing, the part dwindles to nothing – not even a good death speech ('Enter Richard and Somerset to fight. Somerset is killed.') My eventual solution in 1977 was to play him as very stupid, which turned out to have great comic potential – he was always one step behind everyone else – but it was a gesture born of despair.

STRONG SUPPORTING PARTS. These usually have a life and character of their own. They include parts like Horatio in *Hamlet*, Maria in *Twelfth Night*, Albany and Cornwall in *King Lear*, the Provost in *Measure for Measure*, and Poins and Justice Silence in the *Henry IV*s. They can be rewarding, but also frustrating to play. They may not be central enough to the plot, or Shakespeare, having announced them strongly, may not have found room to develop them. Albany takes over the ordering of the kingdom in the last act of *King Lear*, but his relationship with both Lear and Goneril is underwritten. Horatio is very active in the first act of *Hamlet*, but is then largely absent for the middle of the play (doing his PhD in Elsinore library?), only to re-emerge strongly at the end. I found it a sympathetic, but oddly broken-back part to play. Maria, I am sure, would like a scene where Sir Toby proposes to her, and Poins a scene that marks his break-up with Hal. These parts, however, do have a number of colours to play, whether of tension, grief or comedy, and there are ambiguities, inconsistencies and contrasts to be found. We may need to look harder for them than in leading parts, because they are less obvious or developed, but the search can be very satisfying. They have a journey through the play, and the 'missing' scenes can be filled out in the mind if not on stage. Just as Hamlet seems more mature after his return from England, so Horatio has developed as a person. It is also important to remember status. Albany and Cornwall rule a kingdom, the Provost runs a prison: they are for a time superior to the abdicated Lear and the Duke disguised as a friar.

Finally, don't assume that only major characters have been given interesting soliloquies. I was less than excited to be asked to take over at short notice the small part of Sempronius, third flattering lord, in *Timon of Athens* at the RSC. Being a GCM (Good Company Member) I did agree, but then found that he has the most demanding of speeches. Every performance became a challenge to think my way though this man's ironies and hypocrisies. It's a wonderful piece of writing (though possibly by Middleton). The bankrupt Timon sends his servants to borrow money from three different senators, and they have been twice denied. Sempronius muses:

> How, have they denied him?
> Has Ventidius and Lucullus denied him,
> And does he send to me? Three? Hmh!
> It shows but little love or judgement in him.
> Must I be his last refuge? His friends, like physicians,
> Thrive, give him over; must I take th' cure upon me?
> He's much disgraced me in't. I'm angry at him,
> That might have known my place. I see no sense for't
> But his occasions might have wooed me first,
> For, in my conscience, I was the first man
> That e'er received gift from him.
> And does he think so backwardly of me now
> That I'll requite it last? No.
> So it may prove an argument of laughter

To th'rest, and I 'mongst lords be thought a fool.
I'd rather than the worth of thrice the sum
He'd sent to me first, but for my mind's sake.
I'd such a courage to do him good. But now return,
And with their faint reply this answer join:
Who bates mine honour shall not know my coin.

                    (3.3.7–26)

ACTING ON FILM

There are very few guidelines to acting Shakespeare on film, since every director seems to experiment with a different method, but of course everything already said about preparation and rehearsal still applies (though you will find little time is given over to rehearsal). The camera requires a different use of energy, but not a totally different style of playing. The attempt to film Shakespeare has been going on for over a century, starting with Beerbohm Tree's death as King John in 1899. Early efforts (there were over 400 silent film adaptations and excerpts) tended to be based on theatrical performances, though the hour-long Forbes-Robertson's *Hamlet* (1913) shows an impressive degree of naturalism. There were various Hollywood spectaculars in the 1930s, including Max Reinhardt's *A Midsummer Night's Dream* (with James Cagney as Bottom and Mickey Rooney as Puck), but filmed Shakespeare really comes of age with Laurence Olivier and Orson Welles. Olivier's *Henry V* and *Richard III* are his most successful realisations, partly because they acknowledge their theatrical background in an imaginative way – his *Hamlet* as black-and-white *film noir*, with soliloquies as voice-overs, has worn less well. Olivier's Richard III beckons the camera towards him in order to drop in his asides. Henry V's 'Once more unto the breach' is given full throttle, but the camera draws right back to make it seem less stagey. Welles fights against the theatrical with a very visual style and frenetic editing, but at times speech gets lost in the melee. *Chimes at Midnight* (or *Falstaff*) is an exciting experiment, and allows Welles, John Gielgud, Jeanne Moreau, Keith Baxter and Norman Rodway to show off a range of styles.

The BBC TV Shakespeares (1978–84), now reissued on DVD, are a mixed bag and, though well spoken, rarely find a compromise between stage and screen. The modern director who turned Shakespeare into good box-office is Kenneth Branagh with his *Henry V* (1989), *Much Ado About Nothing* (1993) and, to a lesser extent, *Hamlet* (1996) and *Love's Labours Lost* (2000). They allow the actors full dramatic scope and, though theatre-based, have a strong eye for cinematic style. Branagh takes Hamlet's soliloquies in one take or one shot, and whispers 'To be or not to be' into a mirror. To whisper or not to whisper? This dilemma seems to lie at the heart of modern filmed Shakespeare: the idea that by speaking very quietly the character will seem more natural and the verse less like 'poetry'. Even Peter Brook advocates speaking quietly into a microphone as more truthful. This is fine when the speech is a form of interior thought, but not when the line is clearly intended for general consumption or when the speaker gives the impression that he's alone rather than addressing someone else. Often a semi-whisper has to be enhanced by the sound department, making it appear strangely unworldly.

There are many acting problems with modern filmed Shakespeare. The text is usually so heavily cut that Shakespeare's instinctive flow is disrupted. Most film actors don't go in for flow, their whole naturalistic instinct is to break lines up, and it tends to be only experienced stage and screen actors like Branagh, Al Pacino, Derek Jacobi, Judi Dench – and even Marlon Brando in *Julius Caesar* – who can maintain the flow and make it seem real. Heavy cutting also destroys ambiguity, though ambiguity is anathema anyway to most film directors intent on making things clear for a mass audience. In film the visual always takes precedence over the aural. In fact the two compete on unequal terms – how can Lorenzo's description of the night sky compare with an enormous shot of the Milky Way? Most of these problems are evident in Baz Luhrmann's *William Shakespeare's Romeo + Juliet* (1996), set on modern Verona Beach, which reached a wide audience through imaginative updating and startling visual effects, some akin to pop videos. The bold performances, however, are short-changed by heavy cutting of the text, restless editing and some very dodgy verse-speaking. All this said, however, there have been some very impressive performances in recent films: Al Pacino's Shylock, Ian McKellen's Richard III, Laurence Fishburne's Othello, Paul Scofield's King Lear.

Four-century old language remains a difficulty on screen, and it can't be coincidence that the most admired Shakespeare adaptations have been in other languages, most significantly from Japan and Russia. Grigori Kozintsev's *Hamlet* (1964) and *King Lear* (1970) are grounded in society, with Elsinore as a prison and Lear's kingdom as a bleak landscape peopled with suffering peasants. Akira Kurosawa's *Throne of Blood* (*Macbeth*) and *Ran* (*King Lear*) are very free transpositions into Japanese medieval society (Lear's children become male), using pure cinema narrative and as little speech as possible. Kurosawa also led the way by setting *Hamlet* (*The Bad Sleep Well*, 1960) in modern corporate Tokyo, an idea adopted by Michael Almereyda's *Hamlet* (2000) with Ethan Hawke in contemporary Manhattan. It may be that the plays should be completely rethought and refashioned for film, and that Shakespeare would have been the first to agree to this.

For our purposes, however, there are still some very helpful examples of how to handle Shakespeare's text on film. Two readily available videos are the *Macbeth*s directed by Trevor Nunn and Gregory Doran, both filmed after long runs at the RSC. In the former Ian McKellen gives an internalised performance, speaking his soliloquies quietly to camera. Judi Dench is particularly successful at keeping the language moving and exploring a wide range between conversational naturalism and frenetic breakdown. In Doran's more recent version Antony Sher is very intense and busy, reverting to a whisper in the more internal moments. On occasions a soliloquy continues on the soundtrack while Macbeth is doing other things, and this is particularly effective in 'If it were done when 'tis done'. Harriet Walter as Lady Macbeth also uses a wide dynamic range, and demonstrates the virtues of playing very close to her partner. The contrast between these two productions will, I think, give you more pointers to playing on film than any written critique.

Two final recommendations: Penny Woolcock's *Macbeth on the Estate* (BBC, 1996) shows how well the play can be adapted to a modern Birmingham housing estate and how naturalistically the text can be spoken. Al Pacino's *Looking for Richard* (1996), a film-within-a-film of *Richard III* set in New York, shows a fascinating range of acting styles from Pacino's flamboyance to Kevin Spacey's containment, and Penelope Allen as Queen

Elizabeth shows that the camera can take a heartfelt emotional display. Don't think you have to whisper everything . . .

CHARACTER

David Mamet writes that 'the preoccupation of today's actor with character is simply a modern rendition of an age-old preoccupation with *performance*, which is to say, with oneself'. Hamlet doesn't exist outside the play and there's no way of knowing 'who he is'. The only thing an audience wants is to know 'what happens next'.[45]

There are broadly two ways for an actor to approach CHARACTER. (I) The character is not real, it is an assemblage of a certain number of lines and actions (Mamet would agree so far); and from this patchwork of evidence we deduce a certain individual. It is detective work, and appeals to the actor who likes to work slowly, put off choices and wait for a character to emerge. The drawback can be that we reach a stage where we know the lines, moves, motives and intentions, but still don't know who this person is – no individual has appeared. (2) The character was real to the author and, if we trust our instinct and imagination, can become real to us. Out of our experience we construct a person we can relate to, or, to put it another way, we impose a character on the play. This appeals to the actor who likes to make a rapid choice, if necessary discard it, and make another. The drawback can be that our creation may not entirely square with the text and the play as a whole, and other actors may therefore find difficulty in relating to it. Of course few actors take only one path. It's usually some fusion of the two, and, important to stress, the end result may be the same.

Down the centuries Shakespeare has received extravagant eulogies for his creation and understanding of character. There is evidence that Elizabethan audiences went to see Falstaff rather than *Henry IV,* Beatrice and Benedick rather than *Much Ado About Nothing.* Edward Burns sums up a common attitude when he writes, 'Shakespeare, whose "genius" lies in his ability to produce seemingly endless, perfectly individuated, perfectly coherent, and perfectly "real" representations of almost every kind of human being, crucially informs our received conception of character.'[46] Well, yes and no. Actors who have tackled Salerio and Solanio in *The Merchant of Venice* might not agree that his 'seemingly endless' creation of character quite extended to them. He was very good at providing individual speech patterns and rhythms for his major actors (Mercutio), but not always for his minor (Benvolio). He rarely describes personal appearance, so we are given no clue as to how he visualised Iago or Lady Macbeth. He wasn't too concerned about logical motives for action, and this has caused actors much heartache. Why does Edgar take his Mad Tom act to such lengths, and then not reveal himself to his father? Why is Oliver so nasty to Orlando, and why does he then repent? Plot sometimes overrides coherent character.

Shakespeare loved disguise, behind which characters, particularly women, can more fully realise themselves. Disguise also serves to break down the idea of consistent personality. He loved characters mirroring one another – Lear and Gloucester, Hal and Hotspur, Theseus and Oberon – because both sides of the mirror can be reshaped; it's a way of questioning, transforming, opening up new possibilities. He loved creating archetypes and then subverting them. Patrick Stewart argues that the universal nature of Shylock lies not in his Jewishness, but in the fact that he puts money and commercialism before everything (Jewish actors tend to disagree).[47] Simon Callow suggests that an actor should first ask 'what', rather than 'who', a character is. Thus Hamlet is firstly a prince, a scholar, a son and a bereaved man.[48] Others would argue that Hamlet's essence lies in his psychology, and that an unprincely, unscholarly approach can illuminate the part in different ways. Towards the end of rehearsal a central image may emerge for a character, requiring us to go back through the whole part, discarding, reshaping and refining.

Character in Shakespeare comes firstly through the language – the actor's response to the particularity of the words. Asking what the language is doing is as important as asking about motivation and intention. It's not straightforward. As Peggy Ashcroft said, 'You can appreciate a line, but it's no good thinking you know how to say it until you've found the character.'[49] This may seem a Catch 22: we can't inhabit the line till we find the character, but we can't find a character till we inhabit the line. Fortunately it doesn't work quite like that: in rehearsal one rebounds off the other, and we discover things about both, day by day. No two actors will come up with the same performance, however faithfully they observe the language clues. In John Barton's 1974 production of *Richard II* Ian Richardson and Richard Pasco alternated as Richard and Bolingbroke. Richard Pasco, Ian wrote, 'saw his king in an elegiac sense, very much a Christ figure who really believed devoutly in the Divine Right'. Ian saw the King more as an actor, always acting to his court, and only having moments of self-revelation in private. Pasco saw Bolingbroke as entirely reasonable, with Northumberland the villain; while Richardson saw him under thrall to his glamorous king/cousin, but returning from exile determined to seize his moment.[50]

Shakespeare's characters are often remarkably aware that they have a part to play, that existence consists of role-playing: they constantly use words such as 'act', 'perform', 'part', 'play', 'scene', and 'tragedy'. It was an Elizabethan obsession. The Queen was said to be a princess who 'can act any part she pleases'. Her fear of deposition was summed up in her remark, 'I am Richard II, know ye not that.' Hamlet constantly refers to acting: in his very first speech he talks of 'actions that a man might play', and he is so caught up by the Players that he risks everything on their performance. Macbeth sees the nadir of existence as a 'poor player / That struts and frets his hour upon the stage / And then is heard no more'. Cleopatra fears that she 'shall see / Some squeaking Cleopatra boy my greatness / I'th' posture of a whore'. Richard III is the most self-confessed actor in the canon, playing the 'orator', the 'devil', the 'dog', the 'maid's part' and the 'eavesdropper'. He invites the audience to watch him at work and then comment on his performance. This concentration on role-playing is a way into Shakespeare's use of the stage as a kind of laboratory, in which he can experiment with questions of identity. *A Midsummer Night's Dream* is much concerned with the power of transformation; *King Lear* examines the loss of identity in chaos. We should therefore be constantly on the look-out for our character's awareness that they are playing a part, and their ability to stand outside themselves and view themselves at work. Hamlet sees himself as both a private person and a miscast avenging angel. Brian Cox saw Titus Andronicus as a consummate actor, with strong elements of vaudeville. Olivier detected in many of the tragic figures a self-deception and a tendency to self-dramatise: Brutus and Othello see themselves as noble, Lear as badly treated. So many of the heroines spend most of the play in disguise and, though Viola sees this as a 'wickedness', it enables them to experiment with identity in an extraordinarily liberated way. 'I am not what I am' is a good motif to take into any exploration of a Shakespearean character.

How much of the character should be you? Bernard Shaw divided actors into the classical, who become the character, and the romantic, who make the character become themselves. Granville Barker, however, wrote that it is a fallacy that the actor can

> suppress his own personality in favour of the dramatist's invention . . . The character as it leaves the dramatist's hands has to be recreated in terms of the actor's personality; and the problem for the dramatist is how to write it so that he may prevent it – his character – from perishing in the process.[51]

Many actors feel, as Susan Brown puts it, 'as if there are two of us, the character and I, walking beside each other, then overlapping, and then if possible fusing, like a double image coming into focus'.[52] Simon Callow warns that this fusion is 'an incomparable feeling. Another person is coursing through your veins, is breathing through your lungs. But of course, it's not. It's only you – another arrangement of you.' An actor can only play aspects of herself, not some construct of another person. It's only by revealing deep, sometimes intimate, aspects of ourselves that we can really illuminate what Shakespeare has written. Callow argues, 'Only then will the energy spring from within, instead of being externally applied; only then will you have renewed the umbilical connection between the character and the author. Then, indeed, you will feel almost irrelevant, a receptacle, a conduit, because the character will start to follow his own instincts and have his own life, just as he did when he first came flowing out of the author's pen.'[53]

But don't fall into the trap of thinking in that case I can just play myself. Peter Brook warns, 'the worst trap for the actor is simply saying: "It's like me." The whole point is that the natural emanation of themselves is brought into being only through the demands of the character.'[54] Our performance will inevitably be 'another arrangement' of us, but the arrangement will be in reaction to the demands of the playwright. There may come a point where we feel we are no longer ourself but are not (and can never be) the character. I think this can be a healthy position, and Shakespeare is a willing partner in this. The reason that his characters are so barely described, so lacking in backstory, and so open to interpretation may well be that he is deliberately leaving so much to the actor. He was enough of an actor himself to know that the completion of character lies in the actor's ability and personality – or perhaps one should say 'stage persona', since 'personality' is always to some extent a construct, a way of disguising our inner self. Rosalind and Hamlet can be played by actors of every size, age, sex and race. Each brings something individual to the part, and each is to some extent successful. Shakespeare is not only a great, but also a generous playwright. I don't believe audiences go just to see Shakespeare's Rosalind, they go to see *your* Rosalind, and that's the challenge we must take up.

I often feel that Shakespeare, not surprisingly, understood more about his characters as his writing of the play progressed. Lear and Rosalind, Coriolanus and Portia seem to me to get more interesting and complex later in their plays. This was first brought home to me when I played Falstaff in both parts of *Henry IV*. Compare the two big tavern scenes – both Act 2, sc.4 (Shakespeare was not averse to following a template). In the first, Falstaff has to sweat (literally) through the rather laboured knockabout farce of the ever-expanding men in Kendal green. In the second, the Hostess, Pistol, Hal and Poins swirl around him while he sits, communing with Doll Tearsheet about his mortality. There is much debate about whether Shakespeare was a reviser, but I sometimes wish he'd gone back and rewritten the first act or two of, say, *King Lear* or *As You Like It*. When his writing really takes off, usually in Acts 3 and 4, his powers of imagination are electrifying.

Three final points: first, a way into any part can be through the Elizabethan proportions of choler, phlegm, melancholia and sanguinity. In other words, what makes my character angry, how much does she control herself and what cools her down, what is she afraid of and what depresses her, and what fires her up and makes her hopeful, courageous and loving? We can immediately see how much Shakespeare examines these, and how much variety it can give our performance. Second, we shouldn't feel we have to defend our character too much. Naturally we need to understand her and see things from her point of view, but don't gloss over her faults, and above all don't crave to be liked or play for sympathy. Rosalind, Richard II, Cressida, Falstaff, Helena and Othello will all emerge as more rounded characters if we observe the weaknesses and unsympathetic traits that Shakespeare has written in. Third, play 'winners' as long as you can. Just because things turn out badly doesn't mean your character isn't confident of success. Claudius may think he's going to get away with it until the very last moment, perhaps until Gertrude drinks the poison. Queen Katherine and Hermione both go into their trials confident that their case is unanswerable. Turning points and reversals are the stuff of drama: how late do Iago, Edmund, Lady Macbeth, Antony and Cleopatra realise the game is up?

IMAGINATION, ENERGY, INTERPLAY AND ENJOYMENT

What is the most important muscle in the body? According to the great mime teacher Lecoq, it's the IMAGINATION. It may seem unnecessary emphasising the imagination to actors, since we spend our working lives imagining ourselves to be someone else living in an imagined world, but nothing is more central to Shakespeare and nothing is more difficult to write about.

> The poet's eye, in a fine frenzy rolling,
> Doth glance from heaven to earth, from earth to heaven,
> And as imagination bodies forth
> The forms of things unknown, the poet's pen
> Turns them to shapes, and gives to airy nothing
> A local habitation and a name.
> (*A Midsummer Night's Dream*, 5.1.12–7)

It's dangerous to deduce Shakespeare's attitude from a speech he gives to a character (Theseus), but in this case it makes for a marvellous incentive to the actor. Your mind and senses need to be in a fine frenzy rolling, glancing from sky to earth, to meet the shapes which Shakespeare's imagination conjures up. It's partly a matter of the language; not just a response to the words, but to the ideas. Can you see pity as a 'naked new-born babe striding the blast', rage as 'tiger-footed', youth as 'blasted with ecstasy', memory as 'the warder of the brain', or peace as 'naked, poor and mangled'? As director Declan Donnellan writes:

> In the beginning was not the word. In the beginning was the imagination, which longs to communicate with others. Words are one means of doing this. But no word is ever properly understood unless it has been spontaneously created by the imagination . . . What I love to see is the actor's imagination making various events and words inevitable.[55]

The plays are full of 'events' which challenge the imagination. Can we imagine how Macbeth might respond to the witches, Rosalind to being accepted by Orlando as a male tutor, or Henry V, Williams and Bates to overwhelming odds at Agincourt? Do we have an image of Elsinore, Rome or Arden that might help us into the world of the play? Can we imagine why Juliet might agree to take the potion, Portia to plead Antonio's case, Edgar to dress as Poor Tom, or Leontes to be jealous of Hermione? Our imaginations need to be finely tuned if we're to communicate these ideas to the audience as rich and credible. Almost inevitably in rehearsal a gap will become apparent between what we are imagining and what we are delivering. One of a director's functions is to understand what we have in mind and tell us when it is not being expressed, when it is still trapped in our heads. Shakespeare had this extraordinary ability to release his imagination into the language and the action of the scene. We need somehow to follow suit.

A choreographer once defined dance as 'the decisions the dancer makes as the energy leaves the body'. It's a good description of acting. We rightly place emphasis on determining the character's intentions, and on accessing our emotions. But neither of these is an end in itself: the actor has to reproduce them. This reproduction has to be energised, and that's where the art lies. The inner impulse is there, how do we express it? Playing Shakespeare's major characters requires great physical and mental ENERGY, not to mention courage. Sometimes it pushes us to our

limits – but not often. What audiences respond to in an actor is
relaxation. If we appear relaxed, we can take an audience anywhere. It's not easy. As Spencer Tracy said, 'I listen, I think, and
I speak. And if you think that's easy, try it.' As the energy leaves
the body it has to shape a welter of decisions, both physical and
vocal. These decisions may be prepared, intuitive or subconscious, but they all have to be energised. I have been on stage
with great actors like Paul Scofield, Judi Dench, Michael Bryant
and Vanessa Redgrave, and watched them just stand quite relaxed, say a line and make the moment achieve an extraordinary
clarity and significance. For a time I marvelled how. I now know
it's because they understood how to control their energy.

Most Shakespeare plays start with a high-energy scene. Sometimes, as in the case of *Romeo and Juliet, Coriolanus* or *The Tempest,*
the play erupts from the first line. Sometimes, as in *King Lear* or
The Winter's Tale, there is a short conversational introduction
before the action boils over. First scenes can appear merely
expositional, but don't be deceived. Just because the first scene
of *The Merchant of Venice* starts with the line 'In sooth, I know
not why I am so sad', and the second scene with 'By my troth,
Nerissa, my little body is aweary of this great world', don't be
fooled into thinking sadness and weariness are the tenor of the
opening. Both Antonio and Portia, in their different ways, are in
a desperate state, the one thwarted in both love and business,
the other fearing she may be forced to marry a man she cannot
stand. Their plights need energising from the start, or there is no
play.

Central to the inner energy we need is the ability to think
quickly. Events in plays are always compressed, thought has
often to be faster than in normal life, and this is especially true
of Shakespeare. Virginia Woolf talks of the speed of his images,
poring out in 'the volley & volume & tumble of his words . . .
Even the less known & worser plays are written at a speed that
is quicker than anybody else's quickest; & the words drop so fast
one can't pick them up.'[56] In fact Shakespeare is nearly always
easier to understand when taken at speed, rather than
laboriously spelt out. Quick thinking drives the action forward,
and we constantly need to be heading for the end of the line or
sentence. Look at Hamlet's impassioned reaction to the Player
King's Hecuba speech:

What's Hecuba to him, or he to Hecuba,
That he should weep for her? What would he do
Had he the motive and the cue for passion
That I have? He would drown the stage with tears,
And cleave the general ear with horrid speech,
Make mad the guilty and appal the free,
Confound the ignorant, and amaze indeed
The very faculty of eyes and ears. Yet I,
A dull and muddy-mettled rascal, peak
Like John-a dreams, unpregnant of my cause,
And can say nothing – no, not for a king
Upon whose property and most dear life
A damned defeat was made. Am I a coward?
Who calls me villain, breaks my pate across,
Plucks off my beard and blows it in my face,
Tweaks me by th'nose, gives me the lie i'th' throat
As deep as to the lungs? Who does me this?

(2.2.536–52)

Shaw was a great advocate of this tumble of thought. He wrote of Forbes-Robertson's Hamlet: 'He does not utter half a line; then stop and act; then go on with another half line; and then stop and act again, with the clock running away with Shakespeare's chances all the time. He plays as Shakespeare should be played, on the line and to the line, with the utterances and acting simultaneous, inseparable and in fact identical.'[57]

Speed, however, will come, hopefully, in run-throughs and performance. In rehearsal we need to stay in the moment, extracting as much juice as we can – as Trevor Nunn is fond of saying. Whenever possible try to have each new idea as the scene develops, one thought leading to another. Surprise yourself. If that's not feasible in context, then mint the new thought just before entering, never way back in the dressing room. Time and again actors playing Richard III and Iago have found there is no grand plan; Shakespeare makes you react to events and think of new schemes as you go along. The same applies to Rosalind, Viola, Helena, Hamlet, Macbeth. Portia may have prepared a speech about mercy, but it's more interesting if she improvises in reaction to Shylock. See how Viola works things out moment by moment. Take it quite slowly at first, examining each new thought: speed will come later.

I left no ring with her. What means this lady?
Fortune forbid my outside have not charmed her.
She made good view of me, indeed so much
That straight methought her eyes had lost her tongue,
For she did speak in starts, distractedly,
She loves me, sure. The cunning of her passion
Invites me in this churlish messenger.
None of my lord's ring! Why, he sent her none.
I am the man. If it be so – as 'tis –
Poor lady, she were better love a dream!

(*Twelfth Night*, 2.2.15–24)

Stephen Boxer told me that the director John Dexter used to demand that you brought at least one new idea into each rehearsal, and he would then say, 'Don't talk about it, *show* me it.' Demonstration was always the key. Stephen said what was remarkable was that if you had one idea and it worked, the knock-on effect could be to infuse the whole scene with freshness, spontaneity and possibilities that you had never considered.

One of the most important things in rehearsal is to work out who, at any moment, is driving the scene. This can be a tricky negotiation. Sometimes the actor who should be driving refuses to do so, preferring to react off, or undercut, what others are doing. Sometimes everyone is determined to drive the scene, and this can result in a metaphorical pile-up centre-stage. In many cases the character with the strongest objective starts by driving the scene, and then hands over when her objective is reached. Once Iago has Othello strongly hooked into jealousy he needs to step back and let Othello's emotions dominate. The important thing is to be ready to hand over. It's a relay race, the baton needs passing on.

Theatre is essentially collaborative. There has to be trust and a good co-operative feeling in the rehearsal room and on stage. Good productions and performances rarely come out of tension and disharmony. From the start of rehearsal, INTERPLAY with other characters is crucial. Shakespeare doesn't start out with a fixed idea of character: it grows as situation and interplay develop it. The plays have to be understood dynamically. We need to experience what everyone else is doing: Gertrude has to wait on Hamlet and Claudius, the Nurse on Juliet, Belch on Aguecheek, Petruchio on Kate – and vice-versa. Characters largely reveal themselves by how they are with other people: Rosalind with Celia, Orlando, Phoebe and Jacques; Hamlet with almost everyone in the play. Comedy often depends on a balancing of the double act – Trinculo and Stephano, Portia and Nerissa, Beatrice and Benedick – but tragedy also has its two-handers: Brutus and Cassius, Othello and Iago, Lear and the Fool. At the same time never forget your own objectives. You have a course to set, don't be blown about by every gust that comes your way. Working with other actors is the key, and the most rewarding part of the job. No actor is an island. As Harriet Walter says, Lady Macbeth is a great part if you see her 'as dark twin, mirror, partner in crime to Macbeth'.[58]

The final quality an actor needs is to ENJOY what she is doing, Lady Macbeth included. There are times in rehearsal when the problems may seem insuperable and anxiety is all we're conveying, but as we come to run the play we begin to feel a delight in what we're doing that is the hallmark of good acting. With enjoyment comes relaxation; they feed off one another and immediately communicate with fellow actors and audience. Directly an audience feel that any performer is unhappy, effortful, overparted, they lose empathy. Shakespeare has given such joy down the centuries – enjoy it when you get the chance.

THE DIRECTOR

The actor should look to the DIRECTOR:

- To know the play thoroughly, and have an understanding of how it works and the significance of each part. But not to have done extensive pre-planning with the intention of fitting everyone into a preconceived scheme. The director should be 'thinking on his feet' (Peter Hall).

- To have cast the play as thoroughly, suitably and imaginatively as possible.

- To create a good working environment where actors feel free to experiment and be creative.

- To understand what the actor is trying to do with a part and help her to facilitate that. To question, suggest choices, recognise where the actor is blocked and help her to go further. To determine the needs, strengths and weaknesses of one actor as opposed to another.

- To choose the right moment to criticise and to praise. Nearly all actors act better when they are both challenged and encouraged.

- To leave choices and possibilities open as late as possible, rather than closing down avenues and constantly tidying up. But to be able to pull things together as performance looms.

- To be a tactful leader and ensure that everybody feels they are working towards the same end. To have the passion and enthusiasm to motivate the cast.

- To be the most tasteful audience you will ever have.

No director could possibly fulfil all these criteria, but five would be a good start. In turn the actor should feel generosity towards the director. The director needs the actor's confidence, help and encouragement.

CONCLUSION

Rehearsal is the time to examine all the aspects we've covered: the language, shaping the story, objectives, ambiguity, politics, sex, character, passion, temperance and imagination. Don't be hurried. Shakespeare productions are usually given extra weeks of rehearsal so that we can examine the detail and not feel that we have to reach conclusions too early. It's a rare oasis in an industry driven by ever-diminishing rehearsal periods. It's an opportunity for thought and experiment, for balancing the animal and the rational. The pianist Alfred Brendel said recently: 'Feeling and intellect have to go together. Even if the feeling is the origin and the goal, there is the intellect as the controlling and filtering factor, and it is the intellect which makes the work of art possible. Without the intellect what one does is amateurish; it may be full of love and passion, but it's amateurish.'[59]

One of the hardest things for an actor is to decide when to run with gut instinct, and when to shape and clarify. Something unexpected may happen in rehearsal which your instinct is telling you is true and your intellect that it is unwise or ridiculous. But if your gut is telling you the same thing when you next run the scene, then hang on to it for a while. It may lead to further leaps of the imagination, or it may become clear that it's not rooted in character or situation. Sometimes it can be as simple as a stress which you have intuitively placed on a certain word. The director may point out that to clarify the sense the stress should surely lie elsewhere. You then have to decide between apparent clarity of meaning and the instinct that you/your character had to stress something unexpected. The particularity of Shakespeare's language is of course an enormous help here, not just with stresses but with whole scenes. Your intellect may have directed you to be calm and considered in a certain passage, only to find that the language keeps pushing you in an opposite direction – and vice-versa.

When I was a student, the great director Tyrone Guthrie gave me this definition of good acting: 'It should be convincing, illuminating and compelling.' Any three-word definition is reductive, but these adjectives have rattled round in my mind ever since, and I was interested to notice that Harold Guskin, in his 2004 book *How to Stop Acting*, uses three very similar words: 'The actor's job is to make each moment of the character in the play believable, interesting and thrilling. I think of our work, the actor's, as exploding the moment.'[60]

The bottom line is CONVINCING/BELIEVABLE. Does the audience suspend its disbelief? The actor claims to be Hamlet, Cleopatra, Achilles. Do we, as audience, at some level accept that? It's not simply a matter of appearance. The Hamlet may seem too old, the Cleopatra too English, the Achilles too little of a warrior. But if they accept the challenge, feel the stretch, and inhabit the language and the situation, we may, whatever our initial misgivings, accept them as 'believable'.

ILLUMINATING/INTERESTING is where the hard work of rehearsal comes in. All Shakespeare's plays take place during a crucial period in the lives of a group of people, whether *Othello* or *Much Ado About Nothing*. We have two or three hours to show how and why a character has reached this crisis, and how and why they deal with it in the way they do. What, in short, have we got to *say* about this character in this story? It's an enormous act

of compression, but every intention, every word, every movement is a potential act of 'illumination'. Each moment can be in
some way 'exploded'.

COMPELLING/THRILLING is the hardest to quantify. Is it
innate, or can it be acquired? Is it a life force, a suggestion of
hidden depths, or just luck? Some actors strive very hard to be
compelling, but only succeed in drawing attention to themselves
– not the same thing at all. Some believe that truth will out, that
depth and sincerity are enough – only to find that this hasn't
been communicated. It's obviously to do with imagination,
truthfulness, energy, focus, self-belief, courage, openness – but
ultimately there's no formula. 'Compelling' is unpredictable.

As late run-throughs approach, the words should be coming
automatically, the language should seem part of us, objectives
should be ingrained, and interplay with other actors should be
assured. This is our foundation. Can we now take off? My
inspiration for this is Judi Dench. I watched Judi work on a part
in enormous detail, and then at a second run-through drop at
least a third of the detail, jettisoning moments I really loved, and
go for the emotional centre. Most actors aim to retain and polish
the detail they've worked on when they get it to performance
pitch. The high-risk actor is the one who's prepared to drop
much of the work and go for the scene's jugular. It doesn't always
work. I've seen actors ruin their performance by taking off at the
last moment into some generalised limbo. But in late run-
throughs if I had to choose between playing safe and taking off,
I know which I'd go for. Rehearsal is the time for experiment –
that's what makes it so interesting.

5

PERFORMANCE

A play is what happens in the air
between the stage and the audience.
David Hare

The play in performance before an audience is the ultimate
act of discovery. Everything in preparation and rehearsal has
been leading to this moment. As actor Gemma Jones says, 'The
shell, the shape and form have been rehearsed, but the flesh and
blood are revealed in front of an audience.'[1] The actor is now
central to the process, as he must have been at the Globe, but
the work is not complete. Rehearsal should have left room for
development. Juliet Stevenson records how she and Fiona Shaw,
as Rosalind and Celia,

> never stopped working on it, chipping away, seeking new
> developments, encountering our resistances and trying to
> battle with them, changing choices and experimenting . . .
> We were lucky that the production gave us, finally, the
> space in which to draw upon our own experience, our
> own humour, and our own lunacies, passions, and
> sensibilities – and, primarily, upon our own friendship.[2]

The performance is the tip of the iceberg. All the detailed work,
some of it useful, some of it not, has been done: the audience
aren't interested in being shown it. We may have worked out
what is meant by Cassio being Othello's 'lieutenant' and Iago his
'ancient', and that it was uncommon for wives to follow their
husbands to war. All that has been very useful to us, but the
audience may not want to know, and anyway how would we
communicate it to them? We should by now have narrowed
down our choices. If we haven't decided on our main objectives
when we get into performance, it's not going to work (though we
may find in the course of the run that objectives shift). We have

to try to rid ourselves of worries – about age, shape, appearance, accent, costume. The audience are disposed to accept what we present them with. I have known actors to cripple their performances through fears which they can't/won't admit, and which turn out to be quite unfounded (nobody insists Romeo has to look like a Greek god or Juliet to appear fourteen). Don't keep telling yourself to 'Concentrate', that will just make you tense. Clear your mind, keep focused, and remember: relaxation is your biggest ally. Above all, don't be dominated by remembering the lines: if the work has been done, the words are securely there. The only way we're going to forget them is by putting up obstacles of our own invention.

Though we've narrowed down our choices, our performance is, after all that rehearsal, inevitably very detailed. The director will probably now be plying us with small, but hopefully very telling, changes. One thing I discovered early on with the RSC is that there's no point giving a performance in which you triumphantly feel that you've got all the director's 187 notes right, if he's sitting out front saying, 'Shame he couldn't make the part his own.' The audience have come to see and hear what *we* have to say about the part – so tell them. We should by now have made up our mind what we're going to do. Certain things should have become habitual: objectives, words, moves, physical actions, pieces of business. There's quite enough to occupy us in front of an audience without having to think which hand do I hold the letter in, or should I say 'sullied' or 'solid'. Of course space should have been left for further growth, but a definite 'performance' should have developed.

There are interesting accounts by fellow actors of Richard Burton's New York Hamlet in 1964, in which he refused to make up his mind about the part, regarding it as unknowable. He therefore fell back on his own stage personality which, however impressive for the first few scenes, never amounted to a consistent characterisation.[3] Hopefully we've arranged the bits of us that make up a consistent personality, and have the right to call the part our own. Alan Rickman said of his Jacques, 'Tiredness sometimes brings a freedom which lets you know how much the "work" has been pushed into the background and the character just behaves. These are discoveries I only really make in performance.'[4] That is a kind of ideal, that we get on stage and 'just behave'; that we take off, secure in the knowledge of who we are. It may be a partial view of the character, but it's what we, at this moment, have to offer. Don't stay objective, aloof, commenting – as if in some way we were above the character, the play, even the whole business of acting. Surrender yourself to your material; let it take you over. As Brian Cox said of his Titus Andronicus:

> It is so economic, this point of the play, that you have to pull the audience through it, really pull them, as though through the eye of a needle. They're waiting for it, but they don't know when it's going to be. From the greeting to the pie, through the killing of Lavinia, to the astonishing rapidity of the trio of deaths, it is all profoundly theatrical, and you've got to go for it and not be afraid of it; be bold and audacious, because you've earned it. You can always be audacious in the theatre if you've earned it.[5]

TELLING THE STORY

Shakespeare chose strong, relatively straightforward stories. Hamlet discovers that his father has been murdered by his uncle, who has seized the crown. He succeeds in killing his uncle, but dies himself. Beatrice and Benedick spark one another off, but are constantly at loggerheads. Their friends trick them into thinking, or finding out, that each is in love with the other, and this finally brings them together. Shakespeare then introduces a whole array of subplots and complications: Rosencrantz and Guildenstern's treachery, the Mousetrap play, Polonius' murder, Ophelia's madness; Don John's villainy, the Claudio-Hero plot, Dogberry and his watch. These add immeasurably to the richness and breadth of the play, transforming a bare, sometimes hackneyed plot into a subtle, many-layered examination of humanity. Shakespeare was a master at intriguing, questioning and finally controlling his audience. The actor's job is to make every twist and turn clear and compelling. Once the audience 'loses the plot', then the play is a failure.

This is of course true of any playwright – *Waiting for Godot* and *The Cherry Orchard* have plots, however carefully disguised. But the plotting of the action is central to Shakespeare's art: a story is nothing without its telling. *Romeo and Juliet* opens with a Chorus who announces the plot and theme:

From forth the fatal loins of these two foes
A pair of star-crossed lovers take their life,
Whose misadventured piteous overthrows
Doth with their death bury their parents' strife.

Shakespeare was never quite so blatant again, though 'Time' has to tell us that sixteen years have passed in *The Winter's Tale*, and the audience will think it likely that the witches' prophecies at the opening of *Macbeth* will be fulfilled. The opening scenes of *Twelfth Night* and *As You Like It* make the likely direction of the action clear. More important for the actor, the characters are conscious that they are about to take part in a story. When Romeo discovers Juliet is a Capulet, he immediately says, 'O dear account! My life is my foe's debt'; and Juliet in turn declares, 'My only love sprung from my only hate! / Too early seen unknown, and known too late!' Viola, on hearing that Sebastian may have survived, says, 'Mine own escape unfoldeth to my hope . . . the like of him.' Orlando tells Adam his back-story (which Adam must already know) and concludes, 'The spirit of my father, which I think is within me, begins to mutiny against this servitude.' Each character is conscious, whether outlining their history, their hopes or their fears, that they are announcing their story both to the other characters and to the audience. This is at its most obvious in soliloquy: Richard III, Hamlet, Iago and Macbeth all confide in the audience at the outset. Both actor and character therefore must feel it imperative that they tell their story.

Directors are fond of telling casts on opening night, 'Just go out and tell the story.' I have always found this rather glib: this instruction has to be broken down into its component parts to be of real use. First, plot points have to be made clearly. We need to know that the Turkish fleet is making for Cyprus via Rhodes, or Othello's mission is in doubt; and that Richard II after 'his late tossing on the breaking seas' has arrived back in England. The various changes of heart of the lovers in *A Midsummer's Night Dream* have to be clear or there is no joke; and the plot of the *Henry VI*s becomes unfathomable if the audience can't tell Suffolk from Somerset (earls not counties). Every night there are people in the audience who are seeing *Hamlet* for the first and (crucially) the only time. Second, each character has their own story to tell, and this means being certain of objectives. Each speech and scene has its own story, and the whole kaleidoscopic sweep of the action finally has to make sense. It is alarmingly easy to lose sight of what the story of the play is basically about. Judi Dench recalls how in Africa the audience went wild at the reunion of Sebastian and Viola, much to the surprise of a cast overfamiliar with the play (see p. 217). Third, we have to make sure that nothing *detracts* too much from the telling of the story. As the run progresses there is a tendency to concentrate on the passages we and/or the audience enjoy and skip through the rest, sidelining important plot points. It's fatal if the audience find a scene moving/funny/horrific but have no idea how it's contributed to the story. The tendency to 'milk our moments' may succeed in the short-term, but cause long-term damage. Fourth, we have to *share* the story with the audience. If we begin to play too internally and exclude the spectators, then the first thing to suffer is usually the story. Character in action forms the plot, but the two have to be kept in balance. If we play 'character' too intensely then *we* may be enjoying ourselves but the play is suffering. As Harriet Walter says, 'The job of the actor is to make the audience believe in their character so as to draw them into the story. We are the bait that lures them into the fake reality of the play.'[6] Fifth, stories are best told with lightness, clarity and flow – good advice for acting generally. Mark Rylance sums it up in a complicated, but I think compelling metaphor:

> My image is that the story is like a boat that is cutting
> through the water, or ice or whatever. The audience's
> imagination is cutting through time and space, and there's
> a kind of prow, a front of the story, which is where the
> particular question of what's going to happen next is . . .
> And it's very important for the audience that the actors
> give that front of the story a sharpness by their attention
> to it, by their need to know whether it's going to cut
> through the water or not and what it's going to find,
> whether it's going to hit an iceberg or not. If they don't
> give their attention to what's just in front of the boat –
> the story – then it's hard to ask the audience to.[7]

THE AUDIENCE

Theatre needs an actor, a space – and a spectator: the arrival of the AUDIENCE is the completion of the process. Theatre is at its best when actor and audience are sharing thoughts and emotions, and it is this act of sharing that essentially gives theatre the edge over film and television. The actor is out primarily to awaken the audience's imagination, to link their imagination to his. As the Chorus in *Henry V* says to the audience:

> Piece out our imperfections with your thoughts:
> Into a thousand parts divide one man,
> And make imaginary puissance.
> Think, when we talk of horses, that you see them,
> Printing their proud hoofs i'th' receiving earth;
> For 'tis your thoughts that now must deck our kings.
> (Prologue: 23–8)

Shakespeare, after a decade of writing history plays, may be despairing at the meagre forces at his disposal, but his appeal to the audience to use their imagination is very real. An actor becomes a king not by putting on a crown, but by first the other characters and then the audience accepting him as such.

An audience won't automatically deck us with their thoughts. It has to be earned. As John Barton says, 'most people [don't] really listen to Shakespeare in the theatre unless the actors make them do so'.[8] The audience need to be hooked right from the start. *The Tempest* starts with a shipwreck, *Macbeth* with three witches, *Coriolanus* with an angry mob. *Hamlet's* 'Who's there?' 'Nay, answer me. Stand and unfold yourself' is as sure a way to arrest an audience as any. Shakespeare's determination to wrong-foot the audience and never allow them to relax continues right through to the final scene – think of Fortinbras' arrival, Jacques' departure and Mercade's tragic news. But these moments won't play themselves. Barnardo's 'Who's there?' isn't a routine formality, it's invested with the fear that last night's ghost may be on the prowl again. Fortinbras' arrival means that every member of the court may be in danger of losing their positions, or even their lives. The audience have to be provoked, jolted and stimulated at each turn of events. But at the same time the actor has to stay temperate, subtle and truthful. As always, it's a balance.

Some parts, some moments can be played directly out to the audience. They are the only confidant Viola has for most of the play; Hamlet and Macbeth depend on them a great deal. As Brian Cox wrote about his Titus Andronicus:

> The sense of the vaudevillian in these opening scenes
> comes largely from the fact that they are played out to the
> audience, with almost no interplay between characters.
> It's all addressed out front; the image of Archie Rice is
> much stronger than the image of Hamlet.[9]

Richard III talks to the audience so much that David Troughton felt he needed them to become an actual character, influencing and guiding his direction. Antony Sher likewise felt that they gave him new insights into the way of playing the character. This might suggest that the audience form a cohesive group. While it's true that there will always be spectators who are bored, inattentive or even hostile, theatre at its best enables individuals to feel they form part of a group consensus. The effect of a neighbour's total concentration or outright laughter can be very potent. Group reaction helps the whole audience to become more uninhibited. The thrill of Iachimo emerging from his trunk or Benedick declaring that 'This can be no trick' can unite an audience in gasps or laughter. Both reactions can actually make an audience breathe together, and there is no more exhilarating feeling than an audience holding and releasing their breath at the same time.

An audience is not necessarily easy to read. I tell myself there are always some people two steps behind me, and others two steps ahead, but it's vital not to play to the lowest common denominator. Audiences are usually taking in more than we, or they, are aware of. The director Andrei Serban (echoing Peter Brook) says that the audience is only going to understand about a fifth of what we say *during* the performance, but by the time the play has ended they will take three or four-fifths away with them. Their silences can mean many things, but in time we begin to interpret even these. Timothy West distinguishes the pin-drop hush; the bored pall of quiet; the puzzled lack of understanding; and the growing awareness that the play isn't turning out as good as they thought.[11] What makes an audience attentive on Tuesday and restive on Wednesday remains a mystery (the weather? the news? the rail strike?). Actors despair as the first exciting moment doesn't bring hush or the first comic moment laughter, and then face the customary dilemma: do I work them extra hard, or do I continue as normal and wait for them to catch up? Both have drawbacks: there is no definitive answer. What is either galling or reassuring is when friends come backstage and, as we tax them with what a terrible audience they have been, they retaliate that they and everyone around them were enjoying it enormously. The mystery remains insoluble. At the Globe if the play didn't seem to take on its first performance ('It pleased not the million. 'Twas caviare to the general'), it was never put on again.

The audience may support, encourage and guide us, but we must remain in charge. Audience taste is not always to be trusted: they tend to endorse the familiar and be puzzled by the new. A comic Shylock and a serious Aguecheek are not in their accustomed terms of reference. When I was a student, that brilliant, idiosyncratic actor Kenneth Griffith told me that, because he found the London audience's taste so limited and predictable, he was never going on a stage again – and as far as I know he never did. That was an extreme reaction: don't let their predictability daunt you. In particular don't pander to them by overemphasising the bits they seem to like, and scurrying through the rest. Don't try to force them to see things our way: their perceptions will vary, and may be more valid than ours. The more we try to *show* Othello as noble, the more they may distrust him. Ideally, as Harriet Walter says, 'the audience should see what is going on inside you without realising that you've *shown* it to them'.[12] That's not to say the audience can't teach you a lot, particularly in comedy. It's a two-way relationship, with give and take on both sides. A piece of comedy that seems obvious in the script may be misfiring because you're not placing it right. Experimenting in front of an audience should steer you towards the best timing. They can also be a guide to pace, mystified when you're going too fast, bored when too slow.

The audience may prove to be different beasts in different spaces. Deborah Findlay found that 'what reads in a small space goes for nothing for somebody far away in the upper circle, so I had to learn how to send my thoughts and feelings winging their way to 1,500 people without becoming too demonstrative or two-dimensional'. Cicely Berry 'taught us that enunciation and intensity of thought carry better than shouting. Particularly at the Barbican I had to learn how quiet I could be and still be understood in order to develop a suitable range and not speak everything in a loud monotone.'[13] In a large theatre the emphasis, sometimes literally the spotlight, tends to be on the speaker and the word. Whatever the scenery surrounding him, the speaker is dwarfed by the size of the stage and the auditorium, and conversely the focus on him is all the more intense. This pressure can be releasing or inhibiting to the actor. I find big ideas and large emotions carry more weight and resonance in grand theatres. But faced by a huge sea of dark faces stretching into the distance, the actor can fall into rhetoric, chanting or a form of stylised non-naturalism. It can take months of experiment to come to terms with it, to be relaxed enough to draw the audience towards you rather than constantly reaching out to them. But it's worth the effort – large spaces are exciting.

The chamber space has obvious advantages. The actor can be more conversational, more immediate and less 'out-front'. He can relate more easily on a one-to-one basis to both actors and audience, and domestic settings register and support him more effectively. Nuances of tone, expression and gesture carry more clearly, and intimate scenes engage the audience more immediately. And yet the small space can minimise, parochialise or diminish the scale of the play. I often think that down the centuries we have built theatres the wrong size: the 1599 Globe and the Barbican too big, the Blackfriars and the Pit too small. No wonder the Stratford Swan and the National Theatre Cottesloe are so beloved by actors. To be both epic and intimate is the ideal for Shakespeare.

A last word on audiences from Michael Pennington on his Hamlet:

> The audience will never desert you, bringing you every enthusiasm for the event; and you now learn everything from them. You and they are carried by the prevailing winds: everyone wants it to be special, and everyone, including you, waits for lightning to strike. This animal

relationship is a wonderful thing, like champagne to tiredness, and more than makes up for the sniffy reservations
of a hundred experts.[14]

IMAGINATION, ENERGY AND INTERPLAY

Plays in the theatre communicate at a deeper level than words
and actions, what Brook calls 'the vibration of a great potential
force'. It must be one of the reasons Shakespeare means so
much to foreign audiences, whether in English or in translation.
Playing *Henry V* and *Coriolanus* on European tours (without
surtitles) I have been amazed how much was understood and
appreciated by audiences with only a basic knowledge of the
language. I had the same experience the first time I saw the
Moscow Art Theatre perform *Three Sisters*. Great plays unlock
the IMAGINATION not just through the text but through the total
performance. It's finally down to the actor. If the play has stirred
our imagination as actors, then that can communicate to the
audience. It needs craft and control, but these are nothing without the creative impulse.

An audience will respond to the actor's ENERGY with an
energy of its own. One of the things we most needed to find out
at the new Globe Theatre was how much energy was needed to
control that space. Some early productions relied on movement,
constant roving about the stage and the pit, to focus the
audience's attention. But Mark Rylance, the artistic director,
soon realised that stillness could also provide focus:

> Every year it's got smaller, and now it seems very intimate
> to me. At times I can be very still, can speak very quietly,
> and it's exactly right. Whereas at the beginning it felt like
> we were going to have to reach out so much to get
> people's attention, now we realise there's the alternative
> magnetic force of creating a vacuum inside, and drawing
> people towards us.[15]

In large theatres – like the Royal Shakespeare Theatre at Stratford, the Barbican and the National Theatre's Olivier – the technique of drawing people towards you is particularly important.
There is nothing more exciting for the actor than speaking
quietly in these spaces and feeling this intense concentration

from 1,200 people – but we need to be centred, energised and to pick our moments. One character's energy may be exterior, another's interior; beware of picking up another actor's energy level. In *1 Henry IV* Vernon comes to tell the rebels of the large royal army approaching. The pumped-up Hotspur rubbishes these fears but wishes Glendower were come to join them:

> VERNON   There is more news.
> I learned in Worcester, as I rode along,
> He cannot draw his power this fourteen days.

This is terrible news, a virtual death warrant, and earns a pause. Shakespeare then keeps the reactions brief and near-monosyllabic.

> DOUGLAS   That's the worst tidings that I hear of yet.
> WORCESTER   Ay, by my faith, that bears a frosty sound.

Though the blood is pumping, these two lines could be taken very quietly, an acknowledgement of disaster. Then Hotspur rouses them again:

> HOTSPUR   What may the King's whole battle reach unto?
> VERNON   To thirty thousand.
> HOTSPUR   Forty let it be.
> (4.1.125–31)

And he's off again, picking up the tempo and the volume. Hotspur's energy is palpable, but the others need just as much inner energy to make the moment work.

Hotspur must be prepared to drive this moment, and this is a vital part of performance. Anton Lesser found that when playing Richard of Gloucester in the *Henry VI*s he felt part of the ensemble, but when he came to play the same character on his way to kingship in *Richard III* 'I was told off in no uncertain terms by Adrian [Noble, the director] for my failure to drive the piece. In *Richard III* Richard must take hold of the play and drive it along.'[16] To a lesser degree Rosalind, Helena and Imogen drive their plays. Lear and Leontes drive their first three acts, others take over in the last two. As Toby Belch you have to be the motor of much of the action, while watching others get most of the laughs. Judi Dench talks of 'finding a sort of fifth gear for the final act of *Antony and Cleopatra*'. As Player King I remarked to Hamlet, Daniel Day-Lewis, that he always seemed so pleased to see me enter. 'I'm just happy someone else is going to talk for a bit,' he replied. I felt the same as Lear, when Poor Tom appeared in the storm.

In fact it can be surprisingly lonely playing Hamlet and Lear. As Michael Pennington noted about his Hamlet, 'I was beginning to taste the famous isolation of the part, feeling the emotional tides of a man adrift from his behaviour, the humour, the very language of his neighbours: a disorientation that in some equivalent way was beginning to separate me from colleagues and friends.'[17] In the same way, Viola, Isabella, Helena and Imogen can begin to feel isolated in their journey through the play. INTERPLAY with other cast members remains crucial. As director Mike Nichols advised his cast, 'If you ever felt you were getting lost, drown in each other's eyes.' Performance should be a time, with so much rehearsed and decided, that you really can lose yourself in your fellow actors. Shakespeare wasn't finally interested in history, philosophy, or even rational argument. He took a story, chose a rich diversity of characters, and put them in action together. His interest lay in the way they interacted, changed one another, or let events change them. Actors often joke that a director's notes boil down to 'Act Better'. Well, the first way to act better is to play with the other actors. If you listen to them, watch them, react to them, then the lines will come out fresh and truthful. It sounds an easy formula, and it should be – but of course it's not. So much gets in the way of our emptying our minds, listening to someone else and staying in the moment. We create so many blocks to our natural instinct to play the play. Without them we would sail free. Michael Redgrave put this more simply than any actor I know:

> The late Michael Chekhov said once that there were three ways to act: for yourself, for the audience, and to your partner. Some of the newer theorists say that if it's true for yourself, it's truthful, which is not so. The majority of actors act for themselves or for the audience. I believe that the only way to act is to your partner. As a partner Edith Evans [Rosalind to his Orlando] was like a great conductor who allows a soloist as much latitude as is needed, but always keeps everything strict. It's strict but free. Never is anything too set, too rigid. The stage relationship always leaves enough room to improvise . . . You don't start acting, she told me, until you stop trying

to act. It doesn't leave the ground until you don't have to think about it. The play and our stage relationship in it always had the same shape. It was entirely well-proportioned and yet, in many respects, it was all fluid . . . For the first time, on stage or off, I felt completely free.[18]

ANTICIPATION AND HINDSIGHT

The great enemy of live acting is ANTICIPATION: knowing what you and others are going to do and say next. My awakening came from the Canadian actor Douglas Rain, who, when I asked him for notes in a long run of *Hadrian VII*, told me I was anticipating him in half a dozen places. I protested weakly that I was not breaking into the ends of his lines. 'No,' he replied, 'but I see in your eyes the next thought forming before I've given you the key words that trigger it.' That's a hard discipline to maintain, especially after 300 performances, but it's central to the acting process. We've all experienced that terrible moment when an actor fails to enter from the right, and yet we've already turned right in anticipation of his (unexpected) arrival. No wonder actors in long runs often change entrances and moves to avoid that kind of staleness. If, as we play, we are consciously aware of what happens next, we will unconsciously transmit this to the audience. They may not notice individual moments, but after a time they will get a general sense that things are tired and predictable. Try to be constantly surprised by what people do: perhaps Claudius won't start guiltily at the play, Orlando agree to be wooed by Ganymede, Othello take advice from Iago, or Beatrice believe her gulling friends? It's not easy, but in our surprise/joy/relief/anger at the way things turn out we may find ourselves saying a line quite differently or reacting quite unexpectedly. The repertoire system is a great aid to this. By not being on the treadmill of the same play eight times a week, we can return to it after a short break with fresh eyes and ears.

HINDSIGHT is more to do with character: it's looking back after the event. As actor Eleanor Bron writes:

> To understand all is to forgive all – hindsight implies forgiveness. Whereas with anticipation you're leaning in towards the action – knowing the end – and you deform it. The effect of hindsight is to make you lean away. You

stand back, make allowances . . . if you do that in
performance it blurs the edges, it robs you of immediacy.
It allows you to know too much too soon about why your
character behaved that way and – which can be worse –
why other characters did. You start to have too much
sympathy, not enough energy. Your batteries lose charge.[19]

You need to understand your character, to appreciate their point
of view (Iago deserved promotion), but not necessarily to sym-
pathise with them (Iago should never have been given any responsibility). Malvolio may end up in prison on a false charge,
but that doesn't excuse his behaviour and ambitions. Volumnia
may lose her only son, but that doesn't excuse her militarist
ambitions. Leave pity to the audience. As Bron says, 'You have
to stay right inside that moment where the future doesn't exist,
where looking back you can't believe you could ever have said
and done that.'

PACE, PAUSES, SILENCE AND STILLNESS

We need to respond to the pacing that Shakespeare has marked
out in the pitch, stress and rhythm of the language, and in the
juxtaposition of actions. The actor has to know when to let rip
and when to hold back. The quarrel between Brutus and
Cassius in Act 4 of *Julius Caesar* is a good example. Like all
quarrels it needs ebb and flow, not to be taken at a consistently
angry and hysterical pitch.

> CASSIUS   Brutus, bay not me.
> I'll not endure it. You forget yourself
> To hedge me in. I am a soldier, I,
> Older in practice, abler than yourself
> To make conditions.
> BRUTUS   Go to, you are not, Cassius.
> CASSIUS   I am.
> BRUTUS   I say you are not.
> CASSIUS   Urge me no more, I shall forget myself.
> Have mind upon your health. Tempt me no farther.
> BRUTUS   Away, slight man.
> CASSIUS   Is't possible?
> BRUTUS   Hear me, for I will speak.
> Must I give way and room to your rash choler?

Shall I be frighted when a madman stares?
CASSIUS   O ye gods, ye gods! Must I endure all this?
BRUTUS   All this? Ay, more. Fret till your proud heart break.
Go show your slaves how choleric you are,
And make your bondmen tremble. Must I budge?
Must I observe you? Must I stand and crouch
Under your testy humour? By the gods,
You shall digest the venom of your spleen,
Though it do split you. For from this day forth
I'll use you for my mirth, yea for my laughter,
When you are waspish.
CASSIUS   Is it come to this?
BRUTUS   You say you are a better soldier.
Let it appear so, make your vaunting true,
And it shall please me well. For mine own part,
I shall be glad to learn of noble men.
CASSIUS   You wrong me every way, you wrong me, Brutus.
I said an elder soldier, not a better.
Did I say better?
BRUTUS   If you did I care not.
CASSIUS   When Caesar lived he durst not thus have moved
  me.
BRUTUS   Peace, peace; you durst not so have tempted him.
CASSIUS   I durst not?
BRUTUS   No.
CASSIUS   What, durst not tempt him?
BRUTUS   For your life you durst not.
CASSIUS   Do not presume too much upon my love.
I may do that I shall be sorry for.
BRUTUS   You have done that you should be sorry for.
There is no terror, Cassius, in your threats,
For I am armed so strong in honesty
That they pass by me as the idle wind,
Which I respect not.   (4.2.80–124)

Cassius first speaks in a straightforward, almost prosaic way.
Brutus then flares up in temper – 'Go to' is indication of that –
and they have a swift interchange, with Brutus twice accusing
Cassius of 'choler', and Cassius almost speechless with rage on
'O ye gods, ye gods' and 'Is it come to this'. Then Brutus slows
things down with his measured 'For mine own part, / I shall be
glad to learn of noble men.' Cassius picks up his tone with 'I said
an elder soldier, not a better', but Brutus pours fuel on the

flames with 'If you did I care not', and they're back to quarrelling outside strict metre. Brutus finally quietens things down by asserting his honesty in rhetorical fashion, though the scene continues in the same roller-coaster fashion. Of course all this is open to question – any line *can* be said in any way – but Shakespeare has given us ample opportunities for light and shade if we'll only respond to the pitch of the language. The key is the pace the thought is running at: speed of thought needs speedy delivery, careful piecing together of an argument needs a slower approach. Speed is not necessarily a virtue. As in music you can drive too hard, detail is lost, and all that comes across is a general wash.

Shakespeare also paces both the alternation of scenes, and episodes within long scenes. In *Macbeth* the long debate in England between Malcolm and Macduff is flanked by the murder of Lady Macduff and her children and Lady Macbeth's sleepwalking scene. Act 1, sc.4 of *King Lear* starts with a domestic scene between Lear and Kent in disguise, then comes horseplay with Oswald, a hard-bitten comedy passage with the Fool, Lear's confrontation with Goneril and his terrible curse, and finally a short coda between Goneril and Albany. It's a wonderful opportunity for changes of direction and pace.

Pace often depends on preserving a balance between simplicity and elaboration. As Cicely Berry writes: 'Having discovered the emotional centre, the action and motive, sometimes you have to let the words go. If the speaker fills them too much with his/her intensity they become didactic, giving us the result of a feeling or motive, so that the words cease to be active and open to question.'[20] Sometimes the line is best stated without any adornment. 'I am very sorry that you are not well,' Desdemona states as simply as possible. Nor need you over-explain physically or conceptually: 'This is an original idea and I'm determined you shan't miss it.' Once the lovers in *A Midsummer Night's Dream* have established that the wood is a cold and frightening place, there is no need to continue remorselessly to highlight their discomfort. Irving famously added a scene of Shylock returning to his empty house, just in case we'd missed the point that he will be bereft without Jessica's company (and his jewels). Few go as far these days, but directors and actors still love to start a play or a scene with a minute's worth of dumbshow to 'help' the audience's understanding. This is rarely worth it: get to the text as soon as possible, many opening lines are clearly written to be spoken while entering.

The great pianist Artur Schnabel said, 'I play the notes as well as anyone else – but it's my pauses that count.' Shakespeare was a master of the PAUSE, the silence, the still moment, all of which draw the audience's energy towards the action. If he'd been able to state 'Beat' or 'Pause', or mark two or three dots, he would have rivalled Pinter in exactness.

MACBETH	My dearest love,
Duncan comes here tonight.	
LADY	And when goes hence?
MACBETH Tomorrow, as he purposes.	
LADY	O never
Shall sun that morrow see.	
Your face, my thane, is as a book where men	
May read strange matters. (1.5.56–61)	

The folio places the start of all four speeches in the left margin. Most editors reorder the text into pentameters, revealing that Shakespeare has marked a clear pause before 'Your face, my thane', by omitting the last two feet of Lady Macbeth's line. The exchange is rapidly taken up on half-lines, because both know what the other is thinking, until Lady Macbeth's categoric 'O never / Shall sun that morrow see.' The notion of murder is out in the open and the pause is finally earned. Shakespeare then tells us what happens during the pause: Lady Macbeth watches Macbeth struggling with the proposition. The writer couldn't be more helpful.

Ted Hughes had thought to call his huge book *Shakespeare and the Goddess of Complete Being*, 'The Silence of Cordelia'. Shakespeare loved the use of SILENCE, and silence can only finally be tested in front of an audience – does the moment hold? Bolingbroke allows Richard II to talk on and on during the deposition scene – Richard calls him 'silent king' – because Bolingbroke knows he has the upper hand. Virgilia is so moved by her husband Coriolanus' return from war, and so upstaged by Volumnia, that Coriolanus calls her 'my gracious silence'. Isabella has a pause and then a silence at the close of *Measure for Measure*. Mariana begs her to plead for Angelo's life, and the Duke insists, 'He dies for Claudio's death.' Peter Brook in his 1950 Stratford production asked the young Barbara Jefford to hold the pause until she felt the audience could take it no longer – sometimes two minutes (see p. 243–4). Brook called it a 'voodoo pole', 'a silence in which the abstract notion of mercy became concrete for that moment to those present'.[21] Fifty lines later the Duke asks for Isabella's hand in marriage and repeats the offer a little later. Isabella's silence is one of the great Shakespearean conundrums, but is surely intentional (see pp. 233, 255).

STILLNESS is probably Isabella's greatest ally at the end of the play. The contrast with high emotion is vital. Antony Sher speaks of the need to punctuate Leontes' fevered rant with 'little islands of stillness, of sanity, of sorrow, of humour'. Stillness can be equated with certainty and power. Bolingbroke only has to sit still on the royal throne to proclaim his new status. Iago watches as Othello gabbles and falls senseless in a fit, before saying 'Work on, my medicine, work!' Prospero observes Miranda and Ferdinand falling in love, just as Oberon sees Titania doting on Bottom, and Aufidius watches Coriolanus give in to his mother. The great asset of stillness is that it is in a sense non-committal, and therefore draws in the audience and allows them to make their own judgement. During Rosalind and Orlando's 'love-prate' the eye is periodically drawn to the still and silent Celia: 'What is she thinking?' is more powerful than playing irritation or boredom. Macbeth is so much a creature of action that his stillnesses read powerfully and enigmatically – perhaps at his first sight of Banquo's ghost or the news of his wife's death. Mark Rylance speaks of 'stillness in the creation of silence for speaking, and the creation of stillness for someone to move into – the polarity of these is very important: actors give focus to their fellow actors, and take focus, through the use of stillness and movement.'[22]

THE CONTROLLED DREAM

One of the best descriptions I know of what acting is actually like comes from Ralph Richardson.[23] In 1967 he said in an interview, *'You're really driving four horses, as it were.'*

'First, going through, in great detail, the exact movements which have been decided upon.' This is your security, your fall-back state: the

pattern that you have worked out in rehearsal and will keep you afloat, however rough the night.

'You're also listening to the audience, keeping, if you can, very great control over them.' The audience are helping, guiding, even perhaps inspiring you, but you must never let them take over. It's your job to lead them.

'You're also slightly creating the part, in so far as you're consciously refining the movements and, perhaps, inventing tiny other experiments with new ones.' 'Refining' is a good word for performance. All the time you're experimenting, digging deeper, monitoring and clarifying. Michael Gambon puts it like this: 'There's a little man in your head looking at you, talking to you all the time, he's coming to you in your brain about how a scene's just gone . . . He's saying, "That went well, that was good. Now bring it up a bit. Now bring it down. No, that's boring. Now, do this . . ." You hit the jackpot, and the thing goes bang! And it takes off. Then you can do that the next night – you can remember what it was like.'[24]

'At the same time you are really living, in one part of your mind, what is happening. Acting is to some extent a controlled dream. In one part of your consciousness it really and truly is happening. But, of course, to make it true to the audience . . . the actor must, at any rate some of the time, believe himself that it is really true.' Some actors would disagree with this. They see themselves as storytellers who don't have to inhabit the character and are only defined by what they do in the play – an attitude close to the Brechtian. But most actors, I think, are drawn to the truth of the moment, where they feel strong emotions towards the person they are playing opposite. At some level Viola has to feel that she's in love with Orsino, and Iago that he hates the Moor – whatever their feelings backstage. Modern audiences are hyper-attuned to naturalism: if they don't sense that Rosalind and Orlando are in love there is no play.

Performance does have a certain dream-like quality to it. You're in familiar territory, you've been this way many times before, and as things happen you recognise them. You think you know how it's going to end. Then something happens – it may be the way you or another character speaks or acts – which seems new and unexpected, and pushes you in a different direction. Night after night you have the same dream, but it's never exactly the same. The dream seems perfectly real to you, but at the same time there's a part of you that knows it's not real and, if you wanted to, you could come out of it at any moment. This is surely true for the audience as well. Coleridge says that a theatre spectator creates in himself 'a sort of temporary half faith', but knows that it is 'at any moment within his power to see the thing as it really is'.

BRINGING IT ALL TOGETHER

Acting is the union of craft and imagination. A book can help you in matters of craft, and it can provoke your imagination, but it can't finally *teach* you either. The craft of an actor is not the same as the craft of the trumpet player because the actor's instrument is his own being. Other people can be very perceptive in helping you to realise your potential, but in the last resort you are the only person who can understand how your brain and body interact. It's up to you to discover where that fine balance lies between your reason and your emotion. As the director Jerzy Grotowski says, 'Spontaneity and discipline are the basic aspects of any actor's work and they require a methodical key. The actor . . . is creator, model and creation rolled into one.' The actor must have the imagination to create, but the craft to become the creation.

One of the main reasons actors respond to Shakespeare is because they recognise in him that union of spontaneity and discipline. Shakespeare at his most passionate still observes the iambic pentameter. The wild imaginer of *A Midsummer Night's Dream* still brings every element of the plot together in the last act. 'In the very torrent, tempest, and as I may say the whirlwind of your passion, you must acquire and beget a temperance that may give it smoothness.' We have developed (perhaps wrongly) an image of Shakespeare as a temperate hard-worker, careful with his money, friendly but watchful, a company man and a loner. But inside him raged some whirlwind that created Lear and Othello, Timon and Cleopatra.

Reading Shakespeare can often be counter-productive: it smells of the silent classroom. The text becomes alive when it is spoken. As Philip Larkin said about poetry, it must communicate at first hearing, but should resonate more and more as further layers are revealed. As you read aloud you have twin objectives. What is my character saying and what is the story? What thoughts, images, associations are being released in me? You're aiming at clarity of thought, and this may take a long time and can't be short-changed. You're also letting your imagination and gut instinct roam free. You're tapping into your emotions and finding a way to let your subconscious invade your mind. Some actors find a way quite quickly to allow thought and instinct, control and abandonment, to dictate performance; others discover it through trial and error, and experience. The two can't be prioritised, the art lies in finding the balance.

Theatre is the acid test of language, and language is central to discovering Shakespeare. His characters have, in the main, a great urge to talk, to express themselves coherently and imaginatively. They think quickly: the actor's energy is vital in serving up the text. Modern editors have spattered the texts with full stops that aren't there in the folio. The actor, driving the argument and the emotion forward, should think colons and dashes. The impulse of the verse is almost always towards the end of the line, the speech, the scene. The caesura, implied or explicit, acts as a springboard to launch the line's second half. Shakespeare had an instinctive feeling for shape, and the actor needs to respond to the shape of each clause, sentence and speech, and to the variations in pace which the language prompts.

We inevitably naturalise Shakespeare in a contemporary way, and a remarkable amount of the language lends itself to this. We go strongly for the sense, thinking this is the best way of communicating with the audience. But there are heightened passages of verse that defy naturalistic delivery. We need to respond to the imagery and make it our own, knowing that poetry taps into the subconscious at a level neither we nor the audience are wholly aware of. It's the words themselves that carry meaning and emotion, not what the actor lays on top of them. At the same time there is a discipline to this. We try to make the verse scan regularly and preserve the underlying beat, knowing that the most intriguing moments for speaker and hearer come when the rhythm changes and we're off the beat. We need to be alive to the wordplay, irony, paradox and essential ambiguity in Shakespeare's writing, but also mark the pauses, silences and stillness that give the text its variety. Language is the key to so much in Shakespeare, but it is not an end in itself. It is the *means* to telling the story, developing character, and setting off one idea against another.

There are a number of tools that the actor in Shakespeare needs to develop. Prime among these is vocal flexibility, and this is dependent on constant exercise and attention to breathing. Breath is freedom. Voice is inextricably linked to movement and, wherever possible, their exercise should be taken together. Research may open up new possibilities, and the invention of backstory may feed the imagination. Preconceptions should be challenged and discarded if necessary, while the making of lists helps many actors to view the evidence more objectively. It is always worth examining family and households, class and money, because they are often central to the detailed societies Shakespeare creates.

Politics, whether of the person or the state, are nearly always lurking beneath the surface. Was Shakespeare a critic or an upholder of society's values: did he side with Caesar or Brutus? Most of his plays are about the aristocracy; the middle and working classes are under-represented – though he could write them well enough in the Falstaff plays. I find him obsessed with the responsibilities and pressures of power. I also find him fascinated by sexual politics. In the comedies, women (though often in male attire) assert themselves and achieve some sort of radical equality; in the tragedies they are routinely exploited and demeaned by the men they have relationships with. His plays appear radical in their structure and experimentation, but conservative in their morality and denouement. It is not easy for the actor to know where to stand politically or philosophically in relation to the plays, but I find Shakespeare a shrewd and determined critic of the lust for status and power.

There are problems in interpreting four-hundred-year-old plays. It is not only a matter of archaic language, though this can be a barrier. 1590–1610 is a foreign country. How do we relate to their attitudes to class, religion, morality, chastity, bastardy, spirits, ghosts, monarchy or divine right? Inevitably we, actors and audience alike, bring our own contemporary attitudes to bear, yet we have to view the plays with something of a historical perspective or they don't make sense. Macbeth has to believe in the witches, Viola has to dress as a man to survive, and Rome has to idolise Coriolanus as a fighting machine. Do we try to recharge the play's first meaning, or do we regard Shakespeare's values as irrelevant, his intentions unknowable, leaving us free to interpret the plays and their characters in any way we choose? Is Kate's 'submission' speech one that seemed acceptable to the 1590s, but now has to appear ironic or duplicitous? The audience in 1604 would assume Isabella would accept the Duke: we no longer do. We have to find ways of bridging the gap, finding a balance, rather than pretending it doesn't exist.

We are more obsessed than the Elizabethans with questions of character, but Shakespeare's language shows how instinctively he created recognisable, but patently diverse, individuals. Archetypes exist, but are constantly subverted by his passion for complexity and contradiction. Never try to iron out the inconsistencies. In fact play them to the hilt, because Shakespeare was the first to realise that the most exciting dramatic conflict lies *within* the individual. Role-playing and disguise are often central to this: 'I am not what I am' is the keynote. Character is not something the actor can apply externally; it is always a rearrangement of yourself, and the art lies in the selection and energising of opposites. Don't fall into the trap of playing a generalised exposition of yourself. Be alive to interplay with others, because so much of character is revealed by what one person does to another, what roles are adopted and what makes objectives shift. But Shakespeare supplies no 'solution' to character, and neither should we. Ambiguity lies at the centre of his art, and we continue to produce the plays, as we do all great playwrights, precisely because their meaning remains elusive. Pinter puts this best in his Nobel Prize lecture:

> Truth in drama is forever elusive. You never quite find it
> but the search for it is compulsive. The search is clearly
> what drives the endeavour. The search is your task . . .
> But the real truth is that there never is any such thing as
> one truth to be found in dramatic art. There are many.
> These truths challenge each other, recoil from each other,
> reflect each other, ignore each other, tease each other, are
> blind to each other. Sometimes you feel you have the
> truth of a moment in your hand, then it slips through
> your fingers and is lost.

In performance we need to lose, or at any rate disguise, the detailed work of rehearsal and act spontaneously, with what Daniel Barenboim calls a 'conscious naivety'. Performance is a balance of craft and transparency. The audience have come not to observe character or marvel at language, but to hear a story. The telling of the story, and Shakespeare loves to complicate his basic storyline, depends on clarity, energy and surprise – and the great enemy of surprise is anticipation. As Judi Dench says, 'Everything finally depends on what the audience are going to get out of it' (see p. 218). We are out not just to please the audience but to stimulate, provoke and question them. We need to be sensitive to their feedback, but at the same time to stay in control and draw them into our reality. To achieve this we need always to be in the moment, but at the same time hold the arc of the whole in our mind.

All this may seem daunting, but Simon Russell Beale is right to say the cardinal rule is 'Don't Worry'. Audiences throughout the world don't come to Shakespeare out of duty or the hope that it will do them good; they come because they enjoy the plays. Enjoyment may not seem the first word to apply to *King Lear*, but it is the quality central to the playing and receiving of Shakespeare. I can vouch for the fact that playing Lear is not just 'satisfying' or 'rewarding', it is a great pleasure. Shakespeare gives the actor so much. It is a gift you should accept with open arms.

APPENDIXES

TWO CASE STUDIES

A scene-by-scene examination of two major characters will, I hope, illustrate many of the points examined so far. Duke Vincentio is one of Shakespeare's most contentious figures, and *Measure for Measure* has become one of his most frequently performed and debated plays. I have played the part and been in two other productions (as Escalus and the Provost), so I understand many of the problems – even though I may have no solutions. Viola is apparently a more straightforward creation, but I have found over the course of three different productions that Shakespeare has written her with a great deal of subtlety and empathy.

You will need to have a text by you, as I haven't quoted at any length (line references are again to *The Norton Shakespeare*). I am not advancing radically new interpretations: in fact I have tried to avoid dictating how the parts should be played or how the production should be staged. I have concentrated on what we should be looking for in the text, and what questions we should be asking.

DUKE VINCENTIO
IN MEASURE FOR MEASURE
(1604)

THE STORY

He is known as 'the Duke': the name 'Vincentio' appears only in the folio cast list. He is the ruler of Vienna, and the period seems to be contemporary (1604). He is unmarried, and appears to have total power. He leaves Vienna on the pretext of a journey to Poland (though Lucio thinks it may be Hungary, 1.2.1–2). He appoints as his deputy, Angelo, a man of unblemished rectitude, whom the Duke may or may not suspect of hypocrisy. Angelo applies the letter of the law in condemning to death Claudio, a young man who has made his fiancée pregnant. Isabella, Claudio's sister, pleads for his life, and Angelo offers to trade that for the deliverance of her chastity. The Duke, who has returned to Vienna to spy out corruption disguised as a friar, hears of this and devises an increasingly complicated plot to expose Angelo and save Claudio. He finally succeeds, Angelo's life is spared upon Isabella's plea for mercy, and the Duke proposes marriage to Isabella.

THE BACKSTORY

The Duke has been ruler for at least fourteen years, but his age is uncertain – he could have inherited at twelve or fifty. He seems something of a recluse, probably bookish, and doesn't relish public attention. He has 'let slip . . . strict statutes and most biting laws' (1.3.19, 21). He does not believe 'the dribbling dart of love / Can pierce a complete bosom' (1.3.2–3). There are a number of possible reasons why he pretends to leave Vienna: first, having failed to enforce the law he wants to see if Angelo can do better; second, he wishes to observe every strata of his dukedom in disguise; third, he wants to test Angelo's apparent inviolability, since he is already aware of his shameful treatment of Mariana. These three are hard to prioritise.

THE SOURCE

'The Disguised Ruler', seeking out the true state of his country's corruption, is a figure of world folklore – certainly from Roman times onwards. It was a popular subject for Elizabethan dramatists, used by Rowley, Marston and Middleton, and Shakespeare had already employed the device in *Henry V* on the eve of Agincourt. It lends itself to both tragedy and comedy, and Shakespeare experiments in *Measure* with combining the two. James I's attempt to visit the exchange in March 1604 in disguise also gave Shakespeare a topical reference.

THE TEXT

The play is only found in the 1623 folio, and the Oxford editors believe that various oddities in the text are the result of an adaptation by Middleton for a performance after Shakespeare's death, possibly as late as 1621 when Hungary was much in the news. This may also account for the removal to Vienna of the play's action which, judging by all the characters' names, was originally set in Italy.[1]

ACT I, SCENE I

A puzzling scene. Escalus seems to know the Duke is leaving. He is given his commission in very fulsome terms and must expect to be the deputy, but the Duke immediately disabuses him. Is this trickery? Does the Duke like springing surprises, leading people on? His preamble to Angelo dwells on:

> For if our virtues
> Did not go forth of us, 'twere all alike
> As if we had them not.   (33–5)

The subtext would seem to be, 'You are very well spoken of, let's see if your deeds live up to your reputation.' Does the Duke doubt right from the start that they will; or is it a rebuke to himself, since his own virtues have clearly not 'gone forth'? What he does tell us here is that he does not 'like to stage me' to the people's eyes, and that he's in a great hurry to leave (to avoid further questions?).

The Duke's language is complex, rich and difficult to interpret. His first line is one of the most teasing openings in Shakespeare. It doesn't scan regularly (it has an eleventh syllable which has to be stressed):

> ˘ — ˘ — ˘ — ˘ — ˘ — —
> Of government the properties to unfold.

This is a deliberate inversion which places the emphasis on 'government' and signals the centre of the play. How should a state be governed, and how should we govern ourselves? The line ends with another key word, 'unfold', because of course all plots unfold, but in this case virtue, vice and hypocrisy will be revealed. Key words abound in the scene: Shakespeare knew exactly what he wanted to examine in the play and announces his themes at once. In appointing Angelo, the Duke has 'lent him our terror, dressed him with our love' (19), and love will be balanced against terror in many ways. The scene is rich in hendiadys (doubles): the Duke counsels, 'Mortality and mercy in Vienna / Live in thy tongue and heart' (44–5). The play is much concerned with death and mercy, and with what is said and what is felt in the heart – Angelo will 'say' many things to Isabella, but only finally reveal his true emotions. The images of 'stage' and 'applause' announce at once the way princes are like actors on a public stage: the play will show what goes 'public' and what goes on 'behind the scenes' (which is where the Duke will mainly operate). We need to make sure the key words are clearly stated, but not coloured or put into inverted commas. The Duke seems anxious not to give too much away: he may want to preserve his authority in his absence, or he may simply not want to hint at his true intention. I don't think you can decide how to play this scene until you have sorted out the rest of the play.

ACT I, SCENE 3

This scene is a device, since Friar Thomas says so little: it's almost a confession or a soliloquy for the Duke, who even supplies the friar with a question, 'Now, pious sir, / You will demand of me why I do this' (16–7). The Duke needs the friar to supply him with a habit and some basic instruction (requests the friar may at first be reluctant to oblige). Shakespeare is also using the scene to explain backstory and motives for the Duke's return. The scene starts with a joke: it's as if Romeo has turned up at a friar's cell to arrange a love affair. The Duke protests that he (like Angelo) is not the slightest bit interested in romance or sex (and both men will duly fall for Isabella). He tells us he's always 'loved the life removed'; that he's strewed in the common ear that he's gone to Poland; and that he's 'let slip' the enforcement of 'strict statutes and most biting laws', as a result of which liberty 'plucks justice by the nose'. This is a very serious admission. The Renaissance believed that a ruler should never be too merciful to enforce the law properly. The friar finally gets a word in, with the key question – why hasn't he unloosed 'this tied-up justice' himself? The Duke's excuse can be variously interpreted. Does he shy away from responsibility? Has he given up trying to govern? Does he genuinely think it would be immoral to change course so completely?

What strikes one about the language is the passionate imagery of the Duke's sense of failure: the 'o'ergrown lion in a cave / That goes not out to prey', 'liberty plucks justice by the nose', 'the baby beats the nurse', and that his enforcement of the law would seem like 'tyranny' (22–3, 29, 30). Later he shows his strength of feeling about Angelo's apparent asceticism, that he 'scarce confesses / That his blood flows, or that his appetite / Is more to bread than stone' (51–3). Is this wry observation, or heartfelt denunciation? There's a central problem with the final lines. The folio punctuates it: 'Hence shall we see / If power change purpose: what our Seemers be' (53–4). The colon makes it a general reflection about the nature of power, with some sort of afterthought about 'seemers'. Most modern editors amend the colon to a comma, and the sense becomes the Duke having a shrewd suspicion that Angelo will fail the test. Should the actor take a firm line, or let the ambiguity speak for itself? It's a crucial decision: has the Duke set the whole thing up to teach Angelo that justice must be tempered with mercy, or, more ruthlessly, to expose Angelo's hypocrisy? Is jealousy lurking – 'I've made a mess of things, let's see if you do any better'? Whatever you decide, don't worry about the Duke appearing unsympathetic.

ACT 2, SCENE 3

The Duke, in his quest to visit 'both prince and people', has come to the prison, possibly because he's heard that Angelo has been sending unprecedented numbers there. He examines Juliet, at first with short, direct questions and statements, and then he gets into his stride with the argument that repentance mustn't be because we've been caught or are afraid of heaven, until Juliet cuts him short. How well does he handle this? It can be played that he's a very convincing friar, or that he's tentative and stumbling. In view of his later speech to Claudio it's probably best to play it very seriously – that he does think fornication a mortal sin and that her sin was 'heavier'. He's quite terse, and pretty unfeeling, in telling her that Claudio dies tomorrow: his apparent intention is to support Angelo and uphold the law. He may also be impatient to find out how Claudio is taking his sentence.

The scene also serves the purpose of breaking up the two long Angelo/Isabella scenes. It's not strictly necessary: 3.1 could start with the Provost explaining to him the Claudio situation, but I think Shakespeare relishes the chance to show the Duke at work, and also to remind the audience of the Duke's quest when the play appears to have been taken over by Angelo. Juliet, whom we might assume is introduced as a potentially important character, does not speak again in the play (Shakespeare is not always actor-friendly). There is a moment of potential comedy, when the Duke hails the Provost, whom he knows, and then hastily says, 'So I think you are.' Knowing that the play is going to end in largely comic vein, it's important to decide how much to work the comic moments in the first half – another decision best left for the moment.

ACT 3, SCENE 1

Shakespeare plunges us almost immediately into the Duke's homily on death (5–41), though there is a sense in which the conversation has been going on for some time. The lights might come up on them, or they might enter in mid-conversation. The speech follows Shakespeare's familiar pattern: there is a headline proposition ('Be absolute for death'), followed by a reason ('If I do lose thee, I do lose a thing / That none but fools would keep') and twelve examples. The conclusion is unexpected ('Yet death we fear / That makes these odds all even'), but Claudio confirms the general argument ('To sue to live, I find I seek to die, / And seeking death, find life'). It's a profoundly un-Christian speech, since the Bible certainly doesn't teach that life is 'a thing / That none but fools would keep', and that breath is 'servile' to natural phenomena, nor the Epicurean atomic theory that life exists 'on many a thousand grains that issue out of dust'. Some of the language is infuriatingly obscure. The modern audience find it very difficult to understand that 'all th'accommodations that thou bear'st / Are nursed by baseness' means 'all the material comforts you enjoy are provided by the working classes' (or, in Jonson's classic phrase, 'the shambles and the dunghill'); that 'worm' means 'snake' and 'bowels' means 'offspring'; or quite what is meant by 'an after-dinner sleep / Dreaming on both'. It's possible the Jacobean audience were similarly puzzled.

Every new proposition starts at the caesura, suggesting that the speech tumbles out remorselessly and that the ideas have been very much on the Duke's mind. Long and short vowels are alternated to great effect: 'breath' and 'skyey influences' are concluded by the terseness of 'keep'st' and 'afflict'; the clipped 'Thy best of rest is sleep' is contrasted with the much slower 'yet grossly fear'st / Thy death, which is no more'; and the sentence that begins with the short monosyllables of 'If thou art rich, thou'rt poor' ends with the long slow vowels of 'Thou bear'st thy heavy riches but a journey, / And death unloads thee.' The speech is rich in alliteration ('bear'st are nursed by baseness'); in paradox ('If thou art rich, thou'rt poor'); and in clashing vowel sounds ('gout, serpigo and the rheum'). He uses the jaggedness of the consonant 's' to enormous effect ('grossly fear'st', 'hast, forget'st'): there are in fact 79 in his 37 lines. It's a virtuoso display of the switch of pace between short and long vowels, and the switch between simple monosyllables and tortured complex images.

It's an extraordinary speech, and you have to decide whether it's central, or in some way peripheral, to the Duke's character. It is entirely bleak, its seeming message that fear of death is the only thing that keeps us alive, since life itself has no redeeming features. It suggests the Duke is full of existential despair, and the whole speech can be interpreted as the key to the three preceding scenes and why the Duke has given up office. Is he talking to Claudio at all? Perhaps the speech is about himself: that the prison and the imminence of death unlock in him a despair he's never fully articulated before. I think the speech works best if it's not a prepared statement, but made up, forced out of him as he goes along. He ticks off the subjects – nobility, valour, rest, self, happiness, certainty, riches, friends, youth, age – and finds nihilistic things to say about them all. There is no spiritual dimension, no mention of God-given attributes.

It is tempting to assume that the Duke is suicidal – and it's possible that, at this moment, he is – but it doesn't square with his determination to discover what is going on in his dukedom. His curiosity is great, or he wouldn't immediately ask to eavesdrop on Claudio and Isabella. What the Duke overhears is the turning point of the play and of his life. He has a choice. He could have immediately taken back the reins of power, dismissed and accused Angelo (despite the fact that he would realise Angelo would claim he only 'made trial of' Isabella). Instead he decides to stay in disguise, and embark on a complex and risky scheme. His motive for this is the key to the part. It's possible that the Duke, as God's deputy on earth (Angelo later refers to his 'power divine'), is in fact a Christ figure determined to sort things out as a humble friar rather than resort to his divine authority. It may be that he decides on a teaching role, to show Isabella, Claudio and Angelo how things can be resolved by active virtue. He may relish the idea that instead of cracking the whip as a ruler he can sort everything out as an ordinary man. He may simply delight in the opportunity to manipulate people's lives. Christ figure, teacher, common man, manipulator: elements of one or more of these will be present in any interpretation of the Duke. At the same time we must remember Shakespeare intended the play to have a happy ending. Like *Troilus and Cressida* and *All's Well That Ends Well* it's an experiment in tragicomedy, but with the most violent, and difficult, of gear changes.

At his first meeting with Isabella the Duke immediately drops into a prose that is balanced, clear-cut and legally exact. His mind is working fast, clearly and optimistically. It's a message of hope, a plan that is both preposterous and essentially comedic. The Duke's first line to Isabella concerns her beauty and her virtue: 'The hand that hath made you fair hath made you good' (181). With his later marriage proposal in view, this could be used to show that he falls for her at first sight. 'Virtue is bold, and goodness never fearful' (205): we are immediately in the world of romantic derring-do. The bed-trick, which Shakespeare had already used in *All's Well That Ends Well*, is common to sixteenth-century romances and folklore, and signals a complete change in the tone of the play. Existential despair is banished by comedic invention. The Duke has found a new role in helping others: 'By this is your brother saved, your honour untainted, the poor Mariana advantaged, and the corrupt deputy scaled' (244–5). This radical change of direction is not easy to play, and requires a boldness which only live theatre affords. Go for it!

The Duke then gets a glimpse through Pompey of the evils of the bottom layer of his society, and his reaction is intense – no 'giving the people scope'. He goes back into verse and works off his anger (at himself? at Angelo?) on Pompey, 'Canst thou believe thy living is a life / So stinkingly depending?' (281–2). Lucio enters, and the Duke now hears something of how the world regards him. So anxious to teach others, he finds himself on a learning process. Interestingly the Duke seems to cope with accusations that he is a lecher and a drunk but is extremely riled by Lucio's assertion that he is 'a very superficial, ignorant, unweighing fellow' (379). The Duke sees himself as a 'scholar, a statesman, and a soldier' (384) – for none of which we have evidence, so this could indicate considerable vanity in the Duke, or a projection of how he would like to be seen. Some actors have chosen to make Lucio recognise the Duke straightaway, which would explain the lengths Lucio goes to, but that also makes him suicidally reckless, which doesn't seem in his nature. It also fatally undermines the comedy of Lucio walking into the trap culminating in his unmasking of the Duke in Act 5. At various points in the play, when the Duke is intent on manipulating, or inventing, the plot, he is harassed by Lucio. Lucio is, of course, almost entirely irrelevant to the plot, but is extremely attractive to audiences. When playing the part, I could almost feel the audience willing Lucio on to further excesses. It can become a battle not just between characters, but between actors.

Escalus' arrival gives the Duke a chance to rail against the world's love of novelty, youth, inconstancy and lying – a very middle-aged rant which shows he hasn't lost his earlier despair entirely. Then he risks asking Escalus' opinion of him, and his summary, 'a gentleman of all temperance' (a very Shakespearean commendation), is a great relief to the Duke and a potential moment of comedy. After each encounter the Duke comes out with a rather sententious choric statement: a wish that we were free from our faults and from seeming; an acknowledgement that no ruler can tie up slanderous tongues; and to round off the act, a strange four-beat rhyming verse soliloquy (seemingly lacking at least two lines, possibly intended for another place in the play and possibly not by Shakespeare at all), which marks a halfway stage and, in the modern theatre, the most usual interval. He starts by invoking his pattern for a ruler, again involving holiness, severity, grace, virtue, and the need for balance – 'More nor less to others paying / Than by self-offences weighing' (485–6). It's possible that all this was put in to appeal to James I. However, what is significant is that the Duke sees 'craft against vice I must apply' (497), and perhaps this is his preferred remedy. Laws and exhortation to virtue will never defeat vice, but 'craft' may and this is the line the Duke has chosen.

The 500 lines of Act 3 form, I think, the real core of the play: Shakespeare's interest in the Duke's education in prison is central. The play, which in Act 2 appears to centre on the theme of 'the corrupt magistrate', now returns to 'the ruler in disguise', who emerges as a symbol of reason and moderation. Everything in the prison surprises the Duke and takes him off balance. It's vital to play this surprise, and to appear to be improvising as he goes along: even the advantaging of Mariana seems to me to be best played as a sudden inspiration, not a long-held plan (though Trevor Nunn's production managed to suggest that it was on his mind in the first scene).

ACT 4, SCENE I

This scene, which begins with a song, feels like the start of a romantic comedy. It's not very plausible, since Mariana says of the Duke/Friar that he 'hath often stilled my brawling dis-content' (9), which is impossible within the time-scheme of the play, but may suggest that the Duke and Mariana have quite a backstory. It shows the Duke and Isabella working closely together in harmony, Isabella seeming as absorbed and excited by the stratagems as the Duke, and this can be used as a sign of a developing romantic relationship. There is potential comedy in the fact that the Duke has 'not yet made known to Mariana / A word of' the bed-trick, and seven lines later tells Mariana that Isabella 'hath a story ready for your ear' (46–7, 53). What it does establish is that the women are conniving *only* because it's all been suggested by a friar, who's busy telling them it's no sin.

While Isabella is explaining to Mariana some lines are needed to bridge the gap, and the six lines beginning 'O place and great-ness' seem to have been lifted from the Duke's final soliloquy in Act 3. Perhaps the whole of that speech belongs here? The Duke now seems lodged in comic, scheming mode, and, though this may seem a difficult transition, I think it helps to see it as a reflection of the Duke's awakening to the possibilities of life.

ACT 4, SCENE 2

This must be the same evening, and the Duke enters in high spirits, confident that Claudio is saved. When the letter arrives it shows that Angelo, who has not yet slept with Mariana, has decided that Claudio had better die anyway – presumably because Claudio knows from Isabella of Angelo's proposition, and might therefore be a witness in a court action against Angelo on the Duke's return. I always feel there is a missing scene, that Angelo should have been allowed a chance to examine all this in soliloquy, and then send the message to the prison. Instead he's palmed off with a fifteen-line soliloquy after the event (4.4.19–33). It's missing I think because Shakespeare has become fascinated by the opportunities presented him by keeping the Duke plotting in the prison. The Duke finds the Provost 'gentle', but then has to lie to him in approving of Angelo's severity. With the shaving of Barnardine to make him look like Claudio we're entering the territory of farce – and we wade further in with the Duke revealing his closeness to himself, which allows the Provost the opportunity of recognising him (which the line 'Yet you are amazed' might suggest). When the Duke is in plotting mode he nearly always speaks in prose, only slipping into verse for this choric aside (100–05).

'All difficulties are but easy when they are known' (187–8) is a key line for the Duke. He has changed from a state of generalised despair in a palace to practical problem-solving on the ground, and this he relishes – in fact 'relish' is a good word for the Duke at this point. He presumably makes up his return 'within these two days' on the spot, yet he has it written in a letter – how? Shakespeare too is relishing making up his plot on the hoof, and not caring about inconsistencies. It makes the idea that he wrote the part for himself awfully tempting . . .

ACT 4, SCENE 3

The Duke's plan to shrive and execute Barnardine founders on Barnardine's determination to live, and the Duke has to admit 'to transport him in the mind he is / Were damnable' (60–1), an odd decision based presumably on the fact that he has become fond of Barnardine. Thematically, Barnardine's uncomplicated attitude to clinging on to life is a contrast to Claudio and the

Duke. The Provost comes up with the conveniently dead Raguzine, and the Duke's line 'O, 'tis an accident that heaven provides' (69) is a good laugh and a further indication that we are in farce territory.

The arrival of Isabella is a risk on Shakespeare's part which, since he could have avoided it, must be there for a purpose. It puts both her and the Duke to a test, and the Duke's reaction is unexpected:

> The tongue of Isabel. She's come to know
> If yet her brother's pardon be come hither;
> But I will keep her ignorant of her good,
> To make her heavenly comforts of despair
> When it is least expected.   (99–103)

Why does the Duke do this, when he could easily have told her the Provost had managed to save Claudio? (a) Experimenter: he wants to see how Isabella will react. (b) Manipulator: he has devised a grand plan to confront Angelo in public and doesn't want Isabella to mess it up by knowing Claudio is alive. (c) Teacher: he wants to teach Isabella and others about mercy. (d) Muddler: he's startled and just extemporises wildly. Is he being cruel only to be kind? Does he genuinely wish that Isabella should have her 'bosom on this wretch, / Grace of the Duke, revenges to your heart, / And general honour' (126–8)? Whichever way you cut it, he's using Isabella to further his own agenda.

The scene, which has started in comic mode and has now darkened, is wrenched back into comedy by the arrival of Lucio. Isabella is by now in tears, and the Duke's lines, 'Trust not my holy order / If I pervert your course. – Who's here?' (138–9) can be used to indicate that Lucio discovers them in some sort of compromising position (hugging perhaps?). Lucio's 'Good even' and his later 'She and that friar, / I saw them at the prison: a saucy friar' (5.1.134–5) can be said in such a way as to leave no doubt about his suspicions of intimacy. I think he sniffs that the friar is not on the level, but if he thought he was the Duke he would hardly have reminded him that he lied about getting a wench with child. The mixture of styles is a deliberate experiment on Shakespeare's part, hard for the actor to handle, but another round in the 'Duke versus Lucio' match, which is such an important part of the play's theatrical energy.

ACT 4, SCENE 5

An odd little scene, which suggests that Shakespeare wrote, or rewrote, parts of the fourth act in a great hurry. Why isn't Friar Peter the same friar as in Act 1, sc.3 (where he's named Thomas)? Who is Varrius? Where do the names Flavio, Valentinus, Rowland and Crassus come from? Is the scene there to build up the Duke's entrance, or to introduce Friar Peter, who's going to be needed in Act 5 to accompany Isabella and speak in 'Friar Lodowick's' defence?

ACT 5, SCENE I

At 532 lines this is the second longest last scene in Shakespeare's comedies (*Love's Labour's Lost*, 912; *Cymbeline*, 485; *Twelfth Night*, 375) – an indication of how important the resolution of every strand in the play was to him. It is not an easy scene to stage, since there is a wide range of characters to deploy and numerous coming-and-goings and shifts of focus. It is central to the Duke's plan that the exposing of Angelo and the tying up of every loose end should be done in public: Angelo and Escalus are to receive 'public thanks' and Angelo's desert merits 'characters of brass'. The verse is very confident, with strong exaggerated imagery ('a forted residence 'gainst the tooth of time / And razure of oblivion' (12–3). This is not the Duke who disliked 'staging him' to the people's eyes; he has discovered his public role and proves both a consummate leader – and dissembler.

He must be aware of the irony of asking Isabella to 'reveal yourself to' Angelo. Isabella goes overboard in her denunciation of Angelo, and the Duke tries to pull her back with 'She speaks this in th'infirmity of sense', and then help her on with 'Her madness hath the oddest frame of sense' (47, 61). All this is potentially comedic, since the audience is in on the Duke's stratagem, and then Lucio yanks the scene into farce with his constant interruptions, which so irritate the Duke and delight the audience – who's running this scene? When Isabella finally tells her story, the Duke utterly refutes it by saying she has been 'suborned' and 'set on', since his plan is to bring himself on as the friar. What he hadn't reckoned is that Lucio will denounce the 'meddling' friar, and he has to get Friar Peter to his rescue.

It's important that the Duke registers that his grand plan keeps getting knocked off course and that he has to improvise – always more interesting to play.

Mariana is introduced as witness and tells her tale, which the Duke immediately denounces and then demands to see the friar, leaving Angelo to try the case. All this time the Duke has been watching Angelo, perhaps giving him space to confess, though at the same time pouring on the praise. The sense of relish and manipulation, however justifiable, is enormous. Angelo is being encouraged to dig himself in as deep as possible. It's cat teasing mouse. He heaps on the irony: 'Do you not smile at this, Lord Angelo? / O heaven, the vanity of wretched fools!' (162–3).

The Duke leaves with the feeblest of excuses – 'I for a while will leave you' (254) – and changes rapidly into the friar. This release from ducal formality seems to super-charge him. He delights in rudeness – 'Let the devil / Be sometime honoured fore his burning throne' (287–8) – and in denouncing Vienna and the laxity of its (his own) rule, a reminder that this is what he set out to remedy. He speaks entirely in verse, despite the fact that Escalus and Lucio have gone into prose, a sign of the thematic importance of what he has to say about the state of Vienna:

> Where I have seen corruption boil and bubble
> Till it o'errun the stew; laws for all faults,
> But faults so countenanced that the strong statutes
> Stand like the forfeits in a barber's shop,
> As much in mock as mark.   (312–6)

The Duke must always have intended to unmask himself, but Lucio's intervention turns what could have been a portentous melodramatic moment into a comedic one. Angelo at once acknowledges the Duke's god-like status (another nod towards James I?), 'when I perceive your grace, like power divine, / Hath looked upon my passes' (361–2). Isabella is also totally submissive, asking pardon 'that I, your vassal, have employed and pained / Your unknown sovereignty' (378–9). But the Duke continues to lie about Claudio's death, which is not strictly necessary as Angelo has confessed and agreed to marry Mariana. It can only be because the Duke has a grand plan which he's determined to take to the wire; and this plan has to involve putting Angelo through torment, and testing Mariana and Isabella to the extreme. More and more the Duke takes on the mantle of divine authority in his speech to Angelo, helped by both rhyme and the repetition of key words:

> 'An Angelo for Claudio, death for death'.
> Haste still pays haste, and leisure answers leisure;
> Like doth quit like, and measure still for measure.   (401–3)

Of course he can't execute Angelo because Claudio's alive, but the theme of Justice, even Retribution, he's determined to hammer home. Mariana's plea for mercy he disregards. Does he intend to ask Isabella if she will plead for Angelo, only for Mariana fortuitously to save him the trouble? Isabella's plea (see pp. 243–4) does free him to change course and demand the Provost bring in Barnardine and, presumably by prearrangement, Claudio. What is striking about the Duke's verse throughout this sequence is its strength and implacability, and this runs counter to presenting him as an opportunistic, comic manipulator. He appears a very different man to the person who talked to Friar Thomas in Act I, sc.3. It is as if he's discovered himself through his direct intervention in his subjects' doings, and these extremes need to be played hard if one is to feel that the Duke learns and changes during the play.

The progress towards Mercy starts with Barnardine, who is pardoned without any reason being put forward (clearly not Justice). The winding up of the play is now very swift. Claudio is pardoned, the Duke proposes to Isabella, and Angelo is pardoned all in the space of eight lines – the denouement of a comedy, even a fairy tale. Lucio has really got under the Duke's skin, and he is first condemned to death and then has that remitted to marrying Kate Keepdown; the theme of life, procreation and death neatly tied up. The Duke has a rapid speech listing his thanks, in which he proposes to Isabella for a second time, and then sweeps everyone off to the palace.

Isabella's silence has now become a *cause célèbre*, and recent productions often end either with Isabella walking off in a different direction or left standing alone on stage. The Jacobean audience would have had no such problem, nor would James I when he saw the play. There is no record of a sixteenth- or seventeenth-century head of state proposing to a non-aristocrat and being turned down. It was also vital to the state that the Duke had an heir. The Duke's two proposals must, I think, have been put in by Shakespeare to give Isabella time to think, with the implication that in the intervening 41 lines (2 ½ minutes?) she has made up her mind to accept. I'm pretty sure in 1604 she wasn't left moodily undecided on stage. The transition from middle-aged Friar/Duke/favourite uncle to lover is too opportunistic, peremptory and paternalistic for most modern tastes, and few Isabellas are now keen to fall into the Duke's arms. Indeed Isabella's silence may suggest that Shakespeare felt doubts about the proposal, and couldn't fashion an appropriate speech of acceptance. There is no direct indication in the text of any growing romantic attachment, though, as noted, upon meeting her the Duke immediately remarks on her beauty, in the ensuing plotting a relationship clearly grows, and Isabella comes to rely on the Friar more and more. It is arguable that Isabella would never before in her life have shared a common enterprise with a man and been drawn so close to him (only made possible by his clerical position), and that this unusual closeness could turn into whirlwind romance. Many productions engineer chaste hugs and kisses in the course of their plotting that make his proposal and her acceptance more feasible, though it could equally be argued that the Duke misreads her relief and gratitude for signs of love. Some recent productions, following John Barton's in 1970 for the RSC, have made the Duke's proposal come entirely out of the blue, leaving Isabella nonplussed and the Duke appearing as lustful and opportunistic as Angelo. In any event, marriage, as exemplified by Angelo and Mariana and by Lucio and Kate Keepdown, is hardly presented by the play as an ideal solution.

CONCLUSION

It is very hard to come to a conclusion about either the play or the Duke. Some think it's the most interesting and pertinent tragicomedy in the canon, others that the first half is the opening of a great tragedy and the second a farcical mess. Did Shakespeare always intend this shift in tone, or did he keep changing his mind? If the play were primarily about the corrupt magistrate, the Duke would only feature at the beginning, to leave the country, and the end, to dispense justice. Shakespeare, however, was so taken by the 'ruler in disguise' theme that he allows the Duke to dominate the play, but whether as symbol or personality is hard to decide. The Duke is often accused of not being a fully rounded character, that he learns nothing about himself and is not changed by the course of the play. I have tried to show that in performance there can be a marked transition from lassitude and despair to action, optimism, and a fresh understanding of the balance of justice and mercy. His public exercise of authority and his proposal to Isabella are signs of a new recognition of what he owes to himself and to the state.

But he remains an ambiguous figure. At the one extreme he is the symbol of divine authority, in which the Stuart kings firmly believed. Tyrone Guthrie wrote of his 1966 production:

> I suspect he is meant to be something more than a glorified portrait of royalty. Rather he is a figure of Almighty God; a stern and crafty father to Angelo, a stern but kind father to Claudio, an elder brother to the Provost . . . and to Isabella, first a loving father and eventually the Heavenly Bridegroom to whom at the beginning of the play she was betrothed . . . And may we not suppose that in showing the Duke's considerable and calculated ruthlessness, as well as his wisdom and humour, Shakespeare is permitting himself a theological comment upon an all-wise, all-merciful Father-God, who permits the frightful and apparently meaningless disasters which unceasingly befall his children.[2]

At the other extreme he is a puppet-master, tacking arbitrarily from position to position and devising situations for his own amusement, impervious to the suffering it causes to others. I think the play is diminished by sticking rigidly to either extreme, but is there a clear middle road to be taken? Kenneth Muir was all for leaving the ambiguities unresolved:

> Any good production of *Measure for Measure* would necessarily present us with the possibility that Duke Vincentio was a symbol of divine providence, or an earthly ruler who was God's steward, or a puppet-master, or a busybody. It is not the business of the director to choose one of these and exclude the others.[3]

But in order to inhabit the role the actor does have to make certain choices: to resolve the Duke's intentions in leaving his rule to Angelo and returning to spy on government and people; his mental state that warrants 'Be absolute for death'; and his intentions in remaining in disguise and devising a plan to save Claudio, advantage Mariana and reveal Angelo. Like so many of Shakespeare's characters the Duke has a plan which he constantly has to adapt to changing circumstances, Angelo's decision to go ahead with Claudio's execution being the major obstacle. Basic intention (to discover and show the balance of terror and love in government) is coupled with farcical improvisation, and I think any performance needs to swing between the two, sometimes in the course of a few lines. It's a huge test for the actor, some would say a near-impossible task. As the actor Stephen Boxer commented to me:

> The Duke drives you nuts if you look for psychological consistency; but relish his twists and turns, play him as God and Devil, as spy and enabler, lover and tyrant, and he becomes – to me – one of the most curious and surprising characters in Shakespeare.

In so many ways the play provides no 'solution' to the problems it poses, particularly in relation to sexual desire. The actor playing the Duke has to find a way to present a fully rounded character, without attempting to 'solve' the play.

VIOLA
IN TWELFTH NIGHT
(1601)

THE STORY

Viola and her identical twin brother, Sebastian, are wrecked off the coast of Illyria (which in Roman times was on the Adriatic coast in modern Croatia and Albania). Viola dresses as a man, takes the name 'Cesario', and offers her services to Orsino, the Duke of Illyria, quickly falling in love with him. Orsino, however, is in love with the Countess Olivia, and sends Cesario to woo her on his behalf. Olivia falls in love with Cesario, while Orsino also finds himself drawn to this 'boy'. This impossible situation for Viola is resolved by the reappearance of Sebastian, whom Olivia promptly, if mistakenly, marries. The confusions are finally laid to rest by the union of Orsino and Viola.

THE BACKSTORY

Viola and Sebastian come from Messaline, which is hard to identify but has an Italian or Sicilian ring to it. Their father was also called Sebastian and died when they were thirteen. No reason is given for their voyage, and they both seem content to stay in Illyria, perhaps out of grief/loyalty/hope that the other may be found. Viola is confident Orsino knew her father, and Orsino will later say of young Sebastian 'right noble is his blood', so it's a fair assumption that the twins are aristocrats. The actors playing the twins may feel the need to invent a more detailed scenario for their voyage's reason and destination. On the other hand, if they feel Illyria is some combination of London and Never-Never Land, and that they have simply been parachuted in to stir up the locals, they won't bother with a backstory at all.

THE SOURCE

There are two main sources. In *Gl'Ingannati* ('The Deceived Ones', 1531) the journey is from Rome to Modena. Lelia dresses as a boy to be near Flamminio, whom she already loves, but who in turn loves Isabella. Isabella falls for Lelia/Fabio, and finally marries her brother Fabrizio. In Barnabe Riche's tale of *Apolonius and Silla* (1581), Silla is already in love with Duke Apolonius. She leaves Cyprus dressed as a boy, is wrecked and ends up at Constantinople in Apolonius' court. Apolonius is suitor to Julina, a wealthy widow, and sends Silla/Silvio to woo her. The real Silvio arrives, Julina is entranced, they sleep together but Silvio runs away. Julina is pregnant and Silla/Silvio is put in prison. Silla reveals herself and the Duke marries her, while Silvio returns and marries Julina. Shakespeare therefore has tightened up the plot, and ensured that Viola is not in pursuit of Orsino from the start.

THE TEXT

The play is only found in the 1623 folio, and is an unusually clean text, including act and scene divisions.

ACT I, SCENE 2

Modern productions often put this scene first, but Shakespeare's intention was surely that we should be introduced first to Orsino, and by description Olivia, and observe the sterile self-induced melancholy and mourning of them both, before introducing the life-force of Viola. It's an interesting choice of Shakespeare's, since the heroine emerging from a shipwreck is a more obviously arresting opening. The country is named as Illyria, which Shakespeare may have picked for its contrast to 'Elysium' in line 3, or because it comes into Ovid's *Metamorphoses*. He may have had no idea it was on the Adriatic coast.

Immediately Viola states Sebastian is in Elysium she posits 'Perchance he is not drowned', showing her optimism, and then takes up the Captain's reiteration of the word 'perchance'. Chance is going to be a key theme in the play. When she tips the Captain, it is 'for saying so': she remains realistic about her brother's chances of survival. It's important to establish the depth of her feeling for Sebastian. As the play develops it may come to seem the truest loving bond on offer. Viola says she's heard of Orsino, and her remark, 'he was a bachelor then' shows her immediate interest in his matrimonial status. Her first thought is to serve Olivia (though as a gentlewoman she might simply have begged protection), but the Captain says she won't admit any kind of suit (petition). She then turns to Orsino and realises that she can only serve him as a eunuch who sings and plays, and for this she'll need male disguise (her first intention was not to be a page or look like Sebastian, though this may be Shakespeare's carelessness). Viola commends the Captain on having 'a mind that suits / With this thy fair and outward character' (46–7), introducing the themes of disguise, deceit and seeming. There's a paradox that immediately after this she asks him to 'conceal me what I am'. The other important theme is contained in 'What else may hap, to time I will commit' (56). Viola is ready to set a plan in action, but then to settle back and see how things turn out. Her verse is direct, even prosaic at times, though not without imagery – 'And though that nature with a beauteous wall / Doth oft close in pollution' (45–6) – and even ends with a rhyming couplet. It has a business-like, no-nonsense air about it, not unlike Rosalind and Celia's early verse. Some of it could be played out front to the audience.

A problem with this scene is the absence of the terrors of shipwreck and of despair at the probable loss of her twin. Shakespeare clearly intends it to be an upbeat scene: 'courage and hope' is linked to Sebastian, and the wreck has a certain unreality to it – the opening of a romance rather than a tragedy – witness the Captain's description of Sebastian 'like Arion on the dolphin's back, / I saw him hold acquaintance with the waves' (14–5). This is no help to the playing of Viola, who somehow has to get some sense of horror and loss without much support from the text. It's possible to start with a scream, and be in tears till the Captain brings comfort. This won't be a problem to those who see this scene simply as a fairy-tale prologue.

ACT I, SCENE 4

A brief scene, with certain elements cut to the bone, as if Shakespeare wants to get on with the plot. Valentine gives us the information that Viola has now chosen to be a page, not a eunuch, and has taken the name Cesario (a very assertive choice, when compared with Rosalind's Ganymede – an emperor rather than Jove's cup-bearer). We learn later that she has dressed herself exactly like her brother, 'for him I imitate' (3.4.348), though we don't discover her name, Viola, till Sebastian tells us near the end of the play (5.1.234). In only three days she has become Orsino's favourite, which of course Valentine and the others may resent.

Orsino enters, dismisses the others, and admits 'I have unclasped / To thee the book even of my secret soul' (12–3). Viola has become his confidant in a way she never could have done as a woman. Orsino then dwells on her youth and feminine qualities. Shakespeare had done this before to validate his boy actors and help the audience to accept them as female (Mark Rylance, who has played both Cleopatra and Olivia, talks of a modern audience taking the first five minutes to get used to the convention), but he had never gone as far as 'all is semblative a woman's part' (33). It may be a way of explaining that Orsino's attraction to Cesario was not primarily homosexual. There is a further irony in 'Prosper well in this / And thou shalt live as freely as thy lord, / To call his fortunes thine'. This is the state that Viola already desires, that Orsino will come to desire, and which is finally achieved. Viola's parting remark is terse – 'I'll do my best / To woo your lady' (39–40) – which she honestly does, unlike Lelia in *Gl'Ingannati*. She then has her first clear address to the audience who, now she's in disguise, is her only confidant. The admission, 'Whoe'er I woo, myself would be his wife' (41), could hardly be shorter and more direct, and sometimes gets a laugh. It's comedy shorthand and a rhyming couplet, but also reflects Viola's no-nonsense approach.

The actor needs to sort out why she immediately falls for Orsino. He seems clearly older than her and a man of action (he had seen 'the smoke of war' in a sea-fight with Antonio, 5.1.47). He is deeply and constantly in love with a woman – the whole court has an air of frustrated romance – and immediately takes Viola into his romantic confidence. He may represent to her, lonely and grieving as she is, security, determination and power, though she must have already realised he is a self-centred obsessive. As a young woman Viola may also never have been so intimate with a man before – a constant theme in the 'breeches' parts.

ACT I, SCENE 5

Viola's determination to be heard is well built up. Olivia is resolved not to admit him, though curious as to 'what kind o' man is he?', until Malvolio describes his youth 'between boy and man' and says he's 'very well-favoured' (133, 141–2). Then she abruptly changes her mind, possibly because she's reminded of her brother, more probably because she's attracted to very young men. The scene has started in prose, and continues in the same, mainly for comedic reasons. Viola is as usual direct, but her naivety comes through in admitting that her speech is 'excellently well penned' and she has taken 'great pains to study it, and 'tis poetical' (154, 172). Olivia asks her if she's a comedian ('actor' in Elizabethan terms), and the pertinence of that question pushes Viola into the wry admission that 'I am not that I play' (164), which could be an aside to the audience. The scene reveals that Viola is good at witty repartee: when Maria says 'Will you hoist sail, sir?', Viola is quick with 'No, good swabber, I am to hull here a little longer' (178–9). It also shows that she is a natural actor, released by her male identity into being more assertive than she ever was as a woman – a constant theme in Shakespeare's exploration of the power of disguise.

What first gets to Olivia is Viola's line, 'What I am and what I would are as secret as maidenhead; to your ears, divinity; to any others, profanation' (189–91). The sexuality implicit in the first sentence is a sentiment much more readily uttered by a woman, and perhaps fires up Olivia's thoughts of her own secret maidenhead, and she abruptly says 'Give us the place alone'. Viola is so curious to see what has attracted Orsino that she asks to see Olivia's face (Olivia has been veiled since Viola's arrival). Olivia would normally refuse, but is clearly keen for Viola to see her beauty and unveils with the boast, 'Is't not well done?', a question her status and modesty shouldn't allow. Viola may well be shifting into verse with the four-beat line, 'Excellently done, if God did all' (207), and this allows a number of choices. It could be delivered straight through as a rather bitchy put-down. The missing beat could allow a pause at the caesura, in which case 'if God did all' could be a half-aside. It could be that Viola is bowled over by Olivia's beauty and immediately wonders what chance has she got with Orsino, in which case the second half could be an attempt to regain her composure.

Viola then goes firmly into verse with a conventional Elizabethan sentiment that beauty has a duty to bear children. Olivia stays in prose while making fun of her, and this pushes Viola into monosyllabic lines that show outspoken honesty and a new seriousness:

> I see you what you are, you are too proud,
> But if you were the devil, you are fair.   (219–20)

Twice Viola mentions the word 'love', and Olivia picks up the half-line with 'How does he love me?' – meaning Orsino, but perhaps also Cesario (223). She wants this attractive youth to talk about love, but Viola retreats into conventional bombast about 'groans', 'sighs' and 'thunder'. Olivia is finally pushed into verse and counters with a firm summary of why she 'cannot love him' (Orsino). Viola feels taunted into revealing her own feelings at this absolute rejection with 'If I did love you in my master's flame' (233). She is way out of her brief by now, and the force of 'With such a suff'ring, such a deadly life' (234) is very personal. Orsino may be suffering, but so is she; his life may be deadly, but so hers promises to be without him. Out pour her feelings about rejected, or in her case impossible, love. The delivery of the speech, 'Make me a willow cabin at your gate' may have been prepared, but seems to me better wild and improvised. The willow image is one that Shakespeare uses several times to denote forsaken love (as in Desdemona's 'willow' song). It's over the top, not in conventional hyperbole, but in searching for images that convey her passion, culminating in the cosmic 'And make the babbling gossip of the air / Cry out "Olivia!"' (237–43). There's a wonderful use of onomatopoeia in 'Halloo', 'reverberate' and 'babbling gossip'. The fewer breaths you can take, the better.

Olivia picks up the half-line with 'You might do much' (usually a good laugh), and then there is the stray half-line 'What is your parentage?' (246), which seems to indicate a prior pause. Olivia is in love; she just needs the safeguard that Cesario is of gentle birth. Viola replies enigmatically, since she mustn't give too much away: 'Above my fortunes, yet my state is well', and then, perhaps after a beat, 'I am a gentleman' (248–9). Olivia reveals her interest by asking him to come again, which Viola doesn't immediately pick up, and then she foolishly offers Viola a tip. Viola gives a stinging reply, well beyond the limits of decorum, again fuelled by the impossibility of her own love, and ends as usual with a rhyming couplet.

This scene is a marvellous acting exercise, and is often used as such. It gives Olivia many choices as to the gradations of her falling in love. It presents Viola with two especial challenges: one, to respond to the changes in language (hyperbolical, heartfelt, wild); and two, to mark the various revelations of her feeling about Orsino. Viola, however, has one advantage over Olivia – the audience understand the duality of her position and empathise accordingly.

ACT 2, SCENE 2

After the preceding scene Shakespeare inserts the Sebastian-Antonio duologue, thus informing the audience early in the play that Sebastian is very much alive. For the first time the audience know something that Viola doesn't, though many productions hold back this information by reversing the scenes and making Malvolio's 'run' continuous. I think you should experiment.

Viola's sense of fun with language comes out in the way she picks up Malvolio's formal tone with 'On a moderate pace, I have since arrived but hither' (2–3). 'She took the ring of me, I'll none of it' (10) shows that Viola has picked up Olivia's indiscretion and is prepared to play along with it – sisterly solidarity? Viola now has a soliloquy which must be addressed, at any rate in part, to the audience. Some of it could be thinking aloud: it's a very good opportunity for experiment. It's important not to be overawed by this speech, 'I left no ring with her. What means this lady?' (15–39), as it is so familiar to audiences and is used so much for auditions (avoid if possible). It has to be thought through, idea by idea, and then it will seem fresh. Keep it simple and direct: it contains the very essence of Viola.

Shakespeare uses a mixture of caesuras and full stops at the ends of lines, which help you to decide where to pause and where to run on. For example, there could be a pause before 'She loves me, sure', but then 'The cunning of her passion' (20) comes tumbling out immediately. 'She did speak in starts, distractedly' (19) is a good note for Olivia in the preceding scene, but also perhaps for Viola, as the enormity of what her disguise has achieved hits home. Not only has she failed in her mission, but she has made Orsino's suit even more unlikely (which, from her point of view, is both a plus and a minus). The simple monosyllabic lines, 'None of my lord's ring! Why, he sent her none. / I am the man', contrast with the more reflective moralising of 'Disguise, I see thou art a wickedness / Wherein the pregnant enemy does much' (22–3,25–6). Shakespeare was intrigued by the vices and virtues of disguise (Kent can help Lear; Edgar, Gloucester; and Portia, Antonio, all through disguise), and Viola joins Hamlet and Isabella in their revulsion at 'seeming'. Women are indeed taken in by handsome deceitful men ('proper false'), but the argument that it's not women's fault if they are made of frailty is harder to sustain, though Viola seems to be trying to argue her way out of admitting women are the 'weaker vessels'.

Viola refers to herself as 'poor monster', neither one sex or the other, and a boy player would have added to this complication. The situation appears insoluble. Should Viola seem solemnly resigned, or does the line 'What thriftless sighs shall poor Olivia breathe!' suggest that she sees its comic side? Rosalind or Helena would have set out to find a solution: Viola is content to leave it to Time – as she did at her first arrival. Is Shakespeare exploring a more passive heroine?

ACT 2, SCENE 4

The fact that Feste sings the song may have been Shakespeare's intention all along; or that Robert Armin, who had lately joined the company, was given the song as a favour; or that the original boy player cast as Viola wasn't a good singer (perhaps the boy who Shakespeare had in mind when he devised the singing eunuch idea was no longer available). The substitution bothers academics more than it does audiences. Orsino turns immediately to the subject of love, which Viola is both delighted and distressed to be discussing, since it is uppermost in her mind too. Viola's brief reply, 'It gives a very echo to the seat / Where love is throned' (20–1), Orsino calls 'masterly', but this is again full of irony since Orsino is presumably himself 'throned'. By likening her loved one to Orsino in complexion and years, Viola is either dicing with danger or cannot stop herself – an interesting choice. When Viola agrees that women's beauty is short-lived, is she genuinely lamenting its transience, reflecting on the sudden change that loss of virginity might bring, or being ironic, since she sees her youth's bloom passing in male attire? The play on 'die' is also ironic since, as Cesario, sexual pleasure is denied her.

This dialogue is terse and jagged, and only just fits the five-beat line. It finally breaks down on 'About your years, my lord' (27): six syllables that stand on their own and suggest that Viola has quite a pause before her daring, or helpless, answer. The pause is earned if the previous cues are picked up. The passage ends with a rhyming couplet from Orsino, which Viola echoes (37–40), showing how much in sympathy they are. Orsino is still doing most of the talking; Viola is circumspect, feeling her way. During Feste's repartee and song, Viola says nothing. Orsino may think it 'dallies with the innocence of love', but its theme of death following unrequited love must seem all too real and painful to Viola.

The song has clearly fired up Orsino, as he immediately wants Viola to go and try Olivia again. Not only does Viola know that Olivia's heart now lies elsewhere, but his reference to her beauty, 'miracle and queen of gems' (83), makes her own chances with Orsino seem hopeless. After a pause, which her eight-syllable line 'But if she cannot love you, sir?' suggests, Orsino tersely replies 'I cannot be so answered', and Viola completes the line with 'Sooth, but you must' (85–6). This is strong talk from a page to a master, and she cannot stop herself comparing, albeit indirectly, her own situation of unrequited love with Orsino's. He replies with a six-syllable line, 'There is no woman's sides', that suggests a pause before it: Viola has hit home. Orsino launches into a familiar Elizabethan homily on men's love being deeper than women's (women were thought to be more lustful, but flighty and inconstant). This misogyny riles Viola, who blurts out 'Ay, but I know – '. Orsino has a short line, 'What dost thou know?' (102–3), which suggests a pause before the line while Viola flounders, or a pause after, while she collects herself. From this point Orsino asks only brief questions, while Viola talks at some length – an interesting reversal of the first half of the scene. Viola protests how 'true of heart' women are, but then has to invent a sister to be the protagonist, even though she can't stop herself saying 'As it might be, perhaps, were I a woman / I should your lordship' (107–8). Does this part-admission give Viola relief or pain?

Orsino at last shows some interest in someone other than himself, caught by the obvious depth of Viola's feelings. So now she has to invent a history for her 'sister', or rather a probable history for herself. Perhaps, as Cesario, she thinks of Viola as dead? There's a wonderful completeness in 'A blank, my lord'. She has seen herself as a 'monster', and now a 'blank'. She's back to the theme of disguise with 'concealment', which now appears not a 'wickedness' but a 'worm i'th' bud' feeding on her flesh. The female Viola is being eaten away from within. The image that follows, 'Patience on a monument, / Smiling at grief' (113–4), is extreme because she can at last vocalise her hopelessness to Orsino, but also catches, almost parodies, his language of love-melancholy. It's another chance to experiment with ironic humour. She can't resist the dig that men's love doesn't match up to their vows, but Orsino's curiosity is now totally aroused, and he puts her on the spot with 'But died thy sister of her love, my boy?' (118). Viola's reply shows the depth of her despair, she feels quite alone in the world and even her gender is now confused – is she daughter or brother, or neither? And then comes the streak of optimism, that echoes her first scene, 'And yet I know not'. A sudden change of mood comes with 'Sir, shall I to this lady?' (121), which could be resigned but is probably abrupt. Orsino's reply certainly seems brisk. Perhaps he realises that he is falling in love with Cesario (though she may be unaware of this). I think, however, that both know their relationship has shifted in this scene, and this needs to be communicated to the audience as it is the last time we shall see them together until the denouement in Act 5. It is possible to reinforce this with some physical contact – brief hugs, chaste kisses, heads in laps, etc.

The scene has a great potential for changes of pace and tone, and can be endlessly re-examined. It seems to me the heart of the play. The boost for Viola is that the audience are on her side, alive to every irony and ambiguity.

ACT 3, SCENE I

The exchange with Feste often starts the second half of the play. It shows Viola's skill in repartee, and offers a contrast to 2.4, but its main purpose seems to be to show off Feste's wit with Viola as the feed. Feste may be hinting that he has seen through her disguise with 'Now Jove in his next commodity of hair send thee a beard' and 'Who you are and what you would are out of my welkin' (39–40, 50–1). This could either make Viola uneasy, or she may perceive she has an ally – or even a rival (Feste seems proprietorial towards Olivia).

It's followed by one of Viola's verse addresses to the audience, again demonstrating her quality of observation. The final rhyming couplet could apply first to herself – 'For folly that he wisely shows is fit' – and then to both Orsino and Olivia – 'But wise men, folly-fall'n, quite taint their wit' (60–1). Viola greets Olivia in grandiloquent language, which is probably to set up the gag of Aguecheek's 'I'll get 'em all three all ready', but demonstrates Viola's grim, almost masochistic, determination to remain Orsino's courtly representative. Once Olivia is alone with Viola they go into verse and resume their previous impasse over Orsino's suit, until Olivia breaks it with a straight declaration of love, which Viola unavailingly tries to cut short. When Viola is finally invited to speak, she says simply 'I pity you', and we feel that the pity extends to both of them. Olivia interprets this as 'a degree to love', and Viola becomes increasingly bold by slapping her down with 'for 'tis a vulgar proof / That very oft we pity enemies' (116–7). Viola tries to leave, and Olivia holds her back with 'Tell me what thou think'st of me.' Viola's reply, 'That you do think you are not what you are', is hard to interpret, though it sets up her next remark, 'I am not what I am' (130, 132). The sense that comes across to the audience is that Olivia wrongly thinks she's in love with a male page.

Olivia persists, and her aside about Viola's 'contempt and anger of his lip' shows that Viola is really shaken by this persistence, and that 'for now I am your fool' is a coded way of saying that they are both being made fools of. She is perhaps also angry either that Olivia can speak her love when she can't, or that Olivia's humiliation is letting down their sex. Olivia is now calling Viola 'thee' and 'thou', but Viola sticks to 'good madam'. Olivia's further declaration goes into rhyming couplets, and Viola picks up both its form and tone. It has the effect of distancing both declaration and refusal, moving it away from naturalism into a heightened formality. These shifts in the verse are a great help to the playing of the scene.

ACT 3, SCENE 4

Viola has returned once more to Olivia at her insistence. She has no relish for it, but she has a job to do. Shakespeare wisely leaves the exchange offstage because it's clearly stalemate, and Olivia has 'said too much unto a heart of stone' (178). The irony is that both women are possessed with the madness of love. Olivia offers a jewelled picture of herself, and, since the text is silent, Viola can choose whether to take it or not. Her impulse is surely to refuse, but perhaps pity gets the better of her.

The duel with Aguecheek is primarily a joke at Aguecheek's expense, but is based on Fabian's observation that Cesario 'bears in his visage no great presage of cruelty' (3.2.55–6). Viola makes no attempt to hide her unwillingness to fight, unlike Rosalind who with her 'gallant curtal-axe upon my thigh' might have tried to bluff it out. Viola's aside, 'A little thing would make me tell them how much I lack of a man' (268–9), could mean that she's near to revealing her gender or that she's bound to show her unmanly fear. 'A little thing' indicates there's a sexual innuendo hovering, especially when Viola was played by a boy. A comic duel between two terrified opponents seems too good a chance for a director to miss, though Shakespeare's intention seems to be that it never gets started (despite the fact the boy player would probably have been quite handy with a sword). Perhaps the audience should feel for a moment that real danger looms. Viola is understandably amazed at being asked to return a stranger's purse, and offering half her 'coffer' (purse) is generous enough. She then gets very moralistic about ingratitude: Shakespeare is echoing a common female complaint, but also reiterating one of his own great obsessions.

Antonio then calls Viola 'Sebastian', and they both fall into rhyming couplets, which gives their exchange a heightened formality. Of course Shakespeare can't have Viola demand an explanation, as that would destroy the final recognition scene, but her lack of immediate reaction poses a problem for the actor and some rationale has to be found. She sees how easily, in feature and costume, she could be taken for Sebastian, but does that prove he's still alive? Is Viola unwilling to believe good fortune, or does it simply take time to sink in? The key seems to lie in the line, 'Prove true, imagination, O prove true' (340): she still thinks Sebastian's survival may lie in her imagination. Perhaps she feels, in her general confusion of identities, that she has become Sebastian? Certainly as Cesario she has been keeping him alive: 'I my brother know / Yet living in my glass' (345–6) has a wonderful simplicity. Disguise and identity confusion have come to dominate the action. Olivia and Orsino think Viola is a man, Antonio thinks Viola is Sebastian, Aguecheek thinks Cesario is a tough fighter, and Malvolio thinks Olivia is in love with him and 'disguises' himself in yellow stockings.

ACT 5, SCENE I

Tyrone Guthrie warned me at university that this scene is a brute to stage: 'Don't leave the blocking too late, people keep arriving, the focus keeps shifting.' He was right; I've known directors despair at its complexities. It starts with a surprise: Orsino has at last deigned to visit Olivia in person, though he is intercepted by Feste, just as Viola was in 3.1. Antonio is brought on, and we learn that Viola has already told Orsino about Antonio saving her from a duel, presumably to mitigate his arrest. 'I know not what 'twas but distraction' (62) could be taken as a motif for the whole play. Antonio's speech makes it clear to Viola that she was mistaken for Sebastian and that he was alive half an hour before the duel. Perhaps she feels the need to hang on to her disguise, since acknowledgement of Sebastian is likely to reveal that she must be his sister? Viola is saved by Antonio's claim that three months have elapsed, though this will be a surprise to the audience since the action seems to have covered about a week (Viola's first visit to Olivia occurs only three days after she's entered Orsino's service, and her subsequent visits only cover two days). Shakespeare avoids further confusion by bringing on Olivia.

Viola is embarrassed by the attention Olivia gives her: it's certainly sufficient to alert Orsino that he 'partly know[s] the instrument / That screws me from my true place in your favour' (118–9). Orsino first threatens to kill Olivia, and then shifts to sacrificing Viola, whom he admits is 'the lamb that I do love'. Though Orsino's murderous threats may be a leftover from the *Apolonius and Silla* source, they do show his almost unhinged confusion about his love for Olivia and Cesario. He has now, perhaps inadvertently, declared his love for Cesario, and she recklessly picks up his passion and his rhyme with the melodramatic couplet:

> And I most jocund, apt, and willingly
> To do you rest a thousand deaths would die.   (128–9)

She then reiterates that she loves Orsino more than both life and wife, which may be a surprise to the onlookers – or is this typical Elizabethan men's talk (cf. Tullus Aufidius and Coriolanus)? At last Viola can stop 'feigning', and this is an enormous relief to her. The sequence when Olivia calls her 'husband' is in rapid half-lines and rhyming couplets, which again gives it a comic formality. Orsino's attack on her with 'O thou dissembling cub' produces real confusion in Viola: they have declared their love for one another, but at the same time he hates her. He is about to leave (for ever?), when they are interrupted by Aguecheek (the last person we expect at this crucial moment) and his claim that Cesario has broken his head. Does she realise that Olivia, the Priest and Aguecheek must all be talking about Sebastian? There's nothing in the text to warrant it, so perhaps she thinks the world has gone mad.

Into this mad world Sebastian enters, and Orsino, Antonio and Olivia comment on the twins for twenty-three lines before Viola speaks. The staging here is crucial, as Sebastian and Viola need to be some way apart for these comments to work, particularly for the line that can bring the house down – Olivia's gleeful 'Most wonderful!', as she gazes at two apparent husbands. Viola cannot allow herself to believe it's her brother – it may be a ghost or a figment of her imagination – and so brother and sister, who have only been parted for three months (or a week), go into the formal checking that they had the same father and that he had a mole upon his brow. It's an interesting decision on Shakespeare's part. He wanted to avoid them rushing wordlessly into each other's arms; in fact Viola tells Sebastian not to embrace her until she's produced her 'maiden weeds' (though this line may indicate Sebastian has moved close to her). The more natural response would have been explanations of how they were both saved from the wreck, but Shakespeare goes for the less naturalistic mole-checking to formalise the fairy-tale nature of their reunion. Viola needs to feel to the very last moment that her brother may not be real. When Sebastian finally calls her by the name 'Viola' (never mentioned in the play before), it is as if her female nature is being called back into existence: it is for me the most emotional moment in the play – and of course the moment when they may finally embrace. The reunion works wonderfully in the theatre, but the doubt, excitement and reserve need to be played to the hilt. Cast and audience need to be reminded that their loving bond has been the spine of the play.

Orsino is now released to 'have share in this most happy wreck', and he reminds Viola that she said a thousand [sic] times that she loved Orsino more than any woman – more men's talk. Viola swears the truth of this in her rich poetic vein with the rather hazy simile, 'As doth that orbed continent the fire / That severs day from night' (264–5). Her sincerity is helped by its not being in rhyming couplets and the richness of the alliteration – 'sayings', 'overswear', 'swearings', 'soul', 'sever'. The mood is again broken by Feste and Fabian, but before Malvolio's entrance Orsino manages to offer Viola his hand. Olivia butts in with 'A sister, you are she', but Viola is silent. Bearing in mind Isabella's similar silence, perhaps the convention was that the woman didn't accept first time?

The Malvolio plot is then cleared up, which would give Viola ample time to change her clothes (as Rosalind does), but Shakespeare decided not to repeat this transformation, using the rather clumsy device of Malvolio's arrest of the Sea Captain. Orsino in fact insists on calling Viola 'Cesario . . . for so you shall be while you are a man' (372–3), so the disguise joke is kept going right to the end. Whether Viola, in a dress, can live up to being Orsino's 'fancy's queen' might be in some doubt, but then Olivia is married to a man she knows nothing about and Maria to a complete alcoholic, so the 'comic' ending is complete. Perhaps Shakespeare is saying love knows no bounds of gender, age or class; or perhaps he is saying that marriage is a lottery and no one should be too optimistic. With Malvolio's final threat, 'I'll be revenged on the whole pack of you' (365), we enter unknown territory. There is no closure: what's to come is still unsure.

CONCLUSION

When aged fourteen I first studied *Twelfth Night* for an exam, I accepted it as a fairly straightforward comedy, but the more I see it and play in it, the denser and more puzzling I find it. Jan Kott saw it as a bitter comedy about the Elizabethan *dolce vita*, but I think the critic Stephen Greenblatt is nearer the mark when he talks about its dark notes being swept away by 'the carnivalesque dance of illusion, disguise, folly and clowning'. The play does seem a carnival, at times a mad world, where everything can be turned upside down, whether Olivia's mourning, Orsino's romantic passion or Malvolio's puritanism. As Frank Kermode says, it's a 'comedy of identity set on the borders of wonder and madness'. It's become a truism to say it's Shakespeare's farewell to comedy, though, oddly, the comedy/love plot has few laughs, since Viola, Orsino and Olivia are all so serious about their unrequited loves, and it's the hate plot, the gulling of Malvolio, that has the comedy. In many ways Shakespeare has pitched us into the tragicomic world of *Measure for Measure* and *Cymbeline*.

Into this mad world steps the very sane Viola. Shakespeare was clearly attracted to the basic story of his sources, but his first crucial change was not to have Viola arriving in Illyria in pursuit of Orsino. She enters Illyria by chance as an innocent, with no objectives beyond survival and finding Sebastian. Indeed she spends most of the play in a state of sorrow over her lost brother. She adopts male disguise as a way of going underground, of not attracting attention to herself. It has the reverse effect, it stirs everybody and everything up, but in her relationship to Orsino and Olivia it allows her to explore emotional areas normally denied to a woman. She is in many ways the opposite of Rosalind, written perhaps a year before. Rosalind finds male disguise a liberation, and she draws close to her loved one by 'pretending' to be a woman. Viola draws close to Orsino by pretending to be a young man, and for most of the play her disguise brings her nothing but distress. Viola is less of a role model for feisty young women, but in her stress and uncertainty she appears closer to Everywoman, and perhaps this is why audiences side with her so much.

Viola, however, is not entirely passive. She puts her trust in Time, and this eventually proves a wise decision, but she also sees Time as her enemy, trapped as a man with her woman's beauty fading. In a sense she puts her trust in the story she finds herself in – a fable about journeys ending in lovers meeting. Accordingly she maintains a basic optimism that things will turn out well, and this keeps her from revealing herself too early. She is also forced into quite daring improvisation as her love for Orsino, and Olivia's for her, gather pace. In fact until Sebastian meets Olivia in Act 4, it is Viola who has to drive the main plot, and much depends on her energy and on her comic and emotional life force. The actor is helped here by her verse, which is regular and direct except when emotionally heightened, and her prose, which shows nimble wit and quickness in repartee. Viola enters a topsy-turvy world in disguise, creates love wherever she turns, suffers for it, feels madness all about her, but finds happiness in the end. No wonder it's an attractive part.

INTERVIEWS WITH ACTORS

JUDI DENCH

I don't like talking about Shakespeare to the public, or even to students – laying it down in black and white. I just want them to see a production that's well done, and then they'll know. See a production that's not well done, and you'll put them off for ever. But I do like talking to fellow actors about the process.

Where do you start in rehearsal?

Telling the story is base camp in rehearsal. Are we telling the story, or are we just messing about being beautiful with the language? Anything you can do that illustrates and enlightens the story is fair game. Sometimes it's only when you do a run-through that you realise that this bit isn't clear at all, and you have to go back and clear it up. Clarity of story and speaking the verse is where you start. You have to mark the verse very carefully, without banging out the iambics.

So how important is the language?

The language! It takes your breath away.

> Methought I heard a voice cry 'Sleep no more
> Macbeth does murder sleep' – the innocent sleep,
> Sleep that knits up the ravelled sleave of care,
> The death of each day's life, sore labour's bath,
> Balm of hurt minds, great nature's second course . . .

And then he goes on about 'Glamis hath murdered sleep . . . Macbeth shall sleep no more'. If you'd written just one of those lines you'd be up all night looking at yourself in the mirror. Always when you go to see a Shakespeare play you know well, you hear something new: like one of those great chandeliers, another facet will shine at you.

Sometimes it's with the simplest of lines – 'We are yet but young in deed.'

That is such a chilling line. But to say a line simply you often have to go through quite a complicated process of experiment in understanding the line before arriving back at simplicity.

Do other texts seem easy after Shakespeare?

It's like coming back home, doing Shakespeare. But other writers can be very hard – Shaw, Coward, Wilde – simply because they're so grammatically exact and complex. We don't pay enough attention to that, we've got careless. But once you have the rhythm and everything in its right place, you hear this wonderful ring. It's like doing David Hare.

Where do you start with character?

When we did *Antony and Cleopatra* [National Theatre, 1987], Peter Hall gave me the best two notes I've ever had. First, remember you don't have to play the whole of the character in each scene. You may only have to play a very small aspect of the character, and then at the end the character should be whole. Second, remember not everybody speaks the truth about your character. As Cleopatra you get worried about the description in 'The barge she sat in', but think of where Enobarbus is when he says that. He's got back to Rome and he's with all his mates in the pub, and they say, 'Go on, what's she like?', and of course he goes, 'Phwoarr! Listen to this . . . '

But there are gaps: sometimes you have to invent backstories.

Yes, as Gertrude I decided with Claudius that we'd fancied one another for years, that Old Hamlet lived by the book and his brother was much more subversive and sexy. Some people say there's something missing in Lady Macbeth, but I don't think there's anything missing at all. Of course she has to disintegrate during the Banquo ghost scene, but at the end she has that clue – 'I am in blood / Stepped in so far'. She knows Macbeth went for his goal, and that she went with him, urged him on, but now he's gone for further goals and left her behind. If she's as strong as some make out, why did she ask the spirits for help in the first place? The resolution is drained out of her, and from there it's easy to do the jump to the sleepwalking.

Did you have problems with Gertrude in the National Theatre production [1989] we were both in?

As you well remember. It was partly family – I never felt I was Dan Day-Lewis' mother. But it was also that Ophelia was the first thing I did at the Old Vic in 1957, and Coral Browne was so magical as Gertrude, and she was so much in my mind, that perhaps I wasn't doing my own Gertrude, I was trying to emulate her.

We did Hamlet *Elizabethan: does choice of period help?*

Well, modern dress can be a very good way of telling the story. I did a modern *Measure for Measure* at Nottingham, and the 'moated grange' [4.1] was a nightclub, with Mariana sitting there after hours with a glass, and that proved to be a very helpful piece of storytelling. But I did Regan in an RSC *Lear*, and the designer set it in Czarist Russia, so the three daughters came on in white dresses and blue sashes and tiaras as if it was the state opening of parliament, and I found that very difficult to reconcile with the wild side of the play. I think in that world you would have to make Regan a kind of psychopath. The amalgam of the play and that period I found very difficult.

Yet you always seem relaxed on stage.

The longer you go on acting, the more you find ways of relaxing. It's actually easier to relax in Shakespeare, because you know the play works and the reasons why it works. In a new play you're so anxious about telling the author's story and making it come across.

I remember you saying how important your early tour of West Africa was.

We went there in 1963 with *Twelfth Night, Macbeth* and *Arms and the Man* – imagine! We only ever played in one proper theatre, in Lagos, and for the rest it was mostly clearings in the open air. When Viola and Sebastian faced one another at the end of the play, the audience were completely spellbound. They came on to the acting area and stood pointing at the two of us. James Cairncross said to me, 'It might have been like that at the Globe.'

Macbeth was the most popular play in West Africa, because they told us it was so funny to see a white man believing in the witches. When I said 'The Thane of Fife had a wife' they all shouted, 'Say that again!' They loved anything that rhymed. When James and I went back in 1969 we saw a lot of drama groups that had sprung up because of our earlier tour. Two fifteen-year-olds re-enacted the scene before Duncan's murder, and just laughed. It was so perverse it was extremely chilling.

The audience can teach you so much.

Sometimes it's only in performance that you make discoveries about a line. In *Antony and Cleopatra* there was a line I knew should get a laugh, and I couldn't get it. We did the hundredth performance and that night the laugh came. That's why the theatre wins over film and television every single time: *you* get more out of it, and the audience teach you so much. You rehearse something for weeks on end, and then at the first preview they tell you so much about what you should be doing.

In *Twelfth Night* the audience don't know she's called Viola, they think her name's Cesario, but they do know well before her that Sebastian is still alive. It's wonderful for the audience to be a step ahead and think they know something the character doesn't. Everything finally depends on what the audience are going to get out of it. Does it illuminate the story?

IAN MCKELLEN

There are two things about Shakespeare that I hold on to: I don't believe the Elizabethan theatre had those two pillars [as installed at the new Globe Theatre in Southwark]. The only evidence is that de Witt sketch [of the Swan Theatre], which is itself a copy. You go to see anything with two pillars in it, and you see the actors absolutely flummoxed as to what to do.

The other point is that Shakespeare could have done anything with words. He could have invented the novel if he'd wanted to; he could have fully explored epic poetry; he could have invented the essay in English form – he must have been aware of Montaigne. His version of the essay is the soliloquy, where he introduces the 'I' into the characters, which is really his great gift to drama. It makes me warm all these years later that the greatest man who ever lived should be in my line of work.

The Elizabethans seemed obsessed by role-playing.

Yes, the image that chimes through the plays is that human beings are acting all the time – 'Life's but a walking shadow, a poor player.' They are pretending whether they're aware of it or not, so that when characters are at crisis point and need to express themselves they frequently do it in terms of the theatre metaphor. Acting, professional acting, becomes the most obvious thing for a human being to do, it's what he's most fitted to do, he spends the whole day acting, why not make a living at it? It's his humanity that I love most about Shakespeare: it gives me, against all my better instincts, a personal relationship with him.

Is there value in looking into Elizabethan theatre?

To get concerned about how they did the plays is frightfully interesting but is not necessarily to the point. The point is to do the plays for the people who are going to come and see it *now*, and their terms of reference are probably not to do with Tudor politics or Elizabethan goings-on of one sort and another. I don't think the Globe was as big as they've made it. The Rose is a small theatre, you don't have to shout there, you can just behave, and that seems to be what Shakespeare was on about –

we're getting into attitudes and characters that modern actors would understand. I think Shakespeare would approve of our bringing in all our modern baggage.

Is the language everything: Shakespeare is enormously popular in translation?

That is a bafflement to me, and I'm not perhaps as sanguine as you, because whenever I do Chekhov I almost weep that I can't read what he wrote. You feel it would almost be worth learning Russian. It's our luck that if you speak English you are immediately closer to the heart of what Shakespeare was particularly good at doing. He could also stage a story wonderfully well, though not invent one. The second feature film ever made is a silent version of *Richard III*, because the story is presumably exciting enough without Shakespeare's words. It was always what he did with the story. But at the same time it's almost impossible to divorce Shakespeare from his language. It's the same with translators. If you do a Tom Stoppard translation of *The Seagull*, which I've done, it is very Stoppardian.

Where do you stand on end-stopping lines?

Well, 'speak the speech trippingly on the tongue' is Hamlet's first instruction. The plays are written in the way they are written to help the actors to act them, so the rhyme is there as an *aide-memoire* and it's easier to learn regular blank verse than anything that's ever been invented. But his late verse is as treacherous as learning Shaw, because if you miss a comma, or a particular rhythm he's after, then you will not be able to learn it. You have to know how he's written it. I don't need a director to conduct me, because you may be off the beat the entire speech. It's like jazz. And whether your mind should be working with a post-Freudian sensibility when you come to do Shakespeare – well, frankly how else can you think and behave? We are what we are.

Who are you talking to in a soliloquy?

I would like at one point during the performance to look at every single member of the audience, and when I was at The Other Place [the RSC's studio theatre in Stratford] I made sure that I consciously did that. I'm not looking out front as if I'm imagining a scene there, I'm always looking at people; it's to them that the story is being told and I'm telling my story in real time. And as far as I know, in any Shakespeare I've done, no character ever lies to the audience. The audience can accept at face value that what the character says is what he knows or believes to be the truth. Iago gives the audience four or five reasons why he hates Othello and wishes him ill – they just come out because they're on his mind – so it's perverse for the critic to say that Iago is motiveless. There may be other deeper motives than sexual jealousy, or lack of preferment, or a colour problem, or a class problem, but actually do we need to look any further?

Have you addressed the audience during speeches, with other characters on stage?

No – but it's a frightfully good idea. Though I don't think characters like Hamlet and Iago, who have so many soliloquies, need have another relationship with the audience beyond that. Their duty is to get back into the play with the other actors and tell the story that way. But Shakespeare's theatre can also accommodate what we might call Chekhovian naturalism, whether in prose or verse. The reward of doing Shakespeare is to attempt the impossible – which is to *do it all.* You're working at your wit's end, the demands made on you are so enormous, and so I'm much less interested in a production that goes for the easy option – paint it all scarlet, do it all naturalistic – than one that says 'where do we start?'

Actors have to be at ease with whatever they're doing, whether it's declamatory or conversational or whispered – hold the mirror up to nature in some sense. Shakespeare invented so many wonderful moments in addition to the language; often the silences are the most telling. The greatest scene in Shakespeare is unarguably the awakening of Hermione, and she doesn't say a word. My God, we've had some words up to that point, but the pay-off is silence.

Do you do much research?

An actor may need to know where his character comes from and what he had for breakfast, but all that naturalism is only to give him confidence to get up in public on stage and open his mouth.

Actors need self-confidence and bolstering, and the illumina-
tory way in which they speak may have no relationship to the
amount of research they've done. I do believe that Elizabethan
actors, who might have only got their parts two hours before,
and a virgin audience who'd never seen the play, could produce
a rewarding experience.

*How much do you decide beforehand that you're going to take a
certain route into a character ?*

Well, sometimes it would be nice if on the first day of rehearsal
you were given that. When you come to do a part in a play that
you know well – say Malvolio, a difficult part that's been played
so well by so many different people – I do think is there anything
I can bring to this, and I think probably I can't. To have a take
on a character is a useful soapbox to stand on. But I try to forget
every other performance I've seen, I just keep reading the text
and talking about it. When we came to do *Macbeth* [RSC, 1976]
we added it up, and we twelve actors had between us seen about
a hundred productions of the play. The one that Trevor Nunn
came up with – and he'd directed it three times before – was a
way of doing Shakespeare that was genuinely new (and remains
looking new nearly thirty years later), and that depended heavily
on the text because there wasn't a lot to look at. If you can get
the audience to listen in an active way – everything that modern
commercial theatre is doing away with by having microphoned
performances adjusted by sound engineers – then we've got
something going there which is intensely human. The
diaphragm is where the emotions first register, the laughter and
sobbing are down there, not in the mind. It's first manifested
down there where the breath starts and is pushed up out there
into the air, where it can be measured and land on the ear of the
audience, which then responds.

Do you find the character and yourself converge on one another?

I think the job of an actor is to stick up for his character, not
excuse or explain. I can take an objective overview, but I can't
be objective about myself, and I can't be objective about the
character. Well, you can be – it's a mixture of these things. In
rehearsal I feel awkward referring to the character in the third
person, I'm very alert if the director suddenly calls me by the

character's name as I don't quite know where I am there. But that's in the nature of acting a part, you don't quite know where you are – you're everywhere. You flit about between being the actor in charge of the audience's response, getting a move on, and being in the situation: you can of course have all those things in your mind at the same time. There can be moments in performance when you're lost in the character, when you're exclusively in their world and, having been there, visited it, you'll be able to make reference back to it. The characters I often play are actually going on a journey, literal or emotional – life-changing parts.

How do you respond to directors who interpret the play through changing the text?

You do have a licence with Shakespeare as the text is not sacrosanct – it can't be. Shakespeare was one of us, a man of the theatre, and we must above all else be practical. His material does respond to a group of people saying, 'Now what is *our King Lear?*' Georgio Strehler's *Tempest*, which took great liberties with the text, is the best Shakespeare production I shall ever see.

What we best do is try to discover the *story*, to chip away the enamel or the old brickwork that has been put up around the play by previous productions that we're in thrall to. I want to illuminate what's actually going on in the scenes as they happen, and of course use the language to tell that story. In *The Merchant of Venice*, for example, we know the nature of Antonio's loneliness – it's a love relationship with Bassanio. When Portia realises Bassanio loves this man she can't wait to go and have a look at him. The trial scene is about a woman saving the life of her husband's lover. Shock horror! That's the situation, it's not a secret, and it's never ever played.

Is changing the period a help or a hindrance?

Modern dress is fine, because this isn't a pageant we're doing. These are recognisable characters and attitudes that we can share – where does he keep his money, does he sign cheques, use credit cards – instead of having some all-purpose purse full of money which he rattles and throws at the other actors. It's what we call naturalism or reality, but it seems to me to be what Hamlet was on to in his advice to the Players.

You can do *Much Ado* any period you like, but it has to be a time when it was easy for men to tell women what to do, and for women to be in a subservient role, and it has to be about a martial society. If these things aren't present, the play is distorted. When we did *Richard III* on stage [National Theatre, 1990] and we decided on the 1930s, Richard Eyre was very insistent that we shouldn't use trappings of modernity – no phone, no wireless set. Otherwise the audience are thinking why aren't they having this conversation on the phone. But you're using twentieth-century fascism to illuminate Shakespeare, not the other way round, because Shakespeare can't illuminate fascism, he prefigured it. Film makes different demands, we want it to be more specific than the theatre. Film wants to be in the place where it appears to be, so you have to find the place. Whereas in the theatre the place is the stage.

HARRIET WALTER

How well does Shakespeare write for women? Can you sense he took his boy players into account?

Now that I sometimes teach actors, I realise what a great tradition there is of actors handing down skills to other actors, and how in so many cultures that's the way to do it, since the intervention of the director, the middle person, is such a recent thing. Suppose the historical coincidence had been different and women were allowed to play themselves, would he have written differently? I like to think he wouldn't. But perhaps there is more of an investment in a male career than in a female. I wonder to what extent a young boy progressed from Viola to Cleopatra and then went on to play Hamlet, so if there was a tradition of handing on there'd be no compromising, you wouldn't patronise them by saying, 'I'm going to give them a less difficult speech to do because they're a boy.'

I think women love playing Shakespeare because you don't feel – apart from length, you don't have such a long part in terms of the burden of taking the play through – that you have any less intricate psychological language and poetry, so the task, even if you're only on for one scene like Lady Percy, is no less. His female characters may be no less complex, but the trouble is you often don't get the scenes to show their development – Lady Macbeth for example [RSC, 1999] disappears from the stage and then reappears mad, and you don't have any soliloquies to the audience to chart her disintegration. I don't know whether that's because Shakespeare thought he didn't know the female mind as intricately as he knew the male mind, or because, as women didn't have so many leadership problems, he didn't feel he had to investigate those particular moral quandaries.

But he investigates women in the comedies.

Yes, women do tend to dominate in his love stories, though in the case of Portia it's often gone down as Shylock's play because, even though he's not at the centre, great actors have wanted to play Shylock and consequently unbalanced the play. It's often possible as a male to dominate the play, and as Macbeth take little notice of your Lady, but as a woman actor you have to devise ways of growing through the other person's performance. It's a survival tactic because we are as devoted to our characters as they are to theirs – as Ophelia you want to put as much into your few scenes as Hamlet does in all his – so we have to develop certain ways of surviving, of making our characters 'read', of satisfying ourselves or preserving our integrity in ways the audience will never know. Even as Isabella you don't have the central philosophical soliloquy – the 'To be or not to be'.

Women also tend to dominate in the so-called 'problem plays' – those with a moral conundrum, like *All's Well That Ends Well*. There's an inverse ratio, whereby the greatest plays often have the smallest parts for women; and the best parts for women are often in the least done plays, like *King John* or *Cymbeline*.

Do you think women playing male parts casts light on the plays?

I've done workshops playing Hamlet, and wondered whether this throws any light on the play or whether it's just me nakedly wanting to play a huge part. But when a woman works on Hamlet's speeches you realise that what you're tapping is a universal humanity – the Oedipal complex may still be there but you don't have to play it strongly. It doesn't destroy the essential humanism of the play to have a woman as Hamlet.

How do you tackle character?

I'm strictly analytical because that's the way I like to work. I like to get all my evidence from the text. I absolutely eschew worrying about what colour was Lady Macbeth's wallpaper, because I take it all those exercises are there to give you a real context from which you can believe yourself and therefore sell yourself out there. Lady Macbeth just appears on stage, she is a creature of theatre not the real world. I can't visualise her in the real world and I don't need to. But I do consider character in the sense that how do I, a nice gentle person, arrive at this demoness? I have to find bridges in my own nature where I'm not so nice, not so gentle. I have to find it from what's written on the page. Burbage and the Elizabethans presumably didn't feel the need to analyse as much as we do, though their performances may have been no less deep than ours. But then you have to consider the audience. The Globe had few competitors, whereas

today with all the film and television available – and comparisons between Hoffman and Pacino, etc. – audience expectations
are much more detailed and domesticated. Audiences can't just
jump in and accept Grand Tragedy; we have to be led there
through much more detailed routes or we risk young people just
thinking we're doing 'posh rant'. One of the reasons I loved
Cymbeline and *All's Well* was that the language goes from terribly
naturalistic and ordinary and conversational to huge imagery
and daring concepts; and what I love is being able to do both.

Shakespeare can be quite specific about character.

Yes, you have to find an Ophelia who will crack up, whereas
Juliet knows her mind and doesn't crack up. They're quite
different characters, and you find this in their language: Ophelia
will say 'I do not know what I should think', whereas Juliet goes
ahead with her marriage to Romeo despite all the obstacles.
There are case histories that R.D. Laing writes about that could
be Ophelia's language. Shakespeare may not have read Freud
but there seems no condition of humanity that he didn't know
something about. Although sometimes we overanalyse Shakespeare and say how clever he was to put in a detail when actually
it was probably done on a whim. Is the remark about Shylock's
ring done to contrast with Bassanio giving away his wife's ring,
or is it just a humanising touch? I think just as Mozart is said to
have written straight on to the page, so did Shakespeare and that
he used language subconsciously.

Mother-daughter relationships are rarely examined.

No, though interestingly he does often examine older men being
in love with a man who loves a woman. I've been that woman in
so many plays – Portia, Beatrice, Helena. There's a strange scene
between Helena and Parolles, which is quite frosty and
competitive over Bertram. If you're playing Portia, in the last act
you get the whole double sexual ambiguity: Shakespeare started
with a story about a merchant of Venice who loved a young man
who wanted to marry a rich girl. I found the trial scene
extraordinary because as a lawyer I was concerned with law not
love, and I had this equal fight – as if I was in a boxing ring, it
was like a match. The first half of *Macbeth* is a little like that,
though I had to persuade and entice and manipulate so that my

man got the power, which is very different from getting it myself. What I discovered about Portia is that you don't suddenly leap from being a spoilt virgin in Belmont to spouting law after having a little bit of training, but that her language in Belmont is quite legal; she's got that kind of mind anyway.

You've talked about working scene by scene, not worrying about consistency, and that character is an accumulation of moments.

If I'm playing Alan Ayckbourn I need to find the character early on – the way she walks and dresses – but in Shakespeare the opposite is true. We can add costume and walk later on, but I don't think 'Is she this sort of a person?', I just do what I have to do moment to moment, I don't behave or think of character. As individuals we do very inconsistent things, and I think that's the way he writes. Judgements should be from the outside from other characters, not from the inside. That means the characters are usually bigger than me, whereas in television the characters can be smaller and you have to make certain selections.

Have you found similarities in the 'breeches' parts?

One year [1987 at the RSC] I was playing Portia, Viola and Imogen, and I wanted to make them different because I thought I've only got one boy in me; but in fact it was resolved by the plays, because the reasons for cross-dressing were different in each play. Viola has a desperate, rather tragic, starting point, because she's partly doing it in the hope of keeping her brother alive and partly as a practical necessity, and she becomes more masculine as a result. Imogen starts off as a princess and gradually gets stripped more and more bare, and her femininity comes out – the boys keep saying what a good cook she is and how sweet and gentle. Rosalind again has a completely different impetus, but she's more confident and full of herself, whereas Viola's more cowed and frightened. I knew as Portia I could be quite convincing as a man, particularly in modern clothes, but as Viola I tried to give her a man's voice, and then found the play doesn't work if you make her too masculine.

Helena in All's Well That Ends Well *is a particularly difficult part.*

Helena is interesting because she achieves her ends without putting on trousers, and Trevor Nunn helped by updating the play to the early 1900s and placing me as a Shavian woman [RSC, 1981]. The part is made difficult because there is a judgement out there in the world against the heroine chasing a man, and therefore playing her can be quite tough. Women do suffer from wanting to be liked, but it's not just that; it's knowing that the engine of the play requires the woman to be sympathetic. Trevor encouraged me to be as diffident and unsure of myself and unmanipulative as possible – though I was still judged a scheming villainess. I tried very hard to play her passion, not her using feminine wiles.

It may be a bit much to expect Shakespeare to see further than the convention of marriage, or the racism, anti-Semitism and anti-feminism of his time. In a way he does seem to be more of a feminist or a non-racist than he would know himself to be. He pleads for a common humanity; Shylock's deserving of respect just because he's a human being.

Where do you stand on the importance of language and, in particular, end-stopping?

Language is not the be-all and end-all, but the method by which I will get to the play; the most direct route to the heart of the play is through the language. I don't regard end-stopping as an absolute orthodoxy. Like all rules it's good to know them and judiciously break them. When you've done quite a lot of Shakespeare you do seem able to highlight a word, lift it, serve up the end of a line without whacking it on the head. You can observe different twists of rhythm and, when you have a long list of things, give weight to all of them without hammering them. These are technical skills acquired through practice. With most acting you have to drive the meaning on to the end of the line. Lines are also usually more understandable if you take them at a lick.

Soliloquies come to life when you argue with yourself, think it out at the time, with one thought leading to another. You can confide in the audience things you can't say to anyone else in the play. Even within speeches you sometimes need to externalise your private thoughts. A very good acting note is that, though on the page there may be 26 lines, you must always start as if you've only got one, and this one line leads to another. With Viola your main protagonist is the audience, and you only find yourself through them: with everyone else on stage you're lying.

Are Shakespeare's women reduced by the importance the Eliza-bethans gave to marriage?

I'm personally bored by the thought of everything leading to happy-ever-after marriage. It doesn't inspire me as the main motive for a character, so as Isabella I would substitute for 'chastity', 'integrity' – what do I believe in, what am I willing to fight for, what is the very heart of me, and when do I stop being me when I'm stripped bare and tortured? For a woman in Shakespeare there seems to be less stamina required. Imogen seems to me the heaviest part (even more than Rosalind, who has more lines). She drives the play, as Helena does. Ellen Terry, Peggy Ashcroft and Judi Dench all said Imogen was the most exhausting part they'd played, and it was so for me. But men have so many more – I'm quite jealous of men sweating at the curtain call.

JOSETTE SIMON

I started off having a fantastic grounding. Straight out of drama school I went to Stratford where, among other parts, I was playing Iras to Helen Mirren's Cleopatra. I used to stand around even on the days I wasn't needed, sponge-like, soaking up all this expertise. I just thought, 'Fantastic – aren't I lucky?' I think nowadays it's quite difficult when people get flung into major leading roles quite young. When I started off it was a real privilege to be around Michael Gambon, Helen Mirren, Derek Jacobi and Tony Sher – they were all in that season [1982–3]. You had a fantastic core of experience. I used to love being on stage with Mirren and Gambon, and thinking why and how it was that they were approaching the scene. At that time the RSC had a way of doing things, whereby if you did well in the smaller parts then you worked your way up, which I think was great because by the time I became an actor you didn't have the rep thing of doing whole seasons, so having that kind of journey and experience of being able to learn was great.

How have you come to approach Shakespeare?

Any approach is made up of a number of different elements. I feel like a detective, I comb that text for all those clues. The great thing about Shakespeare is that on the final day of your final performance you're still doing it, there's so much still there. I start with the text because that tells you so much about character, how they speak, the way they use words gives you such clues to the nature of the person – the way Rosaline speaks to Biron is not the same as the way she speaks to the Princess of France. She's so verbally dextrous that you get a feeling of someone who's highly skilled, highly intelligent. Similarly with Beatrice and Benedick, that kind of jousting with words, the barbed nature of some of their exchanges, underpinned by the feelings they have for each other. It's very clear when they have short lines and catch each other's words or complete each other's sentences. It's such a clue to character and their relationship.

But though I start with the text, I don't subscribe to sticking rigidly to it, in an anal way. If Shakespeare is performed successfully all over the world it must be about more than just the

English text. Changing things is fine, as long as you can justify it truthfully. The whole picture is made up of instinct, sensibility, imagination. Shakespeare was questioning the whole time: if we didn't keep coming up with different answers it would be extremely boring.

How do you cope with the preconceptions about the main characters?

When people heard I was going to play Isabella, they said, 'How are you going to play that line?' ['More than our brother is our chastity'], it's Becher's Brook at the Grand National. Same with Titania; and when I did Ibsen's *Lady from the Sea* people had such memories of how Vanessa Redgrave played it. But I never think: I know it's been done like that, so I'll do it this way. I have to pretend that I've never heard of it, seen it, read it. It's like a fresh canvas.

One of the things I really hate is a device, a clever idea, that is different but has nothing to do with the play – it's so untruthful, so arrogant. I wouldn't want anything to be totally the way I see it, or totally the way the director sees it. You're both mining the text. But in the end I have to have an overview, I have to know what the journey is going to be, so that I can then gauge the temperature of the scenes. Shakespeare gives you the bricks and you build the house.

How well does Shakespeare write for women?

Shakespeare gives his women a great sense of equality, absolutely on a level with men. I find him psychologically very acute about women – how he gets himself inside the mind and psyche of a woman, so that they feel absolutely safe in their emotional make-up, I don't know. It takes my breath away. The way Cleopatra, Iras and Charmian talk to one another is very, very female. Their language is so specific to them, the detail of asking the servant how tall is Octavia is so very female; a man wouldn't ask those questions.

How did you approach Isabella and her relationship with the Duke?

I had to think of her going into the convent as a positive step, that it didn't necessarily have to come out of an adverse situation or that she was running away from something. Then I had to work myself into 'chastity' being what it was about, because that's what it was for her. She did mean it, and she did feel her brother would understand. It was clearly a difficult and painful choice to have to make, and I made it difficult for her to say.

We left the end open almost till the technical, because we could never decide what we thought. Then I realised that for several pages before the end Isabella doesn't speak at all, and, as ever with Shakespeare, there's a reason for everything. We decided that she says nothing because she doesn't know what she thinks. So the production ended with Isabella leaving the Duke and walking upstage, turning round at the last moment, but not doing anything. The lights came down and so no one knew what happened next. Isabella didn't yet know the nature of a journey which she'd been very happy to go on with a friar, and which had held no romantic complication. I like there to be a sense that it's not the end, this is where they've got to thus far.

Kate's 'submission' speech at the end of *The Shrew* is another famous problem. You don't want to go down the tongue-in-cheek route, but clearly it's hard to believe she really does mean it. I feel it says a lot about the two of them and the strength of their relationship. There's been an agreement. It's a kind of joke, it's not for real, she's not going to be that kind of wife, but she's quite prepared to say it boldly and baldly without mocking it. The two of them are close enough to go through it with absolute security.

How did you first come to Shakespeare?

I was a classic case at school. I thought Shakespeare was boring – when you were made to write an essay about 'Why did Mark Antony say that?' You're very rarely up on your feet doing it. So I was rather terrified of Shakespeare, I didn't know what people meant when they said 'you could see it all in the text'.

My whole career has been about wanting to do good work, that's my only criterion. But that meant I was always having to justify why I was doing anything, because of my brown skin. It wasn't something I ever put forward. I used to say to people I'm an actor, not a 'black actor'. I hate that phrase. I don't know what a black actor is, I'm an actor, full stop. But when I was in my last year at drama school I was asked into the principal's office and he said to me, 'I know you love Shakespeare, but you should be prepared for the fact that you'll probably never do it.'

'Why?' I said. 'Well,' he said, 'the RSC has never had a black leading actress', which they hadn't – some male actors like Hugh Quarshie, but never women. Same with the National. And I remember sitting there thinking, with the arrogance of youth, well – so what? I may have a problem, but I'm not going to put it in my head as a negative before I start.

Have you ever been conscious of trailblazing as a black actress?

Not as a trailblazer, but I'm always being made aware of it. For a long time, though fortunately no longer, reviews would always say the part is played by the 'black Josette Simon'. Also I could never do a part without some column inches being devoted to whether I should be doing it in the first place, usually before they'd even seen it. So when I started doing large parts there was always this awful extra pressure that if I didn't do it well people would be saying, 'Well, she shouldn't be in it anyway.'

It's never entered my head in the rehearsal room or during performance; I can't afford to be worrying about what the audience might be thinking. Audiences just want you to do it well. They suspend disbelief on all sorts of levels and that's it – it's not a problem. Having white relations in a play doesn't affect a thing. My family is huge and all of different hues, and nobody bothers. Of course if the character's predicament is that they have lily-white skin and long blonde hair then clearly I'd be an idiot to play the part, but most of the time the part is just a person. The biggest race I belong to is the human race – it's a bit like Shylock's speech. We've moved on, but not far enough. It's been slower than I might have thought.

How did you come to Shakespeare?

I was lucky to be introduced to a lot of Shakespeare at school: I had a whole series of inspired and inspiring teachers. In fact I remember very clearly the first time I was asked to speak Shakespeare's words (I was about eight years old), so it must have made some impact. At university I was influenced by some very brilliant contemporaries, in particular Stephen Unwin [currently director of the English Touring Theatre]. He employed an intense and puritanical approach to the speaking of Shakespeare, which was based on a strict clarity of thought and intention.

A few years later, when I joined the RSC, I was faced, as any young actor is, with a whole barrage of stuff about the technical side of verse-speaking, which I have tried to absorb and observe. But what I learnt at university lingers on. I still feel that, given the choice between making sense at first hearing and observing the rules of verse-speaking, I'd plump for clarity. I think it is overstating the case to say that if you always observe the rules of verse-speaking, clarity will naturally follow. For the most part it follows, but – especially in extreme cases like Leontes in *The Winter's Tale* – not always.

You have the ability – I think to an extraordinary degree – to present a line with great clarity and significance and yet remain in character. It's harder than it sounds.

I now think I spend most of my time in rehearsal (at least with Shakespeare) trying to clarify the sequence of thoughts, trusting that the emotional life of the character will follow. And, as you say, it's harder than it sounds. Very often (at least with Shakespeare), it is a question of finding the simplest reading. In *Richard III* there is a scene late in the play where the king, now tired and disillusioned, tries to persuade his sister-in-law to give him her young daughter as his wife. He says that if such a marriage does not take place, then the country will slip back into violent civil war. This can be seen as a debating device or as a threat (after all, Richard is a supremely clever political manipulator); but I wondered if Richard's awful vision of his country at war could not stem from a genuine fear on his part. In other words, for the first time in the play he is honest with another person, expressing himself simply and forcefully. The irony is that, unlike those moments when he is more devious, he fails to be persuasive.

Similarly, when Iago says: 'O, beware, my lord, of jealousy. / It is the green-eyed monster, which doth mock / The meat it feeds on', the simplest reading is that he genuinely means (and feels) it. It might be in the middle of a scene, and a play, that employs all sorts of lies and devious stratagems, but the power of these lines is that Iago knows and fears jealousy. Indeed, it may be the only moment in the play when Iago is completely honest (and that includes 'I hate the Moor'). The simplest reading seemed to me to be the most powerful.

Did you have a similar moment of revelation with Macbeth?

Before I started work on Macbeth [Almeida, 2005] I hadn't realised how little he says in the first scenes of the play. If we were reading the play with no idea of its outcome, and if we treat with scepticism what other characters say about him, then frankly those first scenes reveal next-to-nothing about his interior life. Astonishingly, he finds a poetry, and perhaps a new language, inside him when he agrees to murder his king. God knows where that comes from, or what precisely it means, but that is the Macbeth that Shakespeare gives us.

If you try to superimpose a character on to the person that we first see – great warrior, loving husband, good friend to Banquo, trusted by Duncan – then that seems to me arse-over-tip, and potentially a barrier to further and surprising discoveries. In other words I tried to work out what he was thinking and saying as precisely and honestly as I could, in the hope that his emotional life would reveal something unexpected.

Don't get bound in by preconceptions?

Yes, and that's difficult because in those vague, subliminal parts of your brain, you think you know who, say, Hamlet is; whereas, more often than not, your responses to the part are bound in by a whole lot of presuppositions that are more to do with history of performance and criticism than with the text itself. When I did Hamlet [National Theatre, 2000] I read a piece that talked about the scene where 'Hamlet sexually assaults his mother'.

There's nothing in the text that warrants that description. Rather, such an analysis is the result of a series of brilliant performances and some imaginative criticism – all perfectly valid. But the Hamlet I played had absolutely no desire to sexually assault his mother, partly from love, respect and fear, and partly because the whole world of sex had, in this Hamlet's mind, become distorted and diseased.

Another example from *Hamlet*: we wondered whether Claudius' attitude to Hamlet had to start as antipathetic. A mutual loathing seems to have become a given, but what if Claudius' opening lines to Hamlet are simply tactless, rather than cruel and aggressive? He has of course done something terrible but, rather like Hamlet himself, could he not want things to return, as far as is possible, back to normal? He wanted his brother's crown and his wife, and now he wants his son too. In saying 'You are my heir', is he also saying 'Love me, as you loved your father'?

A similar thing with Cassius in *Julius Caesar*. He is assumed to be Machiavellian, a wily political operator; but in fact the plot to kill Caesar is, frankly, a bit of a mess. Cassius, far from being coldly logical, is always panicking. In nearly every scene he appears in, he threatens to kill himself. We cannot assume that these threats are simply hysterical posturing or the means to get what he wants. They could be genuine, and of course he does in the end commit suicide. I just wonder whether he is idealistic, romantic in his desire to preserve the principles on which the republic is built – a little naive in fact. This of course ignores any source material that Shakespeare might have used, Plutarch etc., which is always of interest, but which seems to me often to confuse things.

Shakespeare thrives on ambiguity. How much do you guide the audience in this?

Ambiguity – or irony – in a situation can be relatively uncompli-cated, as in the scene from *Richard III* I mentioned earlier. The trouble is that ambiguity is both a blessing and a curse. It leads to complexity, but there is always the threat of confusion or indis-tinctness. The great master of psychological ambiguity is, of course, Chekhov. In *Uncle Vanya* there were moments when I thought, 'Jesus, I could be thinking four directly contradictory things at the same time.' The danger lay in ending up presenting nothing – a generalised unhappiness (or, more rarely in Chekhov, happiness).

When we did *Macbeth* I felt it was important to make a decision about whether or not the Macbeths have or have had children – something that is ambiguous in the text as it stands. After all, children so dominate the play. Emma Fielding [Lady Macbeth] and I took the simplest option, I suppose. The Macbeths had one child that died young, but that backstory became the single most important thing about their relationship, the ultimate source of their behaviour. In his first great soliloquy, Macbeth comes out with this grotesque image of a baby, a giant baby it seems, 'striding the blast', and this is just before the scene when Lady Macbeth says that she has 'given suck, and know / How tender 'tis to love the babe that milks me'. I think both remarks, and the emotional weight behind them, take each character by surprise. At a moment of crisis, the other major crisis of their life together comes to the fore. It's like Iago's 'Beware, my lord, of jealousy'. At those great nodal points of Shakespeare's plays, it's as if the characters are genuinely surprised by what they've just said.

Can you play that surprise – 'Where did that come from?'

Yes, I think you can. I remember producing the baby image for the first time in rehearsal and my hands formed a shape as if holding a newborn child to my chest. For a split second Macbeth thought 'Oh shit!'; and then he went on to nightmarish images of the Day of Judgement, and the idea and memory of the baby expanded, changed, disintegrated.

In soliloquy the headline, but not the development, is often pre-thought. Hamlet must know as he enters that he's going to say 'To be or not to be'?

'To be' is a most extreme example. It's a very odd soliloquy indeed because, as it stands in the texts we have, it doesn't come out of a preceding situation. So it *is* pre-thought in some way, whereas it's always more exciting for an actor to have a thought that is fresh and immediately formulated. To be honest I rather dreaded doing it, and not just because it's so famous. Arrogantly I thought it was rather overrated – yeah, yeah, yeah, we all know death is tricky because we don't know what happens to us. But, in fact, it became centrally important precisely because its heartbeat is so deep and fundamental.

'O that this too, too solid flesh would melt' [1.2], in contrast, just spills out of Hamlet. It's a direct response to what has gone before. It's emotionally fevered and that's exciting; but I love its technical requirements, too. There's something thrilling about knowing that you're doing a complete, single sentence here and it's *this* long. It's an extreme example of thinking on the hoof and he's continually interrupting himself. Often with minor details – like the fact that he notices that Gertrude wore the same shoes at the wedding as at the funeral. I love the precision of that. It's reductive and heartfelt and savage and childish.

How important is Hamlet's interplay with other characters?

He's lonely and he needs a friend, in simple terms. Which is why the soliloquies become so important because the audience is the only person, as it were, he can find to talk to. Rosencrantz and Guildenstern won't do, and even with Horatio it's good only as far as it goes. Their relationship is warm, but oddly formal. And at the end of the play the Hamlet who says 'Let be' is different from the one who praised Horatio as an honourable and loyal man. He's glassier and more removed. It's as if he is saying 'I have no need of you, or indeed anyone, any more'. So many of Shakespeare's characters (or at least some of the ones I've played: Iago, Macbeth, Hamlet, Malvolio) are the loneliest men you are ever likely to meet, though they respond to their loneliness in vastly different ways.

Cassius is also desperate for Brutus' friendship.

But who does Cassius describe as his 'best friend'?

Titinius – I played him once.

That's right. You'd think it would be Brutus, but no. And we know (from source material) that Cassius is married, but we're told nothing about his wife. Describing Titinius [a subordinate soldier] as Cassius' best friend may be carelessness on Shake-speare's part, or it may be deliberate that he produces this nugget of information so late in the day. Either way, I think it's brilliant. He drops in this piece of information which he then fails to follow up . . .

Shakespeare's always doing that . . .

Yes, and it can open up a whole new range of possibilities, a whole new world.

Does Hamlet go mad?

When I began to read the play carefully, there seemed to be only one scene, with Polonius, where Hamlet talks in that strange, seemingly incoherent way that we associate with Shakespeare's 'mad language' [cf. Ophelia, Poor Tom, Lear]. And, significantly, it is only Polonius who defines Hamlet as mad; or rather, he is the first to raise the issue. I decided to take Hamlet at his word: that he is 'mad, north-north-west'.

Perhaps Shakespeare made that clear to Burbage?

I'm sure Burbage must have asked him. As I'm sure the two actors playing the Macbeths must have asked him about the baby. Shakespeare's answers may have been dismissive or help-ful, we will never know. I'm just not convinced that, because of the pressures of a large and varied repertory, Elizabethan actors simply learnt their lines and then spoke them. These were very great actors, who inspired a playwright of genius and elicited responses from audience members that we know were deep and heartfelt. To achieve that, they must have invested in the figures they were playing, and that meant asking questions.

Is there always a degree of the tragic and the comic, whether you're playing Hamlet or Malvolio?

In the greatest, and most complex parts, yes. Hamlet is definitely comedic; and Malvolio has what we would see as a tragically limited life. What defines these characters as ultimately tragic or comic is, of course, how they end their stories. Hamlet dies; and Malvolio, even if he has the potential to become an Iago, is, in the end, too mean and unimaginative to exact any terrible revenge. He probably sells his story to the papers and, after a momentary shudder, the world continues as normal.

I found Malvolio very difficult [Donmar Warehouse, 2002]. It's almost as if there is a missing scene. That's quite normal in Shakespeare. In *Hamlet* we never see him on the boat to Eng-land; but he returns to Denmark a different man. That should be a problem, but oddly it isn't. The change is so profound and mysterious that there is no reason to see it defined. With

Malvolio, I can't help feeling Shakespeare missed a chance. We do not see him between the scene in which he tries to seduce Olivia and his incarceration in a cell. Surely the turning point in his story is the moment when he realises he has been set up?

Do you learn the part before rehearsals start? Can you do it without making decisions?

I do learn, or try to learn, a lot before I start: I don't like to get up on to my feet with a book in my hand. I find getting up and moving scary, as we all do, but I prefer to face most of my fears in one go. There are benefits to learning early, but it can be dangerous. When I did Thersites in *Troilus and Cressida* for Sam Mendes [RSC, 1990], I learnt most of the part at home; and, without realising it, had fixed certain rhythmic gestures without thinking them through. I got into the habit of giving one line, 'The sun borrows of the moon when Diomed keeps his word', an enormous weight. After about two months, Sam turned to me and said: 'Would you stop doing that line as if it is the meaning of the play.' The result of learning it in the kitchen, I suspect.

People have many different systems, and although I tend to stick with mine, I have great respect for those who keep the script close to them for a long time, because by the time they put it down they really seem to know the weight and intention of every line they say.

What advice do you pass on to students?

First, clarity of thought. Find the simplest thought-line, the least emotionally complex. If simplicity is not an option, then follow the complexity through in a logical way. The emotional life of a character will come later.

Second, don't worry. Most of the students I meet are terrified of Shakespeare. I don't know where this fear dropped into the psyche. There are rules, but most of them are quite simple and are broken quite often. And don't worry.

You've played more of the great female roles than any actor alive – do you have favourites?

Cleopatra and Volumnia are probably my favourites. The parts I'm most in love with are the ones I've had several stabs at. I had three goes at Viola and Portia, and two at Rosalind. Coming back to a part after a gap of years is very rewarding. Even though you're not consciously making alterations or wishing you'd done it differently, something has happened, something has grown. You don't come to the new production with preconceived ideas: everything is fresh. You have to be completely open, like an open book, but you know what works and what doesn't. Also the lines are easier to learn, even after a gap of twenty years.

I've enjoyed playing some of the more problematic parts, like Ophelia, Gertrude and Lady Macbeth. I think it makes it more interesting if there's something difficult about a part, as in *Macbeth* because of the huge gap in the middle when you've got to bring on what you've been going through since you were last seen. It's the same with Ophelia. Quite often you have to provide things that aren't in the text – it's skeletal stuff.

Do you think Shakespeare made concessions because of his boy players?

Yes, quite a lot. I think the strokes are sometimes very broad. As the parts were written for boys you have to provide a certain womanliness, because I think that's often only sketched in. Apart, that is, from Cleopatra, which offers such variety that some people think it's impossible to do. The biggest problem is to join all her characteristics together, otherwise you'd be playing a different person in each scene. Juliet, for instance, doesn't stand up as a character if you play each scene differently. I think the travesty parts are some of the most successful, because they were suited to his boys. Rosalind is wonderfully written because there is so much fun to be had, but for a woman playing a woman, Cleopatra and Volumnia are out on their own. And there's so much comedy there. It's so valuable to get your laughs – it's terribly hard work without them. I do think Shakespeare got better at writing women as he got older, but then, genius that he was, he had an uncanny understanding of everything, which would of course include having an uncanny understanding of women.

What do you think are the essentials of playing Shakespeare?

You need great experience of verse-speaking – that allows you to forget you're speaking verse. The audience need to feel the verse somehow. But at the same time the meaning is just as important. What you need is the ability to blend the two together. I think I was very lucky in my early life to have a wonderful teacher at school and then to go to the Bristol Old Vic drama school, which was very verse-orientated and gave me a strong grounding. From nineteen onwards it became a natural way of expressing myself, the only way the character could be couched, which is what I've always striven for. The tendency today is to break the verse down and go for the sense. But it is written in verse; he used prose when it was needed. Not that I believe you should impose a way of verse-speaking. It shouldn't be slavish and unnatural. You always have to go with your own instincts.

How much work do you do on character, as against simply responding to the language?

It's a combination of verse and sense. Reading about a character helps you to flesh it out, even if Shakespeare hasn't stuck to history. It's whatever helps you best as an actor; any tool you can use is valuable. Reading about Coriolanus provides you with an atmosphere, even if it's material Shakespeare didn't know. Some people think up a whole scenario about Gertrude being a lush. I decided she was deprived of sensuality with Old Hamlet, she was absolutely starved, and Claudius gives her that back. It's whatever you can find to make it flesh. But you can't play something that the audience can't understand or you'll just puzzle them.

Tell me about the famous 'pause' in Peter Brook's Measure for Measure, *when Mariana's begs Isabella to plead for Angelo's life.*

Isabella was my first big part, and Peter's first big success. It was at Stratford in 1950, with John Gielgud as Angelo. I trusted Peter completely, and being very young [aged twenty] and inexperienced I did exactly what he told me to do. His instructions about the pause were simple: even though I was weighing things up before making the decision to be merciful, I was not to show any of these thoughts. I was told to hold it longer than I thought was safe – to *dare* in fact. I think you'll agree that courage is one of the gifts of young actors – well, *nerve* really. Peter used to say that the duration of the pause would vary in length according to how well I'd earned it. Imagine him trusting me with that! The length was in fact pretty constant, and I don't believe I was ever tempted to 'snap it up' too quickly. I remember the effect on the audience being of a holding of breath – a sort of tingle and silence.

Have styles changed much since 1950?

I believe good playing of Shakespeare always works. Gielgud as Angelo in 1950 would still hold up, while some of the other actors in the company were from another age and tended to sing it. Fashions have undoubtedly changed, sometimes for the worse because there was some very good verse-speaking around at that time. Not to go with the flow seems harder than going with it.

Glen Byam Shaw said a marvellous thing at our first read-through of *As You Like It*, which was that these characters were larger than life, were more intense than we are, and that you were catching them in a spotlight at this time of their life when they were more vivid and more alive than they had ever been – or you had ever been. It's this intensity that requires magnifying. Antony and Cleopatra are super-beings. Whatever you're playing in Shakespeare it has to be wholehearted. I despise the oblique approach, I think that can be very boring. You have to go for it.

ADRIAN LESTER

The thoughts and feelings that I've had to express in Shakespeare have been so much more complicated and multi-layered than in the modern texts I've worked on. Theatre by its very nature has made my body fitter, my vocal technique stronger, and has engaged me fully as an actor: it's the difference between 1500 metres and a marathon. I've had to use every part of my psyche, and it's made me, quite simply, a better actor.

Tell me about playing Hamlet in Peter Brook's production [2000]?

Peter began from a belief that whoever came to this production had seen the play before. He explained that we were not going to please those people who clung to their favourite bits, because he was going to pare away at the elements that structure *Hamlet*; and the element that interested him was the domestic story of the two families. That was his kernel: it wasn't to be a political piece.

I've never worked with a director who discarded so many brilliant ideas simply because he felt that somewhere the audience would be expecting those. He instinctively wished not to please. He was purely interested in Hamlet's story, of a young man who tries to keep himself from falling apart while all this is happening to him. Because of this concentration, this paring down, I don't feel I want to play the role again in a more conventional production.

What are the pluses of a cut-down chamber Shakespeare?

Peter had an agreement with all the theatres we went to that there wouldn't be more than 600 seats, because once you're playing to larger audiences it becomes a different *Hamlet*. The pluses are that the audience are up for a very revealing *Hamlet* because nothing is covered by any kind of bombast, and the actors can reach the back rows without effort. We could work as if we were on camera. But though for the actors it was truth or nothing, it wasn't a naturalistic production – we didn't have real swords, we simply indicated death. We had different coloured bamboo sticks, so that when Claudius is killed by the poisoned sword I would simply touch him two inches below his heart.

There was a Buddhist-like element to the piece, whereby the deaths were purified and distilled. Peter wanted to see someone who was full of life having the life drained away from him. Sometimes I thought it worked brilliantly, sometimes I thought – Oh, can't we have blood?!

How much did you feel you were talking to the audience in the soliloquies?

Completely. I find it difficult to do soliloquies unless I am looking at someone and see a face. Sometimes I would ask for the house lights to be touched up a few points so that I could see individuals, and perhaps refer back to them. It stops me doing it just for myself, because every face has a different expression.

So what was your experience of doing Henry V's soliloquies in the much larger Olivier Theatre [2003]?

I still found people close to the stage. Further away I had to settle on shapes of people, but there was something very interesting in having to convince a sea of people of Henry's ideas and feelings, even berating them because they didn't have Henry's problems, so how could they understand? I actually enjoyed speaking to the person in the back row because I felt like a politician, which is how Nick Hytner's production was structured in its modern setting. Because war and its problems were current at the time, I felt I could stand and talk to the audience as if we were all in the Olivier Theatre. Don't pretend we're not in the Olivier, don't pretend I don't have to vocalise to reach that person at the back. Even in the night scene before Agincourt when Henry is on his own, and he is praying and panicking and berating God, I felt I could push the speech up to God at the back of the circle.

Declan Donnellan has this great thing about the importance of *changing*, that the impulse for the breath is seeing the lack of what you wish to see in the other character's face. You speak to change – even if it's God.

Did you find Hamlet and Henry V lonely parts?

Completely alone, both as an actor in the company and as the character you're playing. In our 2 ½ hour *Hamlet* I left the stage for only five or six minutes. Actors would enter the stage with different energies, and sometimes they wouldn't be in the same play as the rest of us. So I had to grab them and get them up to the same speed as everyone else. Fortunately, Hamlet can do that, as he's constantly running rings round people. With Henry V too there was just so much on my plate. Offstage actors might be chatting, having a few jokes, and I just could not join in because of the weight of what I had to do. It did keep me separate from the rest of the company.

How do you marry moment-to-moment inconsistencies with the arc of the character?

I think you work out an arc in rehearsal, and then concentrate on moment to moment in performance. You can't consciously portray the subconscious inconsistencies that belong to a human being because you're putting a hat on a hat. As soon as I try to 'explain' this person, I'm consciously putting a cap on his character. What's more interesting is trying to find those peaks and troughs within the character before you get to the end.

There's a scene in *Henry V* where he 'woos' Katherine [5.2] and I began to find a release in him – that he wanted to play and flirt with her, and when that didn't work he would say, 'Look, this is an arrangement, it's about duty and kingship and that will never fade', and then he would go back and use humour again. And at first I felt I couldn't play such different intentions, that it's not part of the king or the play, but then I thought: No, do it to its fullest extent so that the barometer really swings. In drama every character you play is in extraordinary circumstances, and therefore, in order to allow yourself to behave extraordinarily, you have to take the conscious cap off.

Someone wrote about your Hamlet that it was 'a brilliant mixture of craft and transparency'. Is that the vital mix?

I have this big thing about being a chameleon: do one type of role and then take on a different type, run a whole gamut of characters. In Shakespeare I hammer myself to try and understand the five or six layers of meaning and not get in the way of any of them. Don't choose just one. Every character I play is at the mercy of his situation, so that they're always *reacting* to it. If I don't *choose* the reaction, but try to keep myself lost *within* the reaction even as I'm speaking, then I hope that it will always remain clear and transparent.

But if you're not making choices about a line, then what are you doing with it?

Take 'To be or not to be'. We moved the speech to the point where he's killed Polonius. I sat down as Hamlet and thought clearly about killing myself – how would I do it and what would that feel like. I carefully felt my pulse, and whatever my pulse dictated is how I would begin the speech. I wanted to be lost within his indecision. If I say to the audience, 'Here's the line, do what you want with it', that's an attitude already. I was very still when I did the speech and I asked the audience, 'What's the point?'

Peter Brook and I met for a week before the rest of the cast joined. I would go and see him for three hours a day and I would tackle the speeches, whispering them through, and he would sit right next to me and sometimes say very quietly, 'I don't think it's that thought.' He was happy when he was sure it wasn't two things that I was telling him. All the rehearsals were about absolute clarity of thought. To explore all those things honestly is quite scary, because they are all the things that hold a human being together – your relationship to life and death, parents, God.

When you played Rosalind [Cheek by Jowl, 1991] did you find that there's a humanity common to the sexes, or that there are interesting differences?

I was only able to play Rosalind when I realised – and this was halfway through rehearsals – that I shouldn't try to play Every-woman. I was trying to marry my own impulses with a cap that said 'Woman'; my voices and gestures would be mine but with a generalised feminine cap on them. Everywhere I was finding blocks, and I was only completely released when I realised that I had to play not 'Woman' but this particular young girl. She's sixteen, six foot, flat-chested, bookish, quiet, very quick-witted, completely powerless in court, and discovering an attraction to men – that's the person I chose to play. I found there to be a common feeling of love and vulnerability to both sexes, but that the society of that period dictated the appropriate behaviour for women, so that I mustn't show extremes of emotion. When, however, I got into the forest dressed as a man I didn't feel any feminine constraints and suddenly I was released.

How then did you find being a man playing a woman playing a man?

When I was with Orlando I didn't feel I was playing a woman at all, apart from certain mannerisms. I grew my nails long so that I found I couldn't grab him. I had to use my palms, and that changed the way I used my arms, my wrists had to be bent. I had to stand tall, because every tall woman I know gets back problems trying to be shorter than the man.

Any other advice?

I've spent a lot of time rapping – for diction, because with some of the best rhyme artists they hide the meaning of the lines while syncopating the beat and hitting the rhymes as they go. It's helped me find a modern rhythm for the expression of some of the characters. Working with students I've found that when their conscious mind is engaged with finding the metre and fitting the rhyme they surprise themselves with what their unconscious mind comes out with. In *Hamlet* we did a great deal of work on Tourette's, and that was such a help. Hamlet has so much to react to, that speed of thought is everything.

I went to the RSC more or less straight from drama school, and I was there for eight years and had amazing opportunities. But people began to talk about me as 'a classical actress', and I knew I didn't want to get labelled. I'd become very preoccupied with these Shakespeare heroines, but also with the Women's Movement – there were such exciting things being talked and written about in the 80s – and so I became intent on re-examining these parts in quite an iconoclastic sort of way. I felt, coming to each of these roles, that they were a bit like statues in a park that had lost their outline through erosion and bird shit. I wanted to scrub them down and search for their original shape. A lot of the joy was in asking, 'Who is she *really*?' The legacy of literary and dramatic tradition has incarcerated some of these roles more than the male heroes, and they are due for reinterpretation.

Which roles in particular?

Isabella is a classic case of course, because whenever I had read about her she was always described as a frigid hysteric or neurotic: that because she won't sleep with Angelo to save her brother's life, ergo there's something wrong with her. So my starting point was: let's give her choices full value and see why she'd made them, and what it means and how they resonate. Why should we judge this character before we understand her? In life, women and their morals are often judged so much more harshly than men.

Cressida is another case. She's censored for flirting with Diomedes, but what other choices does she have? As a hostage, what other course of action is available to her? She does not make the heroic choice of self-sacrifice, but should we condemn her for that? And once you ask some of these questions, it's very liberating. But some people couldn't bear to see her not played as a quasi-whore.

But Rosalind is different?

It's the same problem of preconceptions. You're expected to find the play a celebratory and romantic rural romp. But when I read it I saw it as an amazingly challenging examination of gender, of what love means to men and women, and of their differing responses to the influence of the heart. It *is* full of charm, wit and delight, but it's also bold and iconoclastic.

I have a very complicated relationship with Shakespeare; the roles are probably unrivalled, but they are so difficult to play well. I can't bear to see productions that are mediocre, clichéd or tired – churned out simply because they're there. My favourite Shakespeare productions have often come from abroad. When you come from a different culture you don't have that sort of idolatry and reverence of the text in your head, and may therefore be freer to interpret, to possess the material with a more passionate subjectivity. I remember the Rustaveli Company production of *Richard III* [from Georgia]. There was a huge map covering the entire floor, and at one point as the characters raged and wrangled, the map rose up through them, as though the whole world was in jeopardy – it was so thrilling. They'd seen the scale and the rawness of it, because Russia was a country that had experienced war and civil war. Shakespeare lived so much nearer the edge, and we've lost our understanding of that – our life is so much easier.

You've been away from Shakespeare for some time: what has he left you with?

I was so lucky to have had that training, because the challenge of those plays is so great. It's a bit like training for a marathon; every part of you is stretched – intellectually, imaginatively, emotionally, physically, technically. The canvas of his imagination is so vast. So with everything you do afterwards, you have this tool bag, this history of working on really demanding material. Rosalind for example – I felt she was dancing on this road ahead of me, and however hard I ran I would never catch up with her. That's a great feeling: that you can go on working on her till the very last performance, and however much you have explored her she'll always elude you. That's the mark of a great playwright: that the excavation is endless.

With Rosalind, were you conscious of changing the shape of what you were doing?

Going out there night after night, you keep hearing new resonances in a line or a monosyllable or a speech, and these discoveries incrementally layer and layer what you're doing. I remember a performance of *Measure for Measure* when I suddenly found, in a speech of Isabella to Angelo, that she was hitting a lot of Gs and hard Cs ['No ceremony that to great one longs, / Not the king's crown . . . Becomes them with one half so good a grace / As mercy does.' 2.2.59–63]. That night, for some reason, I found those hard gutteral consonants just came alive, I felt them in my mouth, my throat, my body. Psychologically, emotionally, I felt the energy of those consonants, and it kicked the speech in a different direction. A little pocket opens up, a bit of air is released in a corner of a scene that you had glided over before, or had pre-decided was about a certain number of things, and suddenly you realise that it might be about something different, and so on that night that choice is your discovery. That's the joy of live performance and of repetition – it's beyond science.

An actor works from moment to moment, and yet there's an arc, a structure you're observing. How do you reconcile the two?

When I started working I held arcs in my head more than I do now, perhaps because I was allowing my brain to lead the work more. I would have a conception of what a scene was, and then the next scene, and therefore what the entire arc was, and I set out to play those arcs. But I have moved increasingly towards working moment to moment, and trusting that the whole journey will reveal itself anyway. At any one moment on stage you know the whole terrain of the play, behind and in front, but all your focus lies on the present, the now. As I've got older I have tried not to let the head dominate the work with quite the same intensity as when I was younger. Of course you always think through the words, but I now realise that in life the bio-chemical, the hormonal, the irrational, the sexual, the instinctive – these things drive you, influence you moment by moment, as much as the mind does.

So Rosalind has no game plan?

When she sees Orlando in the forest she really hasn't got time to think. That scene [3.2] is a classic example of someone who's busking on their feet. You have to ask yourself one question: why doesn't she come out and say, 'Hey, it's me'? But she doesn't, and you have to root that decision deep down in who she is, that she is not going to come out without cover, without her disguise. She may have been dressed as a man for only a few days, but already the freedoms that disguise has yielded her are intoxicating. It's too soon to give them up. So she launches into this display of words, like a peacock fluttering its tail feathers; partly to bewitch him into staying, and partly to remain in control in case her heart or her blood betray her and take her into territory that is too dangerous for her at the moment. So she is basking in the moment, but as the scene develops a game plan emerges – it's a complex combination of the two.

How much of a help, or hindrance, is Shakespeare's language?

It's both a constraint and a liberation. In blank verse you are bound by the rhythms, by where a line ends, where a caesura sits in the thought, etc., but if you yield to that you find yourself freed as never before. It's great when you are on top of it and it's taking you with such speed and precision through a thought, but when you feel you're not on top and the language is running away with you, then it can be grisly.

How important to you is research, and finding, or inventing, a backstory?

For Isabella I went on a retreat to a convent, because never having had a religious faith puts you in quite a tight spot when it comes to playing someone about to join a nunnery. So I did make myself get up at five and go to chapel, and I think I began to understand something of the power of prayer. But the visit was only partially successful. What proved much more helpful was a fantastic book I read by Marcelle Bernstein called *Nuns*, which opened a huge number of doors in my head. I realised that I'd have to find a parallel with their faith within myself; and that parallel would be my attempt to lead a good life, morally and ethically, and decide at what point I would be prepared to sacrifice those ideals to save someone else's life. For 'chastity' I substituted 'personal integrity'. So all that research was a way of bringing her *inside me*, instead of her being someone who was *over there*.

I like to do a lot of work on backstory – some of it from the text, some researched, some invented – so that at the beginning of the play I know what my character needs, what she fears, what she hopes will happen and won't happen in the rest of her life.

Everything that takes place after that is in the moment. With Shakespeare, however, the text does much more of the work for you than with most other writers: it serves as both an inner and outer map.

I especially remember in the first Angelo scene [2.2] the particularity of your verse-speaking (I was playing the Provost). You picked your way with such care, as if you were weighing every word.

Well, that's how precisely she speaks. She doesn't think in clumps, because she reveals she has a lawyer's mind. She says, 'But can you if you would?', and he replies, 'Look, what I will not, that I cannot do'; to which she answers, 'But might you do't?' etc. And she has a special relationship to all those verbs – can, cannot, might, will. It's a brilliant acting opportunity, the stakes could not be higher, she's never had to do this before, never met anyone like this before, never had this responsibility before; absolutely all virgin territory – pardon the pun – but the stakes are huge because she loves her brother, they have no parents so it's her or nobody. Her heart is passionately engaged with her brother, but it's only her mind that will make her plea succeed or fail. She's got one minute to make her pitch, and if she doesn't find a purchase on Angelo in that first minute he'll dismiss her and she will have lost. But as soon as he comes back with his first rebuff, her heart doesn't cloud her thinking; her mind clears once she smells the flaw in his argument, and she immediately latches on to that imprecision. Her mind is the tool that he responds to, and that's why it's so sexy, why it's such an erotic scene – because they're so alike.

Adrian Noble gave you a great note. He said in another age you'd both have been doing law at university, and you'd have sat up till 3 a.m. arguing.

Adrian was wonderful on that show because he set no parameters. I remember one day we were rehearsing the first Angelo/ Isabella scene, and as I got into my stride and felt her confidence flying, I suddenly thought I might go and sit in his chair of office. But I lost confidence or self-censored, and didn't do it. At the end of the scene Adrian said: 'I thought you were going to sit in his chair, so why don't you?' If I bumped up against any parameters in the role, Adrian would be the first to say: 'Let's kick that assumption out of the way, shall we? Why not?'

The Duke's offer of marriage: did you ever feel a growing attachment during the play, or did the offer come out of left field?

It's one of the most difficult moments in the whole canon. You have to address it in rehearsal because you know how the play ends, but I don't think it crosses Isabella's mind during the course of the action. She says nothing in reply to his two proposals. If Shakespeare hasn't made a choice and has given you silence – and silence can go anywhere – then it can mean anything. And so every night Daniel Massey [the Duke] and I re-investigated it – not structurally, but internally. Daniel worked hard at making his offer come from a real love that had grown during the course of the action. We decided we didn't want to go for a shock-horror rejection, because it's too complex for that. I felt she's emotionally exhausted at the end of the play; she hasn't begun to consider her own heart in terms of a lover. So it came to depend on how Daniel and I had played that night; if we'd really connected in the scenes there was a sense that it might be a union that had possibilities for her. If we hadn't been connecting as actors, not listening to one another perhaps, then it became much harder. It varied from night to night.

We tend to go on and on about language, but why is Shakespeare in translation so successful in other countries?

Isn't it the scale that Shakespeare offers? You don't get the exquisite sensuality of the original words, that you glean from the sounds and shapes in your mouth, but you do get the thought. It's the thought, the scale of the ideas, the huge scope of his dramatic imagination that translates – and the inspired juxtapositions. No writer I know is so daring: the fact that in *King Lear* you get absurdity and tragedy of that scale rammed up against one another. No other writer would dare, at the very moment of Cleopatra's death, to bring on a funny little man with a basket of snakes and make people giggle. That's the Picasso, the Mozart in him.

Can we take liberties with the plays and their language?

Liberties are fine as long as they come profoundly out of something deeply rooted in the text. My favourite interpretations have often been the boldest. Some of the early bits of Derek Jarman's film of *The Tempest* are really exciting – I'd always thought Miranda should be played as a wild child, feral, hair unwashed, covered with mud and blood and thorns. Also the first twenty minutes of Lepage's *A Midsummer Night's Dream*: the forest isn't a lovely little dell in Burnham Beeches, it's a chaotic landscape of mud and flood and devastation. Those bold choices I adore.

On the language itself I'm probably a bit of a purist. Don't pull the verse towards you, go towards it. It's like plays – don't pull them towards your reality, go towards their reality and then find the resonances for the times we're living in. I don't like it when the language is simplified to make it 'accessible': let's stretch ourselves to meet it, to inhabit the scale of its exploration. Isn't that what art is for? When I was fifteen I saw a simple and uncut performance of *King Lear*, and I thought it was a play about myself.

NOTES ON SOURCES

Full details of the abbreviated titles given below
are to be found in the Bibliography

ONE: THE ELIZABETHAN ACTOR

1 Coldewey, 'From Roman to Renaissance', 65–7. Happé, 'Drama in 1553', 118–22.
2 Milling, 'Development of a Professional Theatre', 144–9.
3 Korda, 'Labours Lost', 195–220.
4 David Grote, *The Best Actors in the World: Shakespeare and His Acting Company*, Westport and London: Greenwood, 2002, 162, 233.
5 Bruster, 'Birth of an Industry', 224–31.
6 G.E. Bentley, 'Shakespeare and the Blackfriars Theatre'. *Shakespeare: An Anthology of Criticism and Theory, 1945–2000*, ed. R. McDonald, Oxford: Blackwell, 2003, 732–42.
7 Gurr, *Shakespeare Company*, 54–69.
8 Stern, *Rehearsal* and *Making Shakespeare*, passim.
9 Milling, 'Development of a Professional Theatre', 152.
10 Thomson, *On Actors and Acting*, 55–6.
11 Joseph, *Elizabethan Acting*, 1–21, 43.
12 Gurr, *Shakespearean Stage*, 100–02.
13 Smith, 'E/loco/com/motion', 131–7.
14 Joseph, *Elizabethan Acting*, 7.
15 Crystal, *Pronouncing Shakespeare*, passim.
16 Gurr, *Shakespeare Company*, 41–5.
17 Thomson, *Professional Career*, 92, 104. Joseph, *Elizabethan Acting*, 42.
18 Leggatt, 'Richard Burbage', 9–12.
19 Jardine, *Still Harping on Daughters*. Dusinberre, *Shakespeare and Nature of Women*. Orgel, *Impersonations*. Levine, *Men in Women's Clothing*. Rutter, *Enter the Body*. Kathman, 'How Old were Shakespeare's Boy Actors?'.
20 McMillan, 'The Sharer and His Boy', 231–45.
21 Milling, 'Development of a Professional Theatre', 172.
22 Gurr, *Shakespeare Company*, 69–77.
23 Thomson, *Professional Career*, 98.
24 Gurr, *Shakespearean Stage*, 98.

TWO: SHAKESPEARE'S LANGUAGE

1   *Norton Shakespeare*, 3361.
2   Ibid., 3350.
3   Granville Barker, *On Dramatic Method*, 75.
4   Hall, *Advice to the Players*, 28.
5   Barton, *Playing Shakespeare*, 15.
6   Walter, *Other People's Shoes*, 156.
7   Palfrey, *Doing Shakespeare*, 134–67.
8   Kermode, *Shakespeare's Language*, 100–2.
9   Cordner, 'Scripts in Shakespearean Comedy', 4–28.
10 Ibid., 1–3.
11 Wells, *Modernizing Shakespeare's Spelling*, 4–29.

THREE: PREPARATION

1   *The Guardian*, 13.7.05.
2   Berry, *On Directing Shakespeare*, 150.
3   *Players of Shakespeare* (*Players*), iv, 153–9.
4   Arthur Miller, *Collected Plays*, London: Cresset Press, 1958, 21.
5   *Players*, iii, 162.
6   White, 'Working Wonders', 220.
7   Gussow, *Gambon*, 24.
8   *Players*, iii, 135.
9   Ibid., v, 94.
10 Ibid., ii, 181.
11 Miller, *Subsequent Performances*, 109.
12 *Players*, ii, 75; iv, 165–8.
13 Ibid., ii, 45.
14 Luckhurst, *On Acting*, 10.
15 *Players*, i, 169.
16 Miller, *Subsequent Performances*, 160–1.
17 Luckhurst, *On Acting*, 28.
18 Worthen, *Authority of Performance*, 127.
19 Granville Barker, *On Dramatic Method*, 92–3.
20 Thomson, *Professional Career*, 104.
21 Kermode, *Shakespeare's Language*, 125.
22 Holmes, *Merely Players?*, 34–5.
23 *Players*, ii, 137.
24 Ibid., v, 177.
25 Granville Barker, *On Dramatic Method*, 22. Brook, *The Empty Space*, 57. Gaskill, *A Sense of Direction*, 139–40. Berry, *On Directing Shakespeare*, 1. Marowitz, *Prospero's Staff*, 6. Kennedy, *Foreign Shakespeare*, 98.
26 Russell Jackson, 'Shakespeare in Opposition: From the 1950s to the 1990s', *Oxford Illustrated History of Shakespeare on Stage*, 233.
27 Kennedy, *Foreign Shakespeare*, 14.
28 Rutter, *Clamorous Voices*, xxiii. *Players*, ii, 50.

29 *Players*, iv, 194.
30 Luckhurst, *On Acting*, 67.
31 Sher, *Year of the King*, 139.

FOUR: REHEARSAL

1   Max Stafford-Clark, *Letters to George*, London: Nick Hern Books, 1989, 66, 70.
2   Iris Murdoch, *The Black Prince*, London: Vintage, 1999, 189.
3   *Imagine*, BBC TV, 25.11.04.
4   Rodenburg, *Speaking Shakespeare*, 4.
5   Michael Billington, *The Life and Work of Harold Pinter*, London: Faber & Faber, 1997, 148.
6   Berry, *The Actor and the Text*, 82.
7   White, 'Working Wonders', 214, 221.
8   John Gielgud, *Stage Directions*, New York: Random House, 1963, 4–5.
9   Flatter, *Shakespeare's Producing Hand* and Styan, *Shakespeare's Stagecraft*, passim.
10 *Players*, ii, 101.
11 White, 'Working Wonders', 221.
12 Cicely Berry, *Voice and the Actor*, London: Harrap, 1973, 285.
13 *London Review of Books*, 5.12.04.
14 Gussow, *Gambon*, 101.
15 Berry, *On Directing Shakespeare*, 212.
16 *Players*, ii, 78; iv, 120.
17 *London Review of Books*, 5.12.04.
18 Barton, *Playing Shakespeare*, 141.
19 Hall, *Advice to the Players*, 61.
20 *Players*, ii, 47.
21 Kenneth Tynan, *Curtains*, London: Longman, 1961, 217.
22 Taylor, *Reinventing Shakespeare*, 263.
23 Kermode, *Shakespeare's Language*, 125.
24 Russell Brown, *Writing for Performance*, 43.
25 *Players*, v, 215.
26 Ibid., vi, 151.
27 Berry, *On Directing Shakespeare*, 36.
28 Shapiro, *1599*, passim.
29 Jan Kott, *Shakespeare Our Contemporary*, London: Methuen, 1964, 3.
30 *Players*, iv, 192.
31 Kiernan, *Filthy Shakespeare*, 120. Partridge, *Shakespeare's Bawdy*, 60, passim.
32 McLuskie, 'Boy Actresses', 130.
33 Chedezoy, *Shakespeare, Feminism and Gender*, 14.
34 Dusinberre, *Shakespeare and the Nature of Women*, 265.
35 Traub, *Desire and Anxiety*, 25 and 'Gender and Sexuality in Shakespeare', in *Cambridge Companion to Shakespeare*, 144.
36 Jardine, *Still Harping on Daughters*, 3.

37 Rutter, *Clamorous Voices*, xxiv.
38 *Players*, v, 230.
39 Michael Hordern, *A World Elsewhere*, London: Michael O'Mara Books, 1993, 138.
40 *Players*, i, 46–66.
41 Ibid., iii, 165.
42 Ibid., iii, 161. Cook, *Shakespeare's Players*, 156.
43 *Players*, iv, 61.
44 In an all-too-rare article about a supporting part, Gregory Doran writes about Solanio in *Players*, iii, 68–76.
45 Luckhurst, *On Acting*, 63. David Mamet, *True and False: Heresy and Common Sense for the Actor*, London: Faber & Faber, 1998, 109.
46 Edward Burns, *Character: Acting and Being on the Pre-Modern Stage*, London: Palgrave Macmillan, 1990, 8.
47 Barton, *Playing Shakespeare*, 171–3.
48 Luckhurst, *On Acting*, 13.
49 Barton, *Playing Shakespeare*, 209.
50 Cook, *Shakespeare's Players*, 51–4.
51 Granville Barker, *On Dramatic Method*, 29.
52 *Players*, iv, 103.
53 Callow, *Being an Actor*, 165.
54 *The Guardian*, 8.6.05.
55 Berry, *On Directing Shakespeare*, 207.
56 Taylor, *Reinventing Shakespeare*, 277.
57 G.B. Shaw, *Our Theatre in the Nineties*, London: Constable, 1932, 206.
58 Harriet Walter, *Actors on Shakespeare: Macbeth*, London: Faber & Faber, 2002, 63.
59 *Omnibus*, BBC TV, 2001.
60 Harold Guskin, *How to Stop Acting*, London: Methuen, 2004, 97.

FIVE: PERFORMANCE

1   *Players*, i, 164.
2   Ibid., ii, 71.
3   Holmes, *Merely Players?*, 117–22.
4   *Players*, ii, 79.
5   Ibid., iii, 188.
6   Walter, *Other People's Shoes*, 115.
7   White, 'Working Wonders', 212.
8   Barton, *Playing Shakespeare*, 7.
9   *Players*, iii, 178.
10 Luckhurst, *On Acting*, 113.
11 Scales and West, *So You Want to be an Actor?*, 77–8.
12 Walter, *Other People's Shoes*, 201.
13 *Players*, iii, 52–3.
14 Michael Pennington, *Hamlet: A User's Guide*, London: Nick Hern Books, 1996, 193.

15 White, 'Working Wonders', 213.
16 *Players*, iii, 149.
17 Ibid., i, 125.
18 Redgrave, *In My Mind's Eye*, 128.
19 Eleanor Bron, *Double Take*, London: Weidenfeld and Nicolson, 1996, 309–10.
20 Berry, *Text in Action*, 20.
21 Styan, *The Shakespeare Revolution*, 216.
22 White, 'Working Wonders', 212.
23 Hal Burton, ed., *Great Acting*, London: BBC Publications, 1967, 71–2.
24 Gussow, *Gambon*, 127, 193.

APPENDIX: TWO CASE STUDIES

1 Wells, *Shakespeare & Co.*, 190–1.
2 Berry, *Changing Styles*, 40.
3 Kenneth Muir, 'The critic, the director, and liberty of interpreting', *The Triple Bond, Mainly Shakespearean, in Performance*, ed. Joseph G. Price, University of Pennsylvania Press, 1975, 28.

BIBLIOGRAPHY

There are tens of thousands of books on Shakespeare, and this list is of course partial and subjective. It includes all the books quoted in the text and Notes on Sources. For further reading you could refer to the bibliographies at the end of each chapter in *Shakespeare, An Oxford Guide*, eds. Stanley Wells and Lena Cowen Orlin, Oxford University Press, 2003.

SHAKESPEARE BIOGRAPHIES

Park Honan, *Shakespeare: A Life*, Oxford University Press, 1998, and Stanley Wells, *Shakespeare: The Poet and his Plays*, London: Methuen, 1997 are both expert and reliable guides. Racier and more 'imaginative' reads are Stephen Greenblatt, *Will in the World: How Shakespeare Became Shakespeare*, London: Jonathan Cape, 2004; and Anthony Holden, *William Shakespeare*, London: Abacus, 1999. A more sceptical look is provided by Katherine Duncan-Jones, *Ungentle Shakespeare: Scenes from his Life*, London: Arden, 2001. James Shapiro, *1599: A Year in the Life of William Shakespeare*, London: Faber and Faber, 2005 is a brilliant look at the key year of the Globe's opening. Frank Kermode, *The Age of Shakespeare*, London: Weidenfeld and Nicolson, 2004 is an excellent short introduction. If you want all the known facts try S. Schoenbaum, *William Shakespeare: A Compact Documentary Life,* Oxford University Press, 1987. Shakespeare and his contemporary playwrights are enjoyably covered in Stanley Wells, *Shakespeare & Co.: Christopher Marlowe, Thomas Dekker, Ben Jonson, Thomas Middleton, John Fletcher and Other Players in His Story*, London: Allen Lane, 2006.

GUIDES

There are many excellent collections of essays on every aspect of his life and work. Try *The Cambridge Companion to Shakespeare*, eds. Margreta de Grazia and Stanley Wells, Cambridge University Press, 2001; *The Cambridge Companion to Shakespeare on Stage*, eds. Stanley Wells and Sarah Stanton, Cambridge University Press, 2002; or *An Oxford Guide*, as mentioned above.

GENERAL

Jonathan Bate, *The Genius of Shakespeare*, London: Picador, 1998 looks at the origins of his modern reputation; and Gary Taylor, *Reinventing Shakespeare: A Cultural History from the Restoration to the Present Day,*

London: Vintage, 1991 takes a critical look at his fluctuating fortunes over four centuries. Anne Righter [Barton], *Shakespeare and the Idea of the Play*, London: Penguin, 1967 is a seminal work on his attitude to playwriting. Harley Granville Barker, *Prefaces to Shakespeare*, Princeton University Press, 1946, and *On Dramatic Method*, New York: Hill and Wang, 1956 are still worth a read, though some of his ideas now seem wrong-headed. I am fond of Germaine Greer's little book, *Shakespeare*, in the Oxford University Press Past Masters series, 1986. Adrian Brine (who once directed me as Othello) has very shrewd things to say in his and Michael York's *A Shakespearean Actor Prepares*, New York: Smith and Kraus, 1996.

ONE: THE ELIZABETHAN ACTOR

Two key works are Andrew Gurr's *The Shakespearean Stage 1574–1642*, Cambridge University Press, 1992, and *The Shakespeare Company 1594–1642*, Cambridge University Press, 2004. Peter Thomson's *Shakespeare's Professional Career*, Cambridge University Press, 1992 and *On Actors and Acting*, University of Exeter Press, 2000 are very enjoyable. Tiffany Stern is illuminating, if speculative, on the company's rehearsal methods in *Rehearsal from Shakespeare to Sheridan*, Oxford: Clarendon Press, 2000, and *Making Shakespeare: The Pressures of Stage and Page*, London: Routledge, 2004. Alexander Leggatt writes on 'Richard Burbage: A Dangerous Actor' in *Extraordinary Actors: Essays on Popular Performers*, eds. Jane Milling and Martin Banham, University of Exeter Press, 2004, 8–20. There are several interesting articles in *From Script to Stage in Early Modern England*, eds. Peter Holland and Stephen Orgel, Basingstoke: Palgrave Macmillan, 2004, including Bruce R. Smith, 'E/loco/com/motion', 131–7; Natasha Korda, 'Labours Lost: Women's Work and Early Modern Theatrical Commerce', 195–230; Scott McMillan, 'The Sharer and His Boy: Rehearsing Shakespeare's Women', 231–45. A compact overview is given by Jane Milling in 'The Development of a Professional Theatre, 1540–1660' in *The Cambridge History of British Theatre: Origins to 1660*, vol. 1, eds. Jane Milling and Peter Thomson, Cambridge University Press, 2004, 139–77, a book that contains interesting articles on every aspect of Elizabethan theatre, including John C. Coldewey, 'From Roman to Renaissance in drama and theatre', 3–69; Peter Happé, 'Drama in 1553: continuity and change', 116–36; Douglas Bruster, 'The Birth of an Industry', 224–41. B.L. Joseph, *Elizabethan Acting*, 2nd ed. Oxford University Press, 1964 is a pioneer work, though some of his early conjectures are now in doubt.

WOMEN AND BOY PLAYERS

Three important works are Lisa Jardine, *Still Harping on Daughters: Women and Drama in the Age of Shakespeare*, Brighton: Harvester, 1983; Valerie Traub, *Desire and Anxiety: Circulation of Sexuality in Shakespearean Drama*, London and New York: Routledge, 1992; and Juliet Dusinberre, *Shakespeare and the Nature of Women*, London: Palgrave Macmillan, 1996. An excellent recent survey is Phyllis Rackin, *Shakespeare and Women*, Oxford

University Press, 2005. Two books of essays are *A Feminist Companion to Shakespeare, Oxford,* ed. Dympna Callaghan, Oxford: Blackwell, 2001; and *Shakespeare, Feminism and Gender,* ed. Kate Chedezoy, London: Palgrave Macmillan, 2000. On Boy Players try Laura Levine, *Men in Women's Clothing: Anti-theatricality and Effeminization, 1579–1642,* Cambridge University Press, 1994; Kathleen McLuskie, 'The Act, the Role, and the Actor: Boy Actresses on the Elizabethan Stage', *New Theatre Quarterly,* 3.10, 1987; Stephen Orgel, *Impersonations: The Performance of Gender in Shakespeare's England,* Cambridge University Press, 1996; Carol Chillington Rutter, *Enter the Body: Women and Representation on Shakespeare's Stage,* London and New York: Routledge, 2000; David Kathman, 'How Old were Shakespeare's Boy Actors?', *Shakespeare Survey: Writing About Shakespeare,* vol. 58, 2005, 220–46.

TWO: SHAKESPEARE'S LANGUAGE

Frank Kermode, *Shakespeare's Language,* London: Allen Lane, 2000 is fascinating and very readable. Two key works are John Barton, *Playing Shakespeare,* London: Methuen, 1984; and Peter Hall, *Shakespeare's Advice to the Players,* London: Oberon, 2004; and their advice extends to every aspect of acting Shakespeare. An interesting, though more academic, look at language is found in Simon Palfrey, *Doing Shakespeare,* London: Arden, 2004, and *Shakespeare and Language,* ed. Catherine M.S. Alexander, Cambridge University Press, 2004. For the relationship between line-structure and phrasing see George T. Wright, 'The Play of Phrase and Line', *Shakespeare's Metrical Art,* University of California Press, 1991. Several of the first folio texts have recently been reprinted with notes, variants and a modernised text on each opposite page, by Nick Hern Books, edited by Nick de Somogyi.

THREE: PREPARATION AND TEXT

For handling the text, and other matters, consult Cicely Berry, *The Actor and the Text,* London: Virgin, 2000 and *Text in Action: A Definitive Guide to Exploring Text in Rehearsal for Actors And Directors,* London: Virgin, 2001; Patsy Rodenberg, *Speaking Shakespeare,* London: Methuen, 2002; and Barbara Houseman, *Finding Your Voice: A Complete Voice Training Manual for Actors,* London: Nick Hern Books, 2002. For analysing staging clues in the text see Richard Flatter, *Shakespeare's Producing Hand,* London: Heinemann, 1948; and J.L. Styan, *Shakespeare's Stagecraft,* Cambridge University Press, 1967. For words, spelling and punctuation see David Crystal and Ben Crystal, *Shakespeare's Words: A Glossary and Language Companion,* London: Penguin, 2004; Stanley Wells, *Modernizing Shakespeare's Spelling,* Oxford University Press, 1979; and Michael Cordner, 'To Show Our Simple Skill: Scripts and Performances in Shakespearean Comedy', *Shakespeare Survey: Shakespeare and Comedy,* vol. 56, 2003, 167–183. On pronunciation David Crystal, *Pronouncing Shakespeare: The Globe Experiment,* Cambridge University Press, 2005, is challenging and well argued.

ACTORS ON INDIVIDUAL ROLES

The six volumes of the *Players of Shakespeare* series, published by the Cambridge University Press, contain articles written by actors on roles they have performed at the Royal Shakespeare Company over the last twenty years, and I have quoted freely from the following actors:

VOL. 1, ed. Philip Brockbank, 1988: Patrick Stewart on Shylock; Donald Sinden on Malvolio; Geoffrey Hutchings on Lavatch; Tony Church on Polonius; Michael Pennington on Hamlet; Roger Rees on Posthumus; Gemma Jones on Hermione; and David Suchet on Caliban.

VOL. 2, eds. Russell Jackson and Robert Smallwood, 1989: Ian McDiarmid on Shylock; Fiona Shaw and Juliet Stevenson on Celia and Rosalind; Alan Rickman on Jacques; Kenneth Branagh on Henry V; Frances Barber on Ophelia; Ben Kingsley on Othello; and David Suchet on Iago.

VOL. 3, eds. Russell Jackson and Robert Smallwood, 1994: Maggie Steed on Beatrice; Deborah Findlay on Portia; Nicholas Woodeson on King John; Gregory Doran on Solanio; Penny Downie on Queen Margaret; Anton Lesser on Richard of Gloucester; Simon Russell Beale on Thersites; Brian Cox on Titus Andronicus; Philip Franks on Hamlet; and Harriet Walter on Imogen.

VOL. 4, ed. Robert Smallwood, 2000: David Tennant on Touchstone; Richard McCabe on Autolycus; David Troughton on Richard III; Susan Brown on Queen Elizabeth in *Richard III*; Paul Jesson on Henry VIII; Jane Lapotaire on Queen Katherine; Philip Voss on Menenius; Julian Glover on Friar Laurence; John Nettles on Brutus; and Derek Jacobi on Macbeth.

VOL. 5, ed. Robert Smallwood, 2003: Philip Voss on Prospero; Antony Sher on Leontes and Macbeth; Zoë Waites and Matilda Ziegler on Viola and Olivia; Simon Russell Beale on Hamlet; Nigel Hawthorne on King Lear; and Frances de la Tour on Cleopatra.

VOL. 6, ed. Robert Smallwood, 2004: Samuel West on Richard II; David Troughton on Bolingbroke and Henry IV; Adrian Lester on Henry V; and Henry Goodman on Richard III.

In Carol Rutter, *Clamorous Voices: Shakespeare's Women Today*, London: The Women's Press, 1988, Sinead Cusack, Paola Dionisotti, Fiona Shaw, Juliet Stevenson and Harriet Walter discuss Cressida, Helena, Isabella, Kate, Lady Macbeth and Rosalind. In Judith Cook, *Shakespeare's Players*, London: Harrap, 1983, Ian Richardson talks on Richard II, Bolingbroke, Richard III, and Prospero; John Wood on Brutus; Paul Scofield on King Lear; Joe Melia on Touchstone; and Ian McKellen on Macbeth. Antony Sher describes the rehearsal process of his Richard III in *Year of the King*, London: Nick Hern Books, new edition, 2004. I discuss Lear in *Playing Lear*, London: Nick Hern Books, 2003. Mark Rylance talks about playing at the new Globe in Martin White's 'Working Wonders' in *Extraordinary Actors* (see above). In Faber and Faber's series *Actors on Shakespeare*, Harriet

Walter writes on Lady Macbeth; Simon Callow on Falstaff; Al Pacino on Richard III; Corin Redgrave on Julius Caesar; Emma Fielding on Viola; Vanessa Redgrave on Cleopatra; James Earl Jones on Othello; David Oyelowo on Henry VI; Saskia Reeves on Beatrice; and F. Murray Abraham on Bottom. They also discuss their plays in general. *On Acting*, eds. Mary Luckhurst and Chloe Veltman, London: Faber & Faber, 2001 is a series of interviews with an off-beat selection of British and American actors. Prunella Scales and Timothy West, *So You Want to be an Actor?*, London: Nick Hern Books, 2005 is characteristically concise and down-to-earth.

ACTOR BIOGRAPHIES

Simon Callow, *Being an Actor*, London: Methuen, 1984 and Harriet Walter, *Other People's Shoes*, London: Nick Hern Books, new edition, 2003 are very good reads and have a lot to say about acting. Michael Blakemore, *Arguments with England*, London: Faber and Faber, 2005 is fascinating on many subjects, including Stratford in the 1950s. Michael Redgrave, *In My Mind's Eye*, London: Coronet Books, 1984, and *The Actor's Ways and Means*, London: Nick Hern Books, 1995 show a very good analytical mind. John Gielgud, *Acting Shakespeare*, London: Pan, 1997; and Laurence Olivier, *On Acting*, London: Wheelshare, 1986 have interesting insights. Mel Gussow, *Gambon: A Life in Acting*, London: Nick Hern Books, 2004 is a series of random interviews that reflect Gambon's no-nonsense approach.

FOUR AND FIVE: REHEARSAL AND PERFORMANCE

John Russell Brown, *Shakespeare's Plays in Performance*, New York and London: Applause, 2000, and *William Shakespeare: Writing for Performance*, London: Palgrave Macmillan, 1996 are inspiring reads on many aspects of performance. Opposing views on actors' approach to performance are taken by W.B. Worthen, *Shakespeare and the Authority of Performance*, Cambridge University Press, 1997; and Jonathan Holmes, *Merely Players? Actors' Accounts of Performing Shakespeare*, London and New York: Routledge, 2004. J.L. Styan, *The Shakespeare Revolution: Criticism and Performance in the 20th Century*, Cambridge University Press, 1983 is valuable. *Shakespeare: An Illustrated Stage History*, eds. Jonathan Bate and Russell Jackson, Oxford University Press, 1996 contains a whole range of articles from Elizabethan stages to Shakespeare productions in the last fifty years; and Dennis Kennedy, *Foreign Shakespeare*, Cambridge University Press, 1993 is good on performances in other countries.

Eric Partridge, *Shakespeare's Bawdy*, London and New York: Routledge, 2001 is definitive, though Pauline Kiernan, *Filthy Shakespeare*, London: Quercus, 2006 is an even more racy read. Stanley Wells, *Looking for Sex in Shakespeare*, Cambridge University Press, 2004 is interesting, particularly on gay issues. There are excellent essays in *Shakespeare and Sexuality*, eds. Catherine M.S. Alexander and Stanley Wells, Cambridge University Press, 2001.

On film, there are numerous excellent surveys, though they concentrate little on acting problems. Try Kenneth S. Rothwell, *A History of Shakespeare on Screen: A Century of Film and Television*, Cambridge University Press, 2004; or *Shakespeare and the Moving Image: The Plays on Film and Television*, eds. Anthony Davies and Stanley Wells, Cambridge University Press, 1994.

DIRECTORS

Among the many books by directors try Peter Brook, *The Empty Space*, London: MacGibbon and Kee, 1968; Jonathan Miller, *Subsequent Performances*, London: Faber and Faber, 1986; Michael Bogdanov, *Shakespeare: The Director's Cut*, Edinburgh: Capercaillie Books, 2003; William Gaskill, *A Sense of Direction*, London: Faber and Faber, 1988; Charles Marowitz, *Prospero's Staff*, Bloomington and Indianapolis: Indiana University Press, 1986; Ralph Berry, *On Directing Shakespeare*, London: Hamish Hamilton, 1989; and for a look at European directors, Dennis Kennedy, *Looking at Shakespeare: A Visual History of Twentieth-Century Performance*, Cambridge University Press, 2001.

APPENDIX: TWO CASE STUDIES

For Duke Vincentio see Daniel Massey in *Players of Shakespeare*, vol. 2; Roger Allam in *Players of Shakespeare*, vol.3; and Ralph Berry, *Changing Styles in Shakespeare*, London: Allen and Unwin, 1981. There are scores of articles on *Measure for Measure*, which has become one of the most frequently performed plays in the last thirty years.

For Viola see Zoë Wanamaker in *Players of Shakespeare*, vol. 2; Zoë Waites and Matilda Ziegler in *Players of Shakespeare*, vol. 5; and Emma Fielding in *Actors on Shakespeare: Twelfth Night*, London: Faber and Faber, 2002. Michael Pennington, *Twelfth Night: A User's Guide*, London: Nick Hern Books, 2000 is an excellent guide to the play.

INDEX

*Works by Shakespeare and characters in the plays
are indexed under 'Shakespeare'. Matters relating to the plays'
language are indexed under 'Shakespeare's Language'*